MITTERRAND'S FRANCE

Edited by
SONIA MAZEY and MICHAEL NEWMAN

CROOM HELM
London • New York • Sydney

© 1987 Sonia Mazey and Michael Newman
Croom Helm Ltd, Provident House, Burrell Row,
Beckenham, Kent, BR3 1AT

Croom Helm Australia, 44-50 Waterloo Road,
North Ryde, 2113, New South Wales

British Library Cataloguing in Publication Data

Mitterrand's France.
  1. France — History — 1958-
  I. Mazey, Sonia II. Newman, Michael
  944.083'8   DC412

ISBN 0-7099-4648-1

Published in the USA by
Croom Helm
in association with Methuen, Inc.
29 West 35th Street
New York, NY 10001

Library of Congress Cataloging-in-Publication Data

ISBN 0-7099-4648-1

Printed and bound in Great Britain by
Biddles Ltd, Guildford and King's Lynn

MITTERRAND'S FRANCE

The election of Francois Mitterrand as President in 1981 marked the first left wing administration of the Fifth Republic. Due to a massive Parliamentary majority, this administration was soon in a position to implement socialist policies. It was elected on a platform of more equal and democratic society. This book outlines the policy intentions of the French socialists; and contrasts intentions with actual achievements. It considers the key sectors of the economy, social welfare, industry, culture, defence, decentralisation and foreign policy. The different case studies are drawn together by common themes, and background is given on the run-up to the Socialist victory, the economic and political constraints on radical change and the general outline of French political and institutional policy-making.

Edited by Sonia Mazey and Michael Newman, both Department of History, Philosophy and European Studies, Polytechnic of North London

CONTENTS

Notes on Contributors   vii

Abbreviations   ix

Acknowledgements   xi

Introduction Sonia Mazey   1

1. The Parti Socialiste français: socialist
   synthesis or ambiguous compromise?
   David Hanley   7

2. Broken Dreams: Economic Policy in
   Mitterrand's France. Peter Holmes   33

3. Labour and Industry: the demise of
   Traditional Unionism? Martin Rhodes   56

4. A More Equal Society? Social Policy
   under the Socialists. Doreen Collins   81

5. Decentralisation: La Grande Affaire
   du Septennat? Sonia Mazey   103

6. Cultural Policy: The Soul of Man under
   Socialism. Jill Forbes   131

7. Foreign Policy: Business as Usual?
   David A.L. Levy   166

8. Defence Policy under Socialist
   Management Neville Waites   192

Conclusion - The Balance Sheet <u>Michael Newman</u> 218

Appendix One: Election Results   235

Appendix Two: Chronology of major political events in France 1981-1986   240

Index   249

NOTES ON CONTRIBUTORS

Sonia Mazey is a Senior Lecturer in Politics in the Division of European Studies at the Polytechnic of North London. She is currently working on public policy-making and decentralisation in France and has published articles on these subjects.

Michael Newman is a Principal Lecturer in Politics in the Division of European Studies at the Polytechnic of North London. He is the author of <u>Socialism and European Unity: The Dilemma of the Left in Britain and France</u> (1983) and of several articles on British and French politics and contemporary history. He is currently working on a study of the ideas and influence of John Strachey, and on a biography of Harold Laski.

Doreen Collins recently retired from the post of Senior Lecturer in the Department of Social Policy at the University of Leeds. She has written extensively on the social policy of the European Community. Previous work on France has included a study, published in 1984, of the condition of the elderly in France.

Jill Forbes is Head of the Modern Languages Department at South Bank Polytechnic, London. She is editor of <u>INA French for Innovation</u> (1984) and author of the forthcoming <u>French Cinema since 1968</u>. She has a longstanding interest in arts policy, serving on the East Midlands Arts Association for many years, as a governor of the British Film Institute 1976-80, and as a member of its Production Board 1980-83. She is also a film critic contributing regularly to <u>Sight</u>

and Sound, the Monthly Film Bulletin and Framework.

David Hanley is a lecturer in French Studies at the University of Reading. He is the author of Keeping Left: CERES and the French Socialist Party (1986) and co-author of Contemporary France (2nd edition, 1984). He has also published several articles on French and British politics.

Peter Holmes is a lecturer in Economics in the School of European Studies at the University of Sussex. He spent 1984-5 at the University of Grenoble and is now doing research on French industrial policy, sponsored by the ESRC. He has written widely on the French economy including, with Saul Estrin, French Planning in Theory and Practice (1983).

David A.L. Levy is a Lecturer in Politics and Contemporary History at the University of Salford. He was a student at Nuffield College, Oxford where he wrote a D.Phil thesis on the French Popular Front. Thereafter he worked as a current affairs writer and producer for the BBC. He researches on contemporary French History and Politics.

Martin Rhodes is a Lecturer in Politics at the University of Salford, having previously been a Research Fellow at the University of Strathclyde and at the European University Institute in Florence. He is the author of several articles on the steel industry, government-industry relations, and industrial relations in Western Europe, and is the author of Steel and the State in France (OUP forthcoming, 1988) and co-author of Information Technology and the State in Western Europe (OUP, forthcoming 1987).

Neville Waites is a lecturer in French Studies at the University of Reading where he is also Director of the Centre for Advanced Study of French Society and Director of European Studies in the Graduate School. Editor of Troubled Neighbours: Franco-British Relations in the Twentieth Century, and co-author of Contemporary France (2nd edition, 1984), he has published a number of articles on aspects of French foreign and defence policies since World War One.

ABBREVIATIONS

CERES	Centre d'Etudes, de Récherches et d'Education Socialiste - Centre for Study, Research and Socialist Education
CFDT	Confédération Française Démocratique du Travail - French Democratic Confederation of Labour
CFTC	Confédération Française des Travailleurs Chrétiens - French Confederation of Christian Workers
CGC	Confédération Générale des Cadres - General Confederation of Managerial Staff and White Collar Workers
CGT	Confédération Générale du Travil - General Confederation of Labour
CIR	Convention des Institutions Républicaines Convention of Republican Institutions
CNIP	Centre National des Indépendants et des Paysans - National Council of Self-employed Persons and Smallholders
CNPF	Conseil National du Patronat Français - National Council of French Employers
CPG	Programme Commun de Gouvernement - Common Programme of Government (agreed between the PS and PCF in 1972)
DATAR	Délégation Générale à l'Aménagement du Territoire et à l'Action Régionale - Delegation for Regional Planning and Development
Div.G.	Divers Gauche - Non-Communist and Non-Socialist Party left-wing groups
EEC	European Economic Community
EMS	European Monetary System
FEN	Fédération de l'Education Nationale - National Federation of Teachers
FLNC	Front de Libération Nationale Corse - Corsican Nationalist Liberation Front

FN	Le Front National	- National Front
FO	Force Ouvrière	- General Workers' Confederation
LO	Lutte Ouvrière	- Workers' Front (Trotskyist Party)
MRG	Mouvement des Radicaux de Gauche	- Left-wing Radical Movement
PCF	Parti Communiste Français	- French Communist Party
POE	Parti Ouvrier Européen	- European Workers' Party
PS	Parti Socialiste	- Socialist Party
PSU	Parti Socialiste Unifié	- Unified Socialist Party
Rad.	Parti Radical	Radical Party
RPR	Rassemblement pour la République	- Rally for the Republic (Gaullist Party)
SFIO	Section Française de l'Internationale Ouvrière	- French Section of the Workers' International (Socialist Party 1905-1969)
SMIC	Statutory Minimum Wage	
SNPMI	Syndicat National de la Petite et Moyenne Industrie	- National Association of small and medium-sized Industries (employers' association)
UDF	Union pour la Démocratie Française	- French Democratic Union
UIMM	Union des Industries Minières et Métallurgiques	- Union of Mining and Metallurgy Industries (employers' association)

ACKNOWLEDGEMENTS

We would like to thank the Humanities Faculty of the Polytechnic of North London for granting us research relief for this book and also Liz Courquin for her help in typing parts of it. We would also like to thank Peter Sowden of Croom Helm for encouraging the project.

Sonia Mazey
Michael Newman

INTRODUCTION

Sonia Mazey

On the 10 May 1981 François Mitterrand became the first Socialist President of the Fifth Republic. His victory was an impressive one: in the second round of the presidential elections held that day he won 51.75 per cent of the votes cast while his rival, the incumbent right-wing President, Valéry Giscard d'Estaing scored 48.24 per cent. Mitterrand's first act as President was to dissolve the right-wing controlled National Assembly and seek a parliamentary majority. The electorate obliged: in the legislative elections held in June 1981 the Socialists and their non-Communist electoral allies won 285 of the 491 seats in the National Assembly. Mitterrand's own Parti Socialiste did astonishingly well in these contests, winning 262 seats - a clear overall majority. This performance contrasted sharply with that of the Communist Party which obtained just 16.1 per cent of the vote at the first ballot and 44 seats - its worst election result since 1936. Having led his Party to triumph in the National Assembly, the newly elected President was thus under no obligation to seek the support of the Communists. (1)

While several factors contributed to the Socialists' victory in 1981, the fundamental prerequisite to their success was the transformation of the French Left during the 1970s. During the 1960s electoral rivalry between the (then much larger) Communist Party and the ideologically fragmented non-Communist Left had paid regular dividends to the more disciplined Right. (2) As David Hanley explains in Chapter One, the establishment of the Parti Socialiste in 1969 as a national, modern presidential party committed to a formal electoral alliance with the Communists was thus an important first step in building the left-wing coalition which elected

1

Introduction

Mitterrand in 1981. Equally important to the Socialist Party's impressive victory was the decline of the <u>Parti Communiste Français</u>, which failed to respond to the presidential regime and which, since 1974 had for various reasons been unable to stem the steady flow of Communist votes to the Socialists. (3)

It is important to stress, however, that the socialist electorate in 1981 was an extremely disparate one. As is so often the case in national elections, many people voted against the incumbent regime rather than for socialism. In the presidential contest, for instance, the arrogant and imperial manner of the once reformist and republican Giscard d'Estaing alienated many voters who had supported him in 1974. Many people were also disillusioned with the lacklustre conservatism of the former right-wing Prime Minister, Raymond Barre. The failure of his administration to remedy the worsening economic situation convinced large numbers of voters in 1981 that the time had come for a change. More generally, after 23 years of continuous right-wing rule there was a less tangible, but none the less significant feeling of boredom with the Right. In the past, support for <u>l'alternance</u> among uncommitted centrist voters had been curbed by solemn warnings to the electorate that the only alternative to the Right was Communist-led chaos. In 1981, however, confronted with the eminently presidential François Mitterrand and the debilitated Communist Party few people believed the Republic to be under threat from the Left.

Similarly, among those on the Left who voted for the Socialists, different people voted for different reasons. Most Communist voters supported Mitterrand in the second round of the presidential elections (88 per cent of those who had voted for Georges Marchais on the first ballot) and some, offended by the crude nature of the Communist Party's election campaign and impatient to see the Left in power, supported Mitterrand from the outset. In the legislative elections the following month, many Socialist candidates throughout France also owed their success - to varying degrees - to Communist votes at the second ballot. Other groups who associated themselves with the Left, such as regionalist, ecology and anti-nuclear movements, also supported the Socialists. And the French Socialist Party itself is a broad coalition movement which embraces several ideological <u>courants</u>. Thus, while some Socialist voters in 1981 were voting for <u>autogestion</u> - democratic self-government, some hoped for a Marxist

Introduction

transformation of the capitalist economy, while others were pledging their support for social-democratic policies.

In May 1981 the 'long march of the French Left' thus came to a spectacular end and as Jack Hayward declared:

> (We) have in 1981, with the coming to power of a Socialist President in the shape of François Mitterrand and of an overall socialist Parliamentary majority, an invaluable opportunity to observe both the continuity and changes in national policy styles of which France is capable. The key political institutions of the Fifth Republic for the first time will all be controlled by the Left, which has never heretofore had the opportunity to carry out its programme. (4)

Five years later, we are now in a position to assess the impact of the Mitterrand administration upon French society. The exercise is a particularly interesting one since the keyword of the socialist programme was le changement; French society was to be not simply changed at the margins, but totally transformed. The declared intention of the socialist government in 1981 was the creation of a more democratic society, characterised throughout by egalitarianism, citizen participation and a new partnership with the state. The cornerstone of the socialist programme was economic policy: unemployment was to be reduced and the economy revived by a bold reflationary strategy, extension of the public sector and the resurrection of economic planning. This was to be accompanied by redistributive social policies, democratisation of educational opportunities, cultural and mass media reform, political decentralisation and industrial reform designed to increase the influence of employees in the workplace. Finally, French foreign and defence policies were henceforth to conform to socialist principles of support for the Third World, humanitarianism and self-determination.

In the euphoric atmosphere of 1981 the newly-elected government (which included four Communist junior ministers invited by Mitterrand to join the government) embarked upon its radical programme with enthusiasm. Yet as observers of French political life could not fail to observe, all did not go smoothly for the government. 1982 brought a U-turn in economic strategy and the introduction of austerity measures which were further extended in 1983: benefits were cut, taxes were increased, public sector wage increases held down and nationalised industries told to put their finances in order. And as indicated in the following studies of socialist policy-making after 1981, in other policy sectors too, there were problems, delays and trimming.

Meanwhile, the widespread popularity of the socialist President and his government began to evaporate. In local elections in 1982 and 1983 right-wing opposition parties made important inroads into traditional left-wing strongholds. (5) Worse was to follow: car-workers, steelworkers, coal-miners, dockers, university lecturers, teachers, civil servants and doctors who in 1981 had voted in large numbers for the Socialists, began to take to the streets in protest at government policies. In 1984 the opinion polls confirmed that François Mitterrand was the most unpopular President of the Fifth Republic. That summer, the young, highflier in the Socialist Party, Laurent Fabius replaced the avuncular senior Party figure, Pierre Mauroy as Prime Minister. The switch - which prompted the departure of the Communists from the government - was a significant one: ideological debate within the Socialist Party gave way to the more moderate language of social reform while the government began to proclaim the virtues of economic efficiency. Finally, on the 16 March 1986 the French socialist experience came to an end: in the legislative elections held that day, the Socialists were predictably - though not disastrously - defeated by the Gaullist-led right-wing opposition coalition. (6) Mitterrand remained President, but in the new era of <u>cohabitation</u> with the right-wing government of Jacques Chirac, the country could no longer be described as 'Mitterrand's France'.

Looking back, two related questions thus spring to mind: to what extent did the socialist administration actually succeed in implementing its election programme - and why; and how did such a popular regime manage to lose the support of its electorate. This book focuses upon the first of these two questions by examining in detail the formulation and subsequent implementation of socialist policy in areas specifically singled out by the Mitterrand administration for <u>grandes réformes</u>. The picture which emerges is a complex one. Close inspection reveals that some important socialist reforms were indeed accomplished between 1981 and 1986. None the less, as the following chapters confirm, actual

Introduction

policies often fell some way short of election pledges. But as these studies also highlight, there was no single reason for this 'failure'; different factors seem to have been relevant in different policy sectors. International constraints, financial difficulties, electoral considerations and ideological differences within the government were just some of the factors which determined the pace and nature of change in France after 1981.

The book also provides important insights into the second of the two questions posed above - the widespread disillusionment with the regime. On this issue, two general points emerge: firstly, expectations in 1981 were (as in 1936 when the Popular Front came to power) tremendously high - unrealistically so. Secondly, as indicated above, those expectations were extremely diverse: while many on the left were disappointed with the failure of the socialist administration to implement its programme, others who had voted for Mitterrand in 1981 quickly became disenchanted with change. As the French Socialists discovered to their cost, many voters make fickle friends.

In the concluding chapter, Michael Newman pieces together the information and arguments presented in earlier contributions to provide a general assessment of the Mitterrand administration and an appraisal of the reasons for its achievements and failures. In so doing, he discusses a number of important questions about the nature of the French socialist government and French socialism and, more generally, raises the thorny issue of the capacity of socialist parties in liberal-democratic regimes to implement a comprehensive programme of radical change. Overall then, these studies not only provide insights into Mitterrand's France, but also introduce valuable material for international comparisons.

Notes
1. For details of the 1981 election results see 'L'Election Présidentielle: 26 Avril-10 Mai 1981, Le Monde - Dossiers et Documents May 1981; D Goldey & A Knapp, 'Time for a change: the French elections of 1981', Electoral Studies, vol. 1, (1982); P. Hainsworth, 'A majority for the President: the French Left and the presidential and parliamentary elections of 1981', Parliamentary Affairs, vol. 34, (1981); V. Wright & H. Machin, 'Why Mitterrand won the French Presidential elections of

April-May 1981', <u>West European Politics</u>, vol. 6, (1982); H. Machin, 'The third ballot of 1981: the French legislative elections of 14 and 21 June 1981', <u>West European Politics</u>, vol. 6, (1982).

2. For details of the impact of the French Presidential system and electoral system on the nature of the party system during the Fifth Republic see V. Wright, <u>The Government and Politics of France</u>, 2nd Edition, (London: Hutchinson Ltd, 1983); D. Goldey & P. Williams 'France', in V. Bogdanor & D. Butler (Eds.), <u>Democracy and Elections: Electoral Systems and their Consequences</u>, (Cambridge: Cambridge University Press, 1983).

3. For details of the changes in the French Socialist Party during the Fifth Republic see Chapter One. For information on the French Communist Party see M. Adereth <u>The French Communist Party: a critical history 1920-1984</u> (Manchester: Manchester University Press, 1984); T. Judt, <u>Marxism and the French Left</u>, (Oxford: Oxford University Press, 1986); I. Aviv, 'The French Communist Party from 1958-1978', <u>West European Politics</u>, vol. 3, (1979). On the French Communist Party after 1981 see J. Marcus, 'The French Communist Party between government and opposition', <u>World Today</u>, March 1984; A. Antonian & I. Wall, 'The French Communists under François Mitterrand', <u>Political Studies</u>, Vol. 33, (1985).

4. J. Hayward, 'France: the dual policy-style', in J.J. Richardson, <u>Policy-Styles in Western Europe</u>, (London: George, Allen & Unwin, 1982), p.137.

5. For details of the 1982 cantonal elections see C. Dogan and J. Marcus, 'The French cantonal elections: local skirmish or national test?', <u>The World Today</u>, May 1982. For details of the 1983 French Municipal Elections see D. Bell and B. Criddle, 'The French Municipal elections of March 1983', <u>Parliamentary Affairs</u>, vol. 36, (1983).

6. For details of the March 1986 French legislative elections see 'Les Elections Législatives du 16 Mars 1986', <u>Le Monde - Dossiers et Documents</u>, March 1986; D.A.L. Levy and H. Machin, 'How Fabius lost: the French elections of 1986', <u>Government and Opposition</u>, vol. 21, (1986); D.B. Goldey and R.W. Johnson, 'The French General Election of 16 March 1986', <u>Electoral Studies</u>, vol. 5, (1986).

Chapter One

THE PARTI SOCIALISTE FRANCAIS: SOCIALIST SYNTHESIS OR AMBIGUOUS COMPROMISE?

David Hanley

The triumph of François Mitterrand in the presidential election of 1981 was matched if not surpassed by that of his party, the <u>Parti socialiste</u> (PS) in the parliamentary elections held six weeks after. This is no accident for the two successes are linked. Mitterrand's rise accompanying that of his party during the previous decade. Whatever his charisma and political skill, he needed the instrument which any person with aspirations to the presidency requires - a viable party. The PS is thus not just a function of Mitterrand's ambition and it will continue to play a key role in France after he has gone; for by now it has become a major actor in the political system. The following pages will show how the party was built, how it functions, what problems it has faced, and what its future is likely to be.

From SFIO To PS
The modern PS is not so much a rebirth as a transplant onto a somewhat moribund body. This body was the SFIO (<u>Section français de l'internationale ouvrière</u>) which was founded in 1905 and had long since become a key part of the French multiparty system. Despite a revolutionary-sounding rhetoric, characterised by references to class struggle and even, until after 1945, to proletarian dictatorship, SFIO had become, by its actual political practice at local and national level, fairly indistinguishable from the moderate reformist parties typical of North European social-democracy. (1) But by 1969 it was in poor shape, with declining electoral support, a falling membership (mainly ageing public employees) and a dusty, out-of-touch image. Compared to the robust communist party (PCF), it seemed a candidate

7

for demise.

SFIO had suffered for its many years of participation in coalition governments during the Fourth Republic (1946-58). During the Algerian war (1954-62) it had borne major responsibility for governmental failure to check the growing insubordination of soldiers, administrators and settlers in Algiers which would eventually overthrow the Republic.

During the sixties as Gaullism reshaped French institutions, modernised the French Right, sped up economic growth and embarked on a new independent foreign policy, SFIO sat watching, unable to change its leaders, ideas or image. It was true that the party now contained a small nucleus of young, highly educated activists, eager to shake the party up and make it the spearhead of a left unity pact with the PCF; this was the CERES (<u>Centre d'études, de recherche et d'éducation socialiste</u>). But CERES pulled little weight then and the ageing Guy Mollet, general secretary since 1946, tireless in the service of the party, decent and sincere in his ideals but totally without charisma or media appeal, symbolised by now the public face of SFIO. In the presidential election of June 1969 SFIO hit rock bottom, when its candidate Gaston Deferre took a bare 5 per cent of the vote. Renewal was imperative: and in 1969 renewal meant merger.

Even before then attempts had been made to pull together the scattered parts of the non-communist left. In 1965 Mitterrand had stood as presidential candidate against de Gaulle, very much on an individual basis, but with the support of both PCF and other left parties. His 45 per cent in the run-off ballot showed there was a big Left constituency in France, and that much of it might be able to be drawn into one party. Mitterrand himself comes from the Radical tradition, though he never belonged to the party of that name. In 1964 he had begun to organise his supporters, many of whom were active in the political clubs of that time (the surest index of the decline of political parties) (2) into a new party, the CIR (<u>Convention des institutions républicaines</u>). During the rest of the decade, Mitterrand put together a short-lived electoral coalition with other groups of the non-communist left, including SFIO. When this broke up after May 1968, SFIO took up the running by changing its name to the PS and welcoming in smaller groups such as the followers of Alain Savary and Jean Poperen. It remained only to unify these with the Mitterrandists,

The Parti Socialiste Francais

and this operation took place at the famous unity congress of Epinay in 1971.

Table 1.1: Epinay Congress 1971 – Percentage scores obtained by motions presented by participating groups

Savary-Mollet (SFIO Centre-left)	34.0
Defferre-Mauroy (SFIO Right)	30.0
CERES (SFIO Left)	8.5
Mermaz-Pontillon (CIR and some votes 'loaned' by SFIO)	15.0
Poperen	12.0
Left-wing Catholics (allied to CERES)	0.5
Total	100.0

Here the PS took its modern shape. Six groups were concerned in the unity congress, and Table 1.1 shows the weight each represented in terms of the memberships of the various organisations which were about to join up (i.e. the scores each obtained for the general policy motion it presented to congress). What happened was that in this situation where no group had a majority, Mitterrand did a deal (in advance in fact) with both the moderate wing of SFIO (Mauroy and Deferre - see below) and also the left of the SFIO, CERES. By so doing he outsmarted Mollet who had gained the support of the rest. Thus by a short head (43,926 votes to 41,758 - these figures grossly inflate the real memberships) Mitterrand became First Secretary of the PS. The Party also agreed to seek an electoral alliance with the PCF, including an agreed Common Programme of Government (CPG) and it accepted an internal code of rules which would institutionalise fractionalism (see below). At last it seemed that the Left's most plausible national leader had been given the instrument he needed to win office. By a series of transplants the SFIO had been pulled from its death bed to become almost a new being.

From Epinay to the 10 mai
The party leadership, on which all the victorious allies of Epinay were represented, quickly got down to work. Under the CERES leader Jean-Pierre Chevènement, the PS head of research, a draft programme was prepared which the party would approve and publish in 1972 under the title *Changer la vie*. This would serve as a basis for negotiations with the

PCF, and the two parties duly concluded a CPG in June 1972, which committed them to an alliance for the March 1973 elections. The CPG was a compromise between PS and PCF, not least on economic strategy where the PS was forced to agree to a package of nationalisations of major groups (nine in all) that would become famous. This apart, the partners were committed to high economic growth, where demand management and government intervention (nationalisations and control of credit) would play a major role. Redistribution through increased benefits and tax changes also figured prominently. Political differences between the two different views of socialism were just left side by side, and foreign policy disagreements (e.g. over the Atlantic Alliance) disguised as best they could be. A section on liberties included promises to strengthen parliament at the expense of the presidency (e.g. by abolishing the emergency powers of article 16) and to introduce a supreme court as a constitutional watchdog, as well as to bring in proportional representation. The small MRG (<u>Movement des radicaux de gauche</u>), a split from the Radical party which was by now lining up with the Right, also signed the CPG; its support was probably worth another 2 per cent of the vote. Compromise or not, the CPG found favour with the voters, with the Left scoring 46 per cent in 1973 and the PS closing to within 2 per cent of the PCF. There followed the early presidential election of 1974 when Pompidou died suddenly. Backed by all 3 parties, Mitterrand lost very narrowly to Giscard d'Estaing; as he said, the election had come a few months too early.

It may seem odd the PS took seven more years to reach national office after such a surge. The delay is due to worsening relations with the PCF. Aware that electoral results were increasingly favouring the PS, the communists began to question the socialist good faith of their ally; in particular, they raised the stakes for the updating of the Common Programme in 1977 to such a provocative level that the alliance split and the 1978 elections were lost against all expectation. This created some difficulty inside the PS at its Metz congress of 1979 where Mitterrand needed help from his old friends CERES to beat off a challenge from the modernising wing of the party, led by Michel Rocard who had joined in 1974. But Giscard's growing difficulties and the PCF's failure to persuade the public that there was another alternative to Mitterrand on the left eventually opened the door in 1981.

The Parti Socialiste Francais

Retrospectively it could be seen that Mitterrand had easily won his game of poker with the PCF. At the outset the latter seemed to hold many trumps: a mass membership, strength in Parliament and local government, strong union and pressure-group links and above all a discipline whereby members carried out unquestioningly the decisions of a small, self-co-opting leadership of professional politicians. But it also had weaknesses. It was reluctant to criticise the Soviet version of socialism, despite growing awareness of its defects. It was slow to pick up the changes - social, political and cultural - which were taking place in contemporary capitalism and to offer plausible programmes in the light of this. And its vertical decision-making structure of democratic centralism seemed increasingly archaic in a society where more and more people obtained qualifications and demanded inputs into decisions at every level.

Like many socialists Mitterrand admired the PCF's strength and its capacity to defend the working class but feared what he saw as its dependence on the Soviet model. His skill was to realise that the Leninist-Stalinist tradition, which despite its repeated face-lifts the PCF still reflects, was rapidly losing its appeal in those developed states of the West where viable communist parties still hung on. For the moment electoral necessity made a deal with the PCF imperative; but the longer the partnership lasted, the more PCF's implausibility as a serious candidate for government would show through. So it would prove, as during the seventies the PS forged ahead of its rival/partner and indeed after 1981 when the weakened PCF accepted four posts in government. Its presence there for three years made little apparent difference to policy-making, and when it did withdraw it was by then far too compromised for its critiques to carry any weight. The strategist Mitterrand had outsmarted the PCF to make his own party dominant on the Left - a goal unthinkable in 1971.

The Structures of the PS

This section will examine several aspects of the party, beginning with its programmes. We shall then consider its organisation, with particular reference to its fractions, as well as its voters and members. Finally we examine the party in relation to outside forces such as local government and pressure groups, before assessing how it responded to the challenge of office after 1981.

Programmes. <u>Changer la vie</u> (1972) was followed by a number of texts through the seventies (3), which add to and refine the original material. It is possible to extract from these a sort of essence which contains the kernel of the PS approach. We should bear in mind that PS texts are always a result of compromise between the party's sub-groups, which have views of their own; nevertheless, there is a common core, which we attempt to describe here.

In terms of social analysis the PS used a marxist framework, borrowed, despite verbal precautions, from work done by the PCF and popularised by writers such as Poperen. Central was the notion of a 'class-front'. As capitalism developed and the number of wage-earners increased, social polarisation grew: on the one hand a small group at the heads of the multinational corporations and the state apparatus confronted a vast wage-earning mass, whose incomes, working conditions and lifestyle in general lagged far behind what they might be. The interests of most of these people were held by the PS to be similar, and indeed they had much in common with non-salaried social strata like farmers or self-employed craftsmen. All could benefit from changing the monopolistic pattern of growth and ensuring that its fruits were fairly distributed. Hence the message, still subscribed to by the more earnest PS activists, that 'sociologically, France was on the left'. The PS aimed to translate this sociological leftness into political terms, i.e. votes for itself and left unity.

The kind of society towards which the PS wanted to see France develop would increasingly have as its organising principle <u>autogestion</u>. This philosophy of socialism was presented as being distinct from that of the USSR (and thus by implication from the PCF) in that it was less concerned with social ownership of the economy than with decentralisation of power and responsibility. In every sphere of activity - workplace, community, university - power was to be decentralised to the smallest unit practicable. An impression was thus given of PS commitment to a much more libertarian, if not to say individualist ethic, alongside a traditional socialist commitment to fairness and greater equality. Hard to pin down in practice, <u>autogestion</u> was to prove an attractive and very operational ideological mix.

Traces of <u>autogestion</u> emerge in PS economic doctrine, though they had to coexist with traditional socialist maxims, such as nationalisation of the credit system and of major private industrial groups. The rationale for this was to give government the means to plan expansion: the enlarged public sector was to act as a sort of tow-rope for the many smaller firms in the private sector through its policy of subcontracting, purchasing, etc. The commitment to growth became more strident as unemployment increased through the seventies, and the party remained optimistic that statist methods of the above type, plus more Keynesian ones of demand management, would produce it. But <u>autogestion</u> made its influence felt in the theories of 'democratic planning' whereby firms and local authorities would make major inputs into the national indicative plan and also in proposals for running industry, particularly the public sector (see chapter 2) with greater workforce involvement. In its economic thought then, the PS continued both statist doctrine of the past plus the Keynesianism widely used by social-democratic governments since 1945, as well as hinting at a new more participatory approach.

In the area of civil liberties, the party fought what it saw to be the increasingly heavy repression of the Giscardian state, by promising measures to improve the rights of citizens vis-a-vis police and courts. It also favoured greater checks on the executive (cf above) and in the field of sub-central government declared in favour of greater powers and resources for the units, particularly the regions (cf. chapter 5). Only on one aspect of liberty did the party seem unable to change its discourse, and this was <u>laïcité</u> (secularism). The PS remained committed to the old pledge to nationalise all private schools receiving state funds: in Mediterranean countries this is shorthand for Catholic schools. The PS thus confirmed its attachment to the anticlerical traditions of Republicanism which had so marked SFIO: it also demonstrated the not inconsiderable power of the teachers' lobby in its ranks.

Finally in foreign policy and defence, the PS made a major move in 1977-8 by accepting the retention of the nuclear deterrent (see chapter 8). Before, it had been committed to unilateral nuclear disarmament, like the British Labour Party's current stance; and indeed the CPG had been signed on that basis. The switch of the seventies reflects PS awareness that the French public generally supports

13

The Parti Socialiste Francais

the nuclear arsenal and that opposition to it might stop the party from winning office. At the same time, support for the EEC was maintained as in the past, albeit accompanied by increasing notes of criticism about the bureaucracy and waste of that institution.

In short, the party managed on all main policy areas to present an air of boldness and innovation, while remaining aware of what was electorally acceptable. In particular it seems to have catered for both its old working-class constituency (through its growth and redistribution package), while offering openings to the new, salaried middle-classes (essentially through its libertarian and participatory line). And it remained nicely distinct from its PCF ally. To judge by its results, the PS seems to have concocted its programmatic mix with particular shrewdness.

Organisation

Figure 1.1: The Structures of the Socialist Party

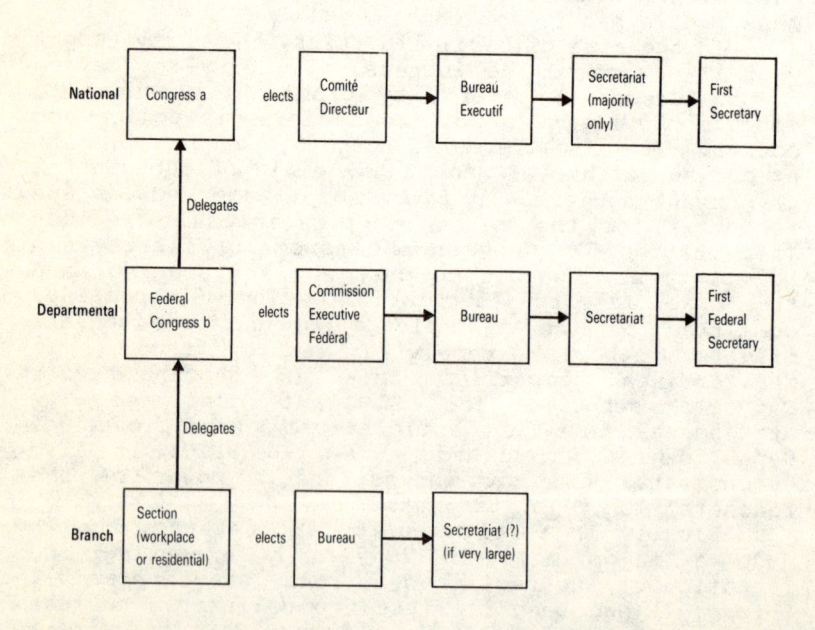

National	Congress a → elects → Comité Directeur → Bureau Executif → Secretariat (majority only) → First Secretary
	↑ Delegates
Departmental	Federal Congress b → elects → Commission Executive Fédéral → Bureau → Secretariat → First Federal Secretary
	↑ Delegates
Branch	Section (workplace or residential) → elects → Bureau → Secretariat (?) (if very large)

Source: D. Hanley, <u>Keeping Left? Ceres and the French Socialist Party</u>, (Manchester: Manchester University Press, 1986).

Article 5 of party rules states that proportional representation (PR) with the highest average is used to elect party organs at every level (see Figure 1.1). The PR applies to the votes which members give to different general policy motions submitted to party congress (two-yearly). These motions are produced prior to congress by the different fractions (see below) and circulated to branches which then vote on them. These branch votes are then counted up at the level of the federation (i.e. the department), and it is on this basis that places are shared out on the <u>commission exécutive fédérale</u> or its smaller <u>bureau</u> which meets more frequently. But the real leadership body in the <u>fédé</u>, as activists like to call it, is the <u>secrétariat</u>; places on this are not given out according to PR but shared only among supporters of the majority motion (and its allies if a deal is done nationally at congress - see below).

Federations send their delegates to congress, duly mandated in favour of the different motions, where the above scenario is repeated, with seats on the <u>comité directeur</u> and <u>bureau exécutif</u> shared out as they are for their federal equivalents. But it may be possible to reach a <u>synthèse</u>, i.e. for the different signatories of motions to agree a common text. If this happens (usually after a hard night's bargaining in the resolutions committee between the fraction bosses) then the agreed text is usually presented to congress and voted unanimously. Every fraction then gets its share of posts on the <u>secrétariat</u>, the key policy-making and executive body. If there is no <u>synthèse</u>, then the <u>secrétariat</u> remains the preserve of the majority motion(s), and it governs the party, with the supporters of the minority motion(s) forming a sort of parliamentary opposition within the <u>bureau</u> and <u>comité directeur</u>.

It is clear that such a formal set of rules absolutely invites members to organise in fractions. This was fully assumed at Epinay, when the decision to have internal PR was taken, and since then there have been, with minor variants on the fringes, four main fractions. Each has its own ideology, organisation inside the party, its own publications and in some cases town premises. Members identify quite strongly with them, particularly CERES and the Rocardians; and in some cases it is a very moot point whether primary loyalty is towards fraction or party. In 1986 we can distinguish:

1. The Mauroyites: often ex-SFIO members, based on the old areas of municipal socialism in the

North and the Mediterranean zones. Generally pragmatic and near to mainstream social-democracy.

Leader Pierre Mauroy (M.P. and mayor of Lille, chairman of regional council of Nord/Pas-de-Calais, Prime Minister 1981-4, former deputy leader of PS).

2. The Rocardians: very 'new left' in approach. Critical of statist socialism, decentralisers and generally looking towards voluntary associations and groups to be the motor of social change. Very pro-Europe and anti-communist. Not fanatical about secularism, and hence have welcomed many of the PS Catholic recruits.

Leader Michel Rocard (ex-leader of leftist PSU party, MP and mayor of Paris suburb, Minister of Planning 1981-3, Minister of Agriculture 1983-5).

3. CERES: Marxist left fraction. Most attached to interventionist socialism and left unity. Has a strong nationalist profile also. Has been split internally by conflict between secularists and Catholics and also <u>autogestionnaires</u> and centralisers. Of late it has played down its marxism in favour of an ideology of Republicanism and national effort, and even changed its name to <u>Socialisme et République</u>. But underneath it remains a mix of dynamic statism and patriotism, each reinforcing the other.

Leader Jean-Pierre Chevènement (MP and mayor of Belfort, Minister of Research and Technology, and also briefly of Industry, 1981-3, Minister of Education 1984-6).

4. The Mitterrandists: this most eclectic fraction includes those from Radical or secularist backgrounds, sometimes with a marxist veneer like Joxe or Laignel. Also ex-communists like Poperen. Many of the post-1971 intake were attracted to this group. The main cement is probably secularism plus the attraction of Mitterrand himself, particularly before 1981. When he disappears it may well break up into a number of sub-groups which will ally with the older more cohesive fractions.

Main personalities include Jean Poperen (deputy leader of PS since 1981, MP and mayor of Lyon suburb); Pierre Joxe (ex-party treasurer, chairman of party's MPs in National Assembly 1981-4, Minister of Interior 1984-6); André Laignel (party treasurer, MP and mayor of Issoudun); Laurent Fabius (MP and mayor of Rouen suburb, Prime Minister 1984-6, previously Treasury Minister and Minister of Industry): Lionel Jospin (MP for Toulouse, party leader since 1981).

The internal life of the PS bubbles away

vigorously, then, beneath its formal structures. The fractions are indeed ideological communities with goals and styles of their own, but over the years they have, with occasional exceptions, managed to coexist in a way which is more competitive than fratricidal. They are certainly more than the presidential launching-pads for ambitious leaders which some see them to be. They are in fact the living symbols of a vital pluralism and as such may well be one of the PS's more original contributions to democratic politics.

Voters and members. Traditionally French socialism drew its electorate from two sources. The first was industrial zones such as Nord/Pas-de-Calais, where the party put down municipal roots early and where increasingly it had to battle with the PCF to hang on to its voters. The second was mainly agricultural zones, south of the Loire, where the party became, during the Third Republic, (1870-1940), heir to the Republican tradition. This means that it was seen as standing not so much for collective ownership as for the defence of the 'small man' (craftsman, farmer, winegrower) against the rich and powerful, especially the landowners and the force perceived as their ally, the church. SFIO managed these disparate electorates as best it could, writing off some parts of France as virtual no-go areas (especially Catholic areas such as Alsace and most of Brittany). One achievement of the new PS is to have broken this deadlock. Today it has a national electorate, scoring respectably in every department in France. The 1986 elections showed an evening-out across the territory. Slight decline in old strongholds like Marseille or Var on the Mediterranean were compensated by growth in previously weak areas, like Britanny or more generally in the Catholic West (Loire region, Poitou-Charentes) (4). These areas tend to be among the more dynamic in economic terms, as well as having a Catholic tradition, so they are areas that bode well for the party's future. (5)

In sociological terms the electorate has also changed. SFIO's original worker and small farmer base had shrunk by 1950 to a hard core of mainly public sector employees. But recent years have seen the party stretch far beyond these limits, to the point where it has become a true 'catch-all' party, with major strength among workers certainly, but also considerable depth among most other groups. The 1981 vote is seen in Table 1.2. We should note the party's high score among workers and white collar workers, superior to both the PCF and the combined Right. It falls behind the Right, unsurprisingly, among retired and non-working people, and among farmers and self-employed, as well as among top wage earners: but there is still a very fair share of such groups (around one-third) who support the PS. This is a very good index of its cross-class appeal.

Table 1.2: Electorates of Major Parties by Social Class, 1981 (Percentage)

	PCF	PS+ Allies	Combined Right (UDF + RPR)
Farmers	6	32	60
Shopkeepers, Craftsmen	10	35	55
Professionals, Industrialists, Senior management	7	38	50
Middle management, lower white collar	16	45	35
Manual workers	24	44	30
Retired, non-working	16	29	54

NB. The horizontal totals do not sum to 100% in view of the omission of the vote for smaller parties.

The 1986 election confirmed many previous features (6). Overall, as Grunberg says, the PS comes across as the party of young people (over 40 per cent of the under 35's) and of the educated (its share of the graduate vote alone equalled that of the combined Right). In particular, the PS appears as the expression of the salaried middle-class, with well over 40 per cent of the vote of lower white-collar workers and middle-management and a similar percentage of the senior managers in the public sector. Yet the PS also kept its footing inside the working class, hanging on to the share of the vote which Mitterrand got in the first ballot in 1981 (though clearly not the record score of June 1981). The PS alone also took 34 per cent of all women's votes. We may say that the party has advanced far beyond its original popular base to become a genuine cross-class force. But there is nothing guaranteed about the loyalty of many of its supporters, particularly among the salaried middle-class, which is the newest and most volatile actor in modern politics. The PS will have to keep working at its

Table 1.3: Party scores at major elections since 1969 (First ballot percentages)

	1969 Pres.	1973 Parlt.	1974 Pres.	1978 Parlt.	1979* Euro.	1981 Pres.	1981 Parlt.	1984* Euro.	1986* Parlt.
PS	5.1	20.7		24.7	23.5	28.3	37.5	24.2	32.8
			43.4+						
PCF	21.5	21.3		20.6	20.5	15.5	16.2	11.2	9.7
Combined Right	44.0	49.5	50.7	44.1	43.9	48.8	40.0	46.4 +11.1 (FN)	44.7 +9.9 (FN)

* Proportional Representation used; + No PCF Candidate - Party supports Mitterrand.

NB The columns do not total 100% as scores of smaller parties are omitted.

policies and at its performance when it returns to office if it wants to keep the support of these people.

In mid-1986 the PS had some 180,000 paid-up members, something of a drop from the 1981 peak of 210,000. 10 per cent were under 25 and only 20 per cent over 55. Geographically, the federations with most members are still the old ones, Nord/Pas-de-Calais and Bouches du Rhône still accounting for a quarter of the total. As with voters, however, there has been something of an evening-out of late across France, so that today there are very few terres de mission where the party does not possess a core of hardworking members.

Increasingly the membership of the PS is coming to resemble that of many social-democratic parties in Europe. (7) It may even be that some of its sociological features are more pronounced than in sister parties. To put it simply, the PS is dominated increasingly by the salaried middle-class. (8)

Over the years its recruitment of manual workers and lower white-collar workers has declined, to the advantage of middle-class professionals, often from the public sector and not infrequently teachers. The party's support can be understood as a series of concentric rings. If the outer ring (the electorate) is more or less a reflection of French social structure at large, then the ordinary members already show a sharp bias towards the salaried middle-class. As one moves to the level of office holders (in party and in sub-central government) the weight of the lower classes declines further, and by the time one reaches national office (in the party itself or as a deputy, senator or latterly a member of the government), the dominance of top public sector elites, often graduates of grandes écoles such as the Ecole Nationale d'Administration, is virtually complete. Significantly, though, many of these elites are themselves from more popular origins, which may help explain their commitment to the Left: to that extent the PS is quite a faithful reflection of the huge social change which has taken place since 1945 in France and which has provided unprecedented opportunities for upward social mobility.

Some 20 per cent of members are believed to be women - not too impressive a ratio in a party which has often been vocal on women's rights. But in practice the PS seems to have been less willing to give chances of office to women than the PCF, prompting an attempt to found a feminist faction in the seventies. Doubtless the patriarchal structures of Latin societies have foundations at least as deep as those of Northern Europe.

Somewhat surprisingly, some 47 per cent of members declare themselves to be Catholics (only 12 per cent practising regularly), as against 39 per cent a-religious. Despite the influx of Catholic activists from the sixties onwards, as the Church's attitude to democratic socialism softened (9), this is a high figure for a party for whom anticlericalism was long a pillar of its identity. In many federations relations were not always easy between the older generation of secularists and the enthusiastic Catholic incomers: they could vary from creative tension to virtual civil war, sometimes even inside party factions.

Local government. French socialism has a long municipal tradition, going back beyond 1905 even. It has been strongest in the North but also in places south of the Loire, where in towns like Marseille, the party seems to have taken a permanent grip on office (10). Much of this implantation was due not just to the administrative skills of socialist mayors or their charisma, but often, especially in the South, to the venerable Mediterranean practice of clientelism (jobs and services in direct return for votes). Since 1971 the PS has spread its control into a number of provincial towns with no previous Left tradition. Today the PS claims 3,212 mayors amongst the 36,000 in France. Of these, 2437 are in communes of less than 1,000, 375 in communes of 2,000 - 5,000, and 173 in those of 5,000 - 10,000. 211 officiate in towns of over 10,000 and 66 in those 227 towns of over 30,000 which are thought of as the major towns. Many of these latter are run by youngish mayors who had joined at Epinay and who in many cases won office in the 'pink wave' of 1977. Such people have often taken root in their cities and are now <u>notables</u> in their own right. Others have taken office in the big suburbs of towns, where services were underdeveloped and problems such as housing, immigration and unemployment high; they have shown how to make the most of local resources and thus made a political name for themselves. It is significant that in 1983, generally a bad year for the PS, most of the young victors of 1977 were returned against the national trend. They showed that the new generation of socialists could, radical discourse notwithstanding, run their towns efficiently and sometimes quite inventively. This was probably one of the major underlying factors in the party's 1981 victories. These municipal elites are clearly one of the PS's assets for the future, as they will doubtless continue to develop their local power bases by using the new powers devolved to local authorities. Some analysts indeed believe that the local government laws of the Mitterrand presidency were primarily put through as a means to give a share of power to such elites and the wider middle-class constituency which they typify.

At the 1985 cantonal elections (where <u>conseillers généraux</u> are elected to departmental assemblies) the PS had over 1040 councillors, nearly 600 of whom doubled as mayors (an elegant testimony to the tradition of <u>cumul des mandats</u> - see chapter 5). The party controlled 20 out of the 96 departmental assemblies in France, plus two in the overseas departments. Ironically the PS strength in this arena was strongest before 1981 when it was in opposition. Since achieving office, it has suffered locally as a result of the effects of its national policies. This means that it is mainly the Right which will be running local authorities with the new powers: and this is especially true of the new regions, for which the socialists had long campaigned. Elections to these authorities were held simultaneously with the parliamentary ones on 16 March 1986 and the PS ended with control of only 2 of the 22 mainland regions, (compared with 6 previously) plus 3 of the 4 overseas ones. Nevertheless with 30 per cent of the vote in these elections the PS still has a firm base in the regions and its turn will no doubt come.

The PS and the unions. Unlike many social-democratic parties the PS has never had a very close relationship to the French labour movement, despite the fact that French unions seem, if their statements of intent are taken at face value, to have a much more explicitly political approach than their British counterparts (12). When SFIO was founded the French unions were strongly tinged with the ideology of 'direct action' or revolutionary syndicalism. This held that workers should organise for power by their own efforts, particularly through the <u>syndicat</u> (union branch) which was seen as the natural form of working class expression. As such it made political parties, with their stress on elections and parliamentary work, redundant. The syndicalist myth died hard in France, surviving until after 1918. But

The Parti Socialiste Francais

by then when the labour movement was ready to think more about its relationship to political parties, there was a new party available, the PCF. Thanks to diligent work before 1939 and during the Resistance, the PCF had become dominant in the main union centre CGT (<u>Confédération générale du travail</u>) by 1945. So much so that the non-communists split off in 1947 to form FO (<u>Force ouvrière</u>); it was then too that the teachers left the CGT to form the autonomous FEN (<u>Fédération de l'Education nationale</u>). But there had also grown up another strand within the union movement, namely Catholic unionism in the shape of the CFTC. After 1945 this centre came increasingly into contact with marxism and other socialist ideologies and radicalised sharply: in 1964 it proclaimed its 'deconfessionalisation' and took the name CFDT (<u>Confédération française démocratique du travail</u>).

Today PS members can be found in all the major centres, with a predilection for the FEN and CFDT, but with a far from negligable presence in the two others. It is far from certain what benefits the party derives from this, or indeed what effect these activists have on their unions. CGT remains very close to the PCF, despite growing resentment at recent attempts to mobilise it as a PCF electoral agent; so PS activists inside the CGT are really bearing witness, as it were. FO remains deeply suspicious of all parties, prefering to bargain on wages and conditions and leave the politics to others. And FO can be a very awkward customer in defence of its members: despite its virulent anti-communism it joined CGT in opposition to the law on flexitime which was the last act of the Fabius government before March 1986. CFDT has a very rich fractional life, is generally open to 'new left' currents of thought, and has strong connections with the Rocardians: but it has never been a candidate for a special relationship with the PS. Both its left wing (typified by men like Pierre Héritier, who maintain in many ways an old-fashioned syndicalist approach) and its more pragmatic leadership (Edmond Maire) mistrust both the PS and any government. They see the union's job as to fight for a long term perspective of <u>autogestion</u> certainly, but in the short term to support workplace struggles while trying to adjust to a time of rapid technological and social change. In short, though most unions would probably prefer to see the PS in office than the Right, none of them is prepared to seek a close relationship with the party, such as exists in states like Austria or Sweden, where social-democracy has governed with success. Here economic policy tends to be run on 'neo-corporatist' lines, with the unions delivering their membership into prices-and-incomes bargains, in return for macroeconomic policies favourable to growth, welfare and employment.

The exception to this rule is the teachers' FEN, in which over a quarter of PS members are unionised. The preponderance of teachers in the intake of deputies in 1981 prompted commentators to refer to 'la République des professeurs'. Teachers have shared historically with the socialists a belief in Republican democracy (in the past, governments always recognised the key role of schools in spreading democratic values), a belief in the role of the state and in the value of secularism, (which teachers tend to espouse more militantly than the average member). FEN has also made considerable contributions to the PS from its vast empire of financial and other services which it offers members. (13) For many years the party HQ in rue Soferino was leased by FEN at a nominal fee. As a consequence of this close relationship, FEN has been able to pressure the government on one issue, namely the attempt to nationalise Catholic schools. It was the Savary Bill of 1984 which brought a million demonstrators out on to the street against what they saw as interference with fundamental rights: as a result Mitterrand simply withdrew the legislation. This crushing defeat for the socialists would never have happened but for the FEN's insistence, though it is probable that Mitterrand gave the FEN its head because he underestimated the opposition to secularist measures. Curiously, then, the one huge example of union pressure on government turned out to be a disaster for both; but it is the exception that confirms the rule, for in general the two go their separate ways.

This is not altogether a disadvantage for the PS. Not having a massive trade union membership with a major financial input and a vote of corresponding weight on the party executive means that PS leaders can elaborate policy without having to secure union assent. Certainly the divided labour movement, without party links and hence without the ability to impose neocorporatist modes of bargaining, was in a poor position to challenge the deflationary policies of 1982 and after. Thus in Lorraine and Northern France, socialist governments undertook with relatively little opposition a shakeout of the steel and mining industries much more brutal than that effected in the UK since 1980, which produced such long and bitter strikes.

Yet in terms of promoting working-class activists and more crucially of propagating socialist values and ideas among working people, the lack of a union base may prove a handicap over time. The advantages of not having one's arm twisted while making policy may be outweighed by lack of real lines of communication to the people who then have to live with those policies. But given the weight of tradition in the unions and the sort of people who now control the PS, there is little chance of this situation changing.

The PS in Office, 1981-6: Elites and Ideology

It may seem from the foregoing that such an articulate party with such a sophisticated organisation would be able to influence government strongly, especially given the comfortable majority enjoyed. The reality proved different, however, with many factors combining to ensure that the PS gave the post-1981 governments a much easier ride than say a British Labour Prime Minister would normally get from his party.

Immediately most of the ablest party elites found themselves in governmental or senior advisory posts. The new recruits, less numerous than had been hoped, seldom had the same quality or experience; hence the PS sometimes seemed at a loss for leadership. Soon also the government ran into problems with its economic strategy, and at the same time international tension mounted; with the Right now recovering and making electoral gains as of 1982, the need for solidarity became paramount. Most of all, the power-system of the Fifth Republic makes in any case for a very centralised type of decision-making; and this system was now in the hands of a master of divide-and-rule (as he had shown in running the PS through the seventies), who could usually find the right mix of stick and carrot to keep dissent within fairly narrow bounds. All of this meant that the party as such did not play a key role in the period 1981-6; but this is not to say that it remained unaffected by the experience of national office enjoyed by its top people.

Initially the PS had to get used to the idea of supporting a government as opposed to criticising the right and being a laboratory for exciting if imprecise ideas. Before 1981 all socialists knew that the executive in France was dominated by the

Table 1.4: Representation of PS fractions in government, 1981-6

	Mauroy I a	Mauroy I b	Mauroy II a	Mauroy II b	Mauroy III a	Mauroy III b	Fabius a	Fabius b	Score at Metz (c)
Mitterandists	26	66.6	23	63.8	25	71.4	27	75.0	47.9
Mauroyites	6	15.4	6	16.6	6	17.1	3	8.3	13.6
Rocardians	3	7.7	3	8.3	1	2.8	1	2.8	20.4
CERES	4	10.2	4	11.1	3	8.5	5	13.9	14.5

(a) = no. of members of that government belonging to that fraction.
(b) = percentage of total posts held by PS alone (i.e. excluding those held by PCF, MRG or non-party).
(c) = Since 1979 there have only been two tests of fractional strength at congress to break the show of unity. In 1983 a CERES motion scored 18.2% and a 'dissident' Rocardian one 5%. In 1985 Rocard's motion scored 28.5%.

President and that it had long ago cut parliament down to size: indeed the party liked to denounce this very fact. But few of them can have been totally surprised to see that Mitterrand continued presidential supremacy in decision-making. (14) He left the party in the care of the loyal Lionel Jospin, a man full of the robot-like reactions and superficial skills which characterise the lesser graduates of the grandes écoles: until 1984 the chief whip of the socialist deputies was the stern and faithful Pierre Joxe, who was then rewarded for his efforts by being made Minister of the Interior. Through these men, who usually breakfasted with the president once weekly, and through the managerial skills of Prime Ministers Mauroy and Fabius, the party in parliament and the country was kept on a firm rein. It is true that Mitterrand also took the precaution of composing his early governments of members from each fraction, more or less in proportion to the scores obtained at the Metz congress. (15) In this way one source of dissidence was muted, even if some of the leaders like Rocard were given virtual non-jobs, and even if the Mitterrandists' share of office rose as that of their rivals shrank (see Table 1.4). Wider pressures also made for unity. As socialist economic strategy was 'blown off course' from 1982 onwards and the opinion polls showed a decline in popularity, the Right stepped up its attacks. This sharply reduced the space for dissent. The incident which shows the limits to dissent occurred in 1982 - the Algerian generals' affair. Mitterrand was desperate to keep the votes of rapatriés (mainly white Algerians who had fled to France in 1962 when Algeria became independent), whose votes had been crucial to his victory in 1981. These votes had been won by offering the rapatriés more financial compensation than the Right was prepared to do, and Mitterrand's aim was to keep their vote for the 1983 municipal elections by offering another concession. This was not more money but an amnesty bill for the four generals who had organised the 1961 Algiers putsch against de Gaulle. These men, who had long been released from prison and who indeed might have been executed for treason, were to be given back their pension rights and full military status. This symbolic gesture was supposed to cleanse the wounds of the past. A number of socialist deputies, including even Joxe, objected to this excess of generosity and blocked the bill. Whereupon Mauroy promptly used article 49-iii which effectively turned the issue into a vote of confidence in the government, forcing deputies to line up for or against it. Of course the bill then passed and the notion of party superiority over government (an old SFIO shibboleth) stood in ruins. This is not to say that the PS was totally without influence over government legislation, simply that its scope is reduced, like that of all backbenchers or party activists in systems with strong majorities. Thus the party could boast of its input into legislation on tax and social security, unemployment benefit, flexitime and reimbursement of abortion costs. (16) This is fair enough, provided we remember that the influence of the party is confined to details and that there is no way it can get the government to budge on an issue that the latter sees as fundamental.

Fractional dissent was contained by the co-optation into government referred to above and by the fraction leaders' awareness that if they pushed demands too far they would be seen as weakening a beleaguered government. The most vocal critic was predictably CERES, which actually put down its own motion at the party's Bourg congress in 1983, soon after Chevènement had resigned from government in protest at the turn in economic policy. (17) The motion criticised the government's obsession with short-term financial orthodoxy, demanding reflation and a more interventionist line, including some protectionism. The point was thus made but not taken too far, as CERES accepted a synthèse, enabling the whole party to make a show of unity (and Chevènement to return to government).

To sum up, we may say that experience of government has made the PS more aware of the need for unity and for greater realism in its programmes and ideology. Recent texts talk very little of autogestion or a 'break with capitalism', or even of social class: if there is a 'buzzword' nowadays, it is probably the rather unsocialist one of 'modernisation', to which the PS devoted a one-day conference in 1984. The texts do stress that the party has learned a lot. Socialism now has to be concerned with investment and production, as well as redistribution; competiton and the market, home and abroad, have a role to play, alongside regulation and planning; the firm is the key unit in the economy, not simply a place where employers extract surplus value from workers. The PS projects itself as a party that will help France to modernise her economy and society in an increasingly competitive world; but unlike the Right, it will see that this is done with the maximum of justice and fairness. It is a more diffuse, less exciting message and it sounds more like that put out by the social-democratic parties of the North. Perhaps then the socialists are right to feel that in talking this way they are making the transition from being a party of opposition to a party of government. (18)

Conclusion
The PS has become a sort of catch-all party. As well as its historic working-class support, it now bites increasingly into that salaried middle-class that has become a major arbiter in Western politics. This it has done by providing these groups with opportunities for political expression and office, as well as by inventing a new discourse in which some old socialist fundamentals were cleverly blended with newer more liberal theories. To some extent the PS was helped by changes in social structure (decline of the agricultural population, and latterly of the old working class), in culture (decline of religion), and in politics (exhaustion of Gaullism and the self-mutilation of the PCF). But these conditions only created a chance, which still had to be seized. This the PS has done. It has shown it can elect a president and indeed any future Left president must have the support of the PS, for it now dominates the ground left of centre. It has sustained a government for five years which recovered well from early setbacks and whose record will in retrospect, as Chirac struggles with rising unemployment, seem quite fair. Indeed the 31 per cent in March 1986 is highly encouraging. The PS has also evolved a novel and vigorous form of internal democracy which does not harm its unity or efficacity.

Quite soon the PS may well return to national office, either through a presidential or parliamentary election, for by now the idea of <u>alternance</u> on Anglo-Saxon lines may well be taking root. It is not our task to say how or when this will occur for there are too many unknowns, not least the ability of Mitterrand to provoke a presidential election before the scheduled date of 1988. The main problem might well be the successor to this man, on whose charisma the PS has leaned heavily. The problem is a delicate one but it is hard to believe that it cannot be solved promptly and efficiently by this party which has managed its tensions so well over the years. If such a solution is found then the PS may well be heading for a period when it will be no longer part of Mitterrand's France, but a party of government in its own right.

Notes
1. H. Portelli, *Le Socialisme français tel qu'il est* (Presses Universitaires de France, Paris, 1980).
2. J. Mossuz, *Les Clubs et la politique en France* (Colin, Paris, 1970).
3. *Quinze Thèses sur l'autogestion* (PS, 1975); *Projet socialiste* (Flammarion, 1980). See also Mitterrand's campaign Manifesto *110 Propositions* (PS, 1981),
4. A. Lancelot, 'Le brise-lame: les elections du 16 mars 1986', *Projet* 199, 1986, pp.7-21.
5. Among Catholics, the party's vote held up better between 1981 and 1986 than it did among the a-religious.
6. G. Grunberg, 'Quelques éléments pour une sociologie du vote en 1986', *Intervention* 16, April-June 1986, pp.9-12.
7. W. Paterson and A. Thomas, *The Future of Social Democracy* (Oxford University Press, London, 1986).
8. P. Hardouin, 'Les caractéristiques sociologiques du PS', *Revue française de science politique*, vol. 28, April 1978, pp.220-56; R. Cayrol, 'Les militants du PS', *Projet* 88, September-October 1974, pp.929-40: 'L'univers politique des militants socialistes', *Revue française de science politique* vol. 25, 1975, pp.23-52; R. Cayrol and C. Ysmal, 'Les militants du PS - originalité et diversités', *Projet* 165, 1982, pp.572-86: H. Rey and F. Subileau, 'Les militants socialistes en 1985', *Projet* 198, 1986, pp.19-34.
9. H. Portelli, *Les Socialismes et le discours catholique* (Le Centurion, Paris, 1986).
10. D. Bleitrach, J. Lojkine et al., *Classe ouvrière et social democratie: Lille et Marseille* (Editions sociales, Paris, 1982); G. Rochu, *Marseille - les années Defferre* (Moreau, Paris, 1983).
11. M. Kesselman, 'The Tranquil Revolution at Clochmerle' in P. Cerny and M. Schain (eds), *Socialism, the State and Public Policy in France* (Pinter, London, 1985).
12. A. Bergounioux, 'Typologie des rapports syndicats-partis en Europe', *Pouvoirs* 26, 1983, pp.125-32.
13. V. Aubert et al., *La Forteresse*

enseignante (Fayard, Paris, 1986).
14. P. Avril, 'Le president, le parti et le groupe', <u>Pouvoirs</u> 21, 1981, pp.115-26.
15. Y. Roucaute, <u>Le PS</u> (Huisman, Paris, 1983).
16. <u>Le Poing et la Rose</u> (official PS magazine) no. 115, November 1983.
17. <u>ibid.</u> no. 104, September, 1983.
18. A. Pelinka, <u>The Social Democratic Parties in Europe</u> (Praeger, New York, 1983).

Official party texts do not (yet?) use the label 'social-democratic' in connection with the party. But one of its most orthodox members now appears to have no qualms about this (see Jean Poperen, <u>Le nouveau contrat socialiste</u>, Paris, Ramsay, 1985, p.144 ff.).

Further Reading
The most useful general works are D. Bell and B. Criddle <u>The French Socialist Party</u> (Oxford University Press, London, 1984), D. Bell and E. Shaw <u>The Left in France</u> (Sokesman, Nottingham, 1982) and N. Nugent and D. Lowe, <u>The Left in France</u> (Macmillan, London, 1981). P. Cerny and M. Schain, <u>Socialism, the State and Public Policy</u> (Frances Pinter, London, 1985) is useful on the work of the socialist government since 1981, and B. Criddle has a study of the PS in W. Paterson and A. Thomas, <u>The Future of Social Democracy</u> (Oxford University Press, London, 1986).

Of the works in French, the sharpest is H. Portelli, <u>Le Socialisme français tel qu'il est</u> (Presses Universitaires de France, Paris, 1980), which cuts through the party's ideological exaggerations. There is an informative account from a 'workerist' viewpoint in J. Kergoat, <u>Le PS</u> (Le Sycomore, 1983) and a briefer one, sympathetic to the socialist Left, Y. Roucaute, (<u>Huisman, Paris, 1983</u>).

For analysis of Left unity, see R.W. Johnson, <u>The Long March of the French Left</u> (Macmillan, London, 1981) and from a PS standpoint, R. Verdier, <u>PS-PC: une lutte pour l'entente</u> (Seghers, Paris, 1976). For a systematically anti-communist line see B. Lazic, <u>L'Echec permanent: l'alliance socialiste-communiste</u> (Laffont, Paris, 1978).

On party sociology, see P. Bacot, <u>Les Dirigeants du PS</u> (Presses Universitaires de Lyon, Lyon, 1978) which tries to play down the middle-class nature of the party, and a more recent study, which does not, M. Dagnaud and D. Mehl, <u>L'Elite rose</u> (Ramsay, Paris, 1982).

Party fractions are treated in M. Charzat et al., *Le CERES - un combat pour le socialisme* (Calmann-Levy, Paris, 1975) which is sympathetic to the PS Left, while a British study which investigates CERES in a wider context is D. Hanley, *Keeping Left? CERES and the French Socialist Party* (Manchester University Press, 1986). To understand something of Rocardism it is probably best to read P. Rosanvallon and P. Viveret, *Pour une nouvelle culture politique* (Seuil, Paris, 1977), or the fairly sympathetic H. Hamon and P. Rotman, *L'Effet Rocard* (Stock, Paris, 1980). A helpful study in English is B. Brown, *Socialism of a Different Kind* (Greenwood, New York, 1982).

Chapter Two

BROKEN DREAMS: ECONOMIC POLICY IN MITTERRAND'S FRANCE

Peter Holmes

The Inheritance
Before 1973 France was renowned for the pace and smoothness of her economic growth, and so the stagnation of recent years stands out more starkly than elsewhere. With the benefit of hindsight, the Giscard presidency appears as a transition period from one phase of economic development to a newer and more problematic phase, whose characteristics emerged fully during the Socialist period.

Unemployment began to rise sharply in the late 1960s and early 1970s, even before the first oil shock. Economic growth remained fast because of the high and rising rate of investment, as a percentage of national income. This capital-intensive development was costly, and even before 1973 the industrial sector of the economy was directly generating a remarkably small fraction of new jobs. When growth slumped the industrial sector became a source of additional unemployment rather than employment.

President Giscard was evidently uncertain how to respond to the post-1973 crisis. After a period of inaction, he authorised Premier Jacques Chirac to expand the economy in 1975, and promised a return to full employment by 1980 in the Seventh Plan covering 1975-80, despite forecasts showing the policies proposed could not ensure this. Then in 1976 Giscard replaced Chirac with Raymond Barre, who implemented a severe counter-inflationary programme, and denounced both interventionist industrial policies and the use of budget deficits to stimulate the economy. Drawing attention to German success, he argued that the economy had to be made more efficient to face international competition. Despite the free market rhetoric, Barre used state subsidies and state controls to achieve his aims, notably in continuing to promote industrial concentration and in subsidising huge government-backed export contracts in armaments, telecommunications etc. In this period the government also gave considerable help to the biggest French firms, who profited from the high levels of public investment in the late 1970s, notably in telecommunications and nuclear power, while private investment slumped.

Partly inspired by German policy, Barre tried to keep the franc strong and in 1978 France joined the European Monetary System, hoping that a fixed exchange rate would prevent French inflation from exceeding the German rate.

Economic performance in the late 1970s was mixed. Much as the more optimistic forecasts made in 1975-76 had predicted, GNP growth resumed to 3-4% pa over the whole period 1975-80, but was slowed down to almost zero in 1980-1. Unemployment rose from 400,000 in 1973 to 800,000 in 1975 and then reached 1.4 million in 1980. Inflation remained static between 1976 and 1978 but rose sharply again after the entry into the EMS under the influence of higher oil prices in 1979. With German inflation more tightly regulated, this boded ill for French competitiveness. Exports to OPEC had helped the balance of payments move back into surplus in 1979 but big deficits returned in 1980-81.

Table 2.1: Economic Performance 1974-81 (1)

	France	W Germany	UK
Unemployment % 1974	2.8	1.6	2.9
Unemployment % 1981	7.3	4.4	9.9
Increase over period 1974-81	4.5	2.8	7.0
Inflation average rises in consumer prices 1974-81 % p.a.	11.1	4.6	15.4
GDP/GNP growth (2) 1974-81 % p.a.	2.4	2.2	0.9
Balance of payments current account 1981 $bn	-4.7	-5.8	15.5

(1) Source: Federal Reserve Bank of St Louis <u>International Economic Conditions</u> and OECD <u>Economic Outlook</u>.
(2) Figures refer to average rates from 1974 (III) to 1981 (III).

The socialists thus inherited a difficult economic situation. The balance of payments was weak; inflation was over 10%. Perhaps the most serious element of the inheritance were high levels of indebtedness that private companies had built up during the late 1970s; much of this was to finance growth by merger rather than new investment and later on represented borrowing to cover losses.

Socialist Policies

The point of departure for the socialist programme for 1981 was the 1972 Common Programme agreed with the Communists. Though the Communists had formally denounced the pact, the radical vision it embodied remained in the style adopted by socialist spokesmen through the 1970s. François Mitterrand's personal manifesto, his '110 Propositions' explicitly referred back to the Common Programme in places. The capitalist economy was going to be transformed. Barre's pursuit of budgetary austerity and the logic of the international market were to be reversed. The economic crisis of the 1970s was occurring because capitalist policies had been applied: unemployment could and would be brought down. There was to be an expansionary fiscal policy, and national and social priorities were to override the dictates of profitability. More public money was to be spent on re-distribution and social welfare. Whilst there was to be a substantial increase in the government deficit, this was to be strictly contained; as much of the money to finance the new programme as possible would come from soaking the rich, who had allegedly been milking the state in the past. Mitterrand personally promised the nationalisation of nine key industrial groups, and the PS hoped to modernise social relations within industry as well as to provide a 'motor' for a new economic growth. Economic planning was to play a major role in the new economic system. Rising import penetration was to be stopped by a 'recapture of the home market'. While Mitterrand's proposition 11 called for 'strict enforcement of the Treaty of Rome', Proposition 20, somewhat remarkably, promised that the share of trade in Gross Domestic Product (GDP) would be reduced to 20 per cent by 1990, presumably through the use of domestic industrial policy rather than direct protectionism.

The party policy appeared in a variety of guises during the 1970s, much material appearing before the 1978 legislative elections. The main thrusts appear to have been developed from the Common Programme rather newly conceived for the 1980s. The reformists in the party were forced either to admit defeat or keep quiet, and it can be argued that the party came to office with a set of detailed blueprints of what it would like to do but, on finding these ambitions impossible, had no reserve plan to fall back on.

The socialist government inherited both an economic and a psychological legacy from the Barre era. High and rising unemployment was a major feature in the unpopularity of the outgoing regime, but the decision to fix the parity of the franc in 1978 was a poisoned pill for the socialists. The intervening period of higher inflation than in Germany had left French industry severely uncompetitive. The impact of the second oil shock and the deflationary policies pursued in most western countries were just beginning to have an impact. At a psychological level Barre's philosophy had clearly influenced the nature of the political debate. The idea of a strong franc was popular, and the socialists were convinced that they would gain credit by resisting devaluation as long and as strongly as possible. This appears to have been a sad misjudgement, politically and economically, given the inevitability of a parity change, especially if the economy was to be expanded. The socialists were committed to fiscal reflation, but from the outset they intended to make sure that the budget deficit did not become any larger than that of West Germany in relation to GNP. Some ministers and government advisers were wary of the financial constraints they were facing: in particular Michel Rocard advocated 'moderation', so too did Finance Minister Jacques Delors, albeit more discreetly.

It is very clear that the economic policy agenda in 1981 was determined by political criteria. Election pledges meant that antithesis had to come before synthesis. Mitterrand told his ministers that he was committed to an expansionary economic programme, and nationalisation as defined in his '110 Propositions'. Government advisers have subsequently acknowledged that arguments occurred about economic policy in the first weeks of the administration, but that the President insisted that his personal promises had to be adhered to. It can be argued that his programme had been drawn up with an eye not so much on the voters or the economy, but on the factions of the left, both within the PS and in its dealings with the Communists. To secure his hold on the PS, and marginalise Rocard, Mitterrand needed the backing of J-P Chevènement's left-wing CERES faction of the Party. He had to devise a radical-sounding economic programme, and encouraged members of his entourage such as Jacques Attali to express themselves in strong terms, while he himself spoke of 'breaking with capitalism'. The Socialist Party was also keen to outbid the Communists on the left. Though the communists had formally denounced their alliance, the PS felt obliged to ignore this in order to obtain communist votes.

It was thus politically expedient to pay homage to the style and even some of the substance of the Common Programme. With hindsight, Mitterrand's attachment to radical left-wing economics looks somewhat opportunistic.

If the newly elected President personally lacked economic expertise, he had access to a very large number of economic advisers, with administrative as well as academic expertise. Many Socialist (and Communist) economic experts had worked for many years within the civil service, and did not lack experience of the realities of government. Indeed, in the economic policy sphere as elsewhere the new government continued the old practice of making political appointments from the traditional elite of civil servants and graduates of the 'Grandes Ecoles'. This applied as much to Ministerial appointments as to nominations to the Boards of newly nationalised firms.

Government Policy, 1981-83
The economic strategy of the Socialist government fell into two phases - before and after March 1983. On arriving in office the Socialists announced a package of economic measures, increasing public spending, improving welfare benefits and workers' rights. The nationalisation programme was decided in September. A modest boost to public spending was to increase purchasing power through higher government borrowing. Barre had had a slight budget surplus in 1980, and the socialists announced that they would relax this tight policy, although not by very much. Even in 1981 the intention was to reassure the financial community by keeping the budget deficit to a lower proportion of GDP than in Germany, a target which was in fact met. It is estimated that the largest part of the increase in government borrowing between 1980 and 1982 was due to the automatic consequences of the recession, (higher welfare spending, lower tax receipts) rather than deliberate

37

policy changes. The government directly created new jobs in the public sector, estimated at around 140,000 by 1983. The impact of the initial measures on private sector employment was ambiguous however. The most striking measure was to very substantially increase the statutory minimum wage, the SMIC. By increasing the purchasing power of the less well-off this helped promote a consumer spending boom, but it had negative effects on employment. By raising the cost of labour it discouraged employment, particularly of the less-skilled who were most affected by the SMIC. It also reduced profitability and discouraged investment, above all job-creating investment.

The rise in welfare payments also had ambiguous effects on employment. There was an important redistribution to recipients, above all the unemployed, but the method of financing the French social security system required increases in contribution rates, so that the initial boost to purchasing power was offset by a rise in industrial costs and a levy on the incomes of those in work. Finance Minister Jacques Delors wished to see an emphasis placed on social policy combined with the maximum possible financial prudence.

One of the most ambitious devices that the government hoped to use to raise employment, namely work-sharing, hardly involved public spending at all. There had been considerable debate in the 1970s over the effectiveness of shorter working hours, longer holidays, and early retirement as ways to reduce measured unemployment. The issue had been symbolic for the Left since the Popular Front had given three weeks paid holiday in 1936. Most analysts concluded that shorter hours and longer holidays had not had the desired effect in 1936, but in 1981 the debate was alive again. The employers argued that shorter hours (like extra holidays or early retirement) would raise unit labour costs and so actually reduce total hours worked. The unions and a number of socialist academics argued that shared suffering would be less suffering, but they also argued that new work arrangements could be devised which would allow shorter hours with no loss of productivity. President Mitterrand determined that the normal working week should be reduced by law from 40 to 39 hours, but a progressive reduction to 35 hours was largely left to negotiation between workers and employers.

Thus the thrust of the initial wave of macro-economic measures ended up bringing on a modest degree of redistribution and an even more modest expansion of the economy. A similar pattern occurred in the field of industrial policy. Despite talk of comprehensive planning and industrial policy, it rapidly became clear that apart from the rescue of sectors in crisis, the main element in socialist strategy was the nationalisation programme.

This had both political and economic aims. There had been intense debate between the socialists and the communists in the 1970s about how many firms to take over, and whether to buy 100 per cent of the shares and all the subsidiaries of conglomerates. Nationalising the main industrial and banking groups in the nation was intended to shift the balance of social and political power within France, as well as to permit better control of investment and employment. PS economists argued that the big private firms had not invested enough in the 1970s but had taken a short-term view of the economic crisis thereby aggravating the situation. If shareholders would not invest, the state would have to do so, but it must have control of where the money went. At the same time, workers rights were to be improved. The model was Renault which, since the war, had pursued a progressive and expansionary policy without regard to short-term profitability criteria. Some of Renault's methods had been copied by the private sector, but the Socialists accused French employers of unnecessarily sacrificing jobs in the 1970s, by investing in takeovers and overseas plants. There was also considerable talk not merely of improving the quality of long-term corporate planning within state enterprises, but also of coordinating their investment programmes through the National Plan and a National Investment Bank.

In 1981-2, however, battle raged not so much on what was to be done with the enlarged state sector, but about the mechanisms of takeover, each approach having different symbolic meaning. The Communists wanted a 100% nationalisation of all the major private groups and all their subsidiaries. Socialist moderates including Jacques Delors and Michel Rocard wanted a 51% takeover of a smaller number of parent companies only. Mitterrand decided that there should be a 100% takeover by law of the firms he had itemised in his presidential manifesto, but with parent firms only being bought. The legislation covered all privately owned French banks, and the industrial groups Thomson, Péchiney, CGE (Compagnie Général d'Electricité), Rhone-Poulenc, and St-Gobain. In addition certain other firms were to be partially or wholly taken over by negotiation, including Matra's armaments activities, Dassault, and the loss-making CGCT - ITT's last telecommunications subsidiary in France, (which the Chirac government later decided to resell to a foreign firm).

The cost of the nationalisation programme which was determined after a long legal battle by the Conseil Constitutionnel, appeared excessive at the time, at around 40bn FF (about £4bn), given the poor financial state of the industrial firms and even some of the banks taken over. Subsequent rises in stock market values make the 1982 purchases seem a very profitable investment.

The industrial nationalisations had three major consequences for the firms: changes were made in top management, the firms were told to draw up new corporate plans which were to be under-written by a 'planning contract' with the state, and new arrangements were introduced for better consultation with the work-force. Martin Rhodes analyses the law on 'workers' democracy in public-sector companies' in chapter 3; here it suffices to observe that union representatives on the boards (the <u>Conseils d'Administration</u>) of the firms found that their participation provided much better information about the operations of the firm, but that the boards normally acted only to confirm decisions taken by the chair and his/her staff.

French company law concentrates executive authority in the hands of the Président-Directeur-Général (chair and chief executive, or 'PDG'.) Most PDGs were in fact asked to remain or were replaced by their natural internal successors. Mitterrand followed the advice of his Industry Minister Pierre Dreyfus, the former boss of Renault, who argued for maximum autonomy for the new chairs, with respect to both the company boards and the government. This autonomy was assisted by making the Industry Minister the official interlocutor of the firms. This ministry and its minister normally have a low status in the administrative hierarchy, and usually defer to industrialists' views. When there were conflicts between Dreyfus's successor as Industry Minister, Jean-Pierre Chevènement, and the public enterprise bosses, the Elysée backed the latter and Chevènement resigned in March 1983. In retrospect the relationship between state and firms appears quite clearly pre-ordained: even the "contrats de plan" were designed to uphold managerial autonomy, not to oblige firms to conform to the National Plan. The government and the firms ensured that a minimum of formal engagements was undertaken by each side; the form of the contract ensured that, with the obvious exception of the Finance Ministry, only the Industry Ministry was allowed to put pressure on firms. The government wanted the rather ramshackle conglomerate groups that had grown up in the 1970s to draw up coherent corporate strategies, but did not want the responsibility of dictating such strategies itself. As the economic crisis worsened the role of the Finance Ministry increased, but it appears that, contrary to much conventional wisdom, the Finance Ministry was mainly interested in ending the subsidies to loss making firms and not in dictating their strategies. In 1982 the government indicated its willingness to pay for losses during the period of restructuring, but after 1985 the firms had to start making profits: if they did so the management could more or less do what it wanted, but otherwise the PDG would be sacked.

The system of state capitalism that eventually emerged from the industrial nationalisations made sense, but in the first year or so the government was giving somewhat conflicting signals to the firms: promises of managerial autonomy and unrestrictive planning agreements, but pressures to create jobs. The new PDGs, especially those who appeared to be left-wing, therefore adopted an ostentatiously tough management style in order to convince their own staff that they would not be pushed around by the unions or the government. It is evident that Industry Minister Chevènement did not understand the limitations of the role assigned to him.

The Banks. The industrial takeovers took the share of the public sector from 8 per cent to 23 per cent of the industrial sector (excluding energy), and the bank nationalisations took the public sector share of bank deposits from 62 per cent to 92 per cent. Socialist writers in the 1970s had made much of the links between industry and banks, especially the Suez and Paribas groups, which were seen as creating powerful networks of economic social influence. The PS wanted the state to be able to apply selective credit control more effectively than before, preferably linked to the Plan. A National Investment Bank (Banque Nationale de l'Investissement) was to be established, which would be more ready to risk its funds directly for new industrial investment. The existing state-owned banks had enjoyed considerable autonomy and there was talk of the need for their 're-nationalisation'.

Before 1981, the French banking system was highly regulated by the state, but in ways that were so complex and self-contradictory that the state had very little effective leverage. Different classes of banks had a different status, allowing them to accept certain types of deposits and make certain types of loans; some paid tax, while others did not. State control of the credit system prevented competition among the banks, which were widely believed, especially on the Left, to be overstaffed and inefficient. The regulatory apparatus seems to have served the state as an instrument for monetary policy much more than for the control of industrial investment.

The state had owned most of the deposit banks since 1945, notably BNP, Crédit Lyonnais and Société Générale, accounting for nearly two thirds of bank deposits. They typically made loans to industry on a very short-term basis and sought to avoid real industrial risk. Even the big investment banks, Suez and Paribas, increasingly made money through commissions on financial transactions rather than by placing their own money as risk capital. There was an argument however that the two major investment banks, the Paribas group and the Suez group, had played an important role, similar to UK merchant banks, in guiding the merger boom of the 1960s and 1970s, and that control of one or both was a prerequisite for a successful industrial policy. The argument for nationalising the small private deposit banks was less obvious.

Indeed, the government opted for 'rationalisation' of the banks along competitive lines, rather than seeking to make the banks an instrument of industrial policy. There were more personnel changes in the banks than in the industrial firms taken over. The aim was to restructure the system from a technical point of view. Some of the banks were losing money and were merged with others, and staffing was squeezed. Automation was promoted; the only strong link with industrial policy was the socialist government's enthusiasm to use its own banks as a test-bed for French-produced electronic payments systems. The diversity of status was tidied up. The Caissses d'Epargne (similar to Trustee Savings Banks) were encouraged to provide a full range of banking services. Government officials argued that complete nationalisation was the only way to handle the transition problems of making modest steps towards a more competitive deregulated banking system, which was reinforced by the socialist government's moves to replace quantitative credit controls by interest rate mechanisms.

Circumstances seem to have obliged the government to move in this direction, certainly once it had committed itself to managerial autonomy for the state industrial sector. It can be argued that the government had little option but to make its banking reforms along the lines eventually chosen, crisis or no crisis. Many studies were carried out in 1981-2 within the administration which showed the futility of the system of subsidised loans and grants to industry; it had become a jungle from which the wily firm could profit enormously, but from which the government could extract very little power. A very high proportion of all bank loans were subsidised more or less automatically, and so there was little selectivity.

Neither politicians nor civil servants ever had the ability to do more than say no to particular funding requests. All the evidence suggests that the expertise and interests of the Finance Ministry lie in financial matters not commercial or technical matters, and that in fact the Trésor division of the Finance Ministry cared above all about short-term financial management. (1)

The government had enough on its hands coping with its relationship with newly nationalised industrial firms; it simply did not have the resources and expertise to try and direct the borrowing and lending of the rest of the economy in detail, and it rapidly realised this. Nationalisation is reported to have made almost no difference to the workings of the Paribas group. The government made one major effort to force the banks to put money into the <u>Fonds Industriel de Modernisation</u> (FIM) which would be used to promote industrial investment, a small sop to the supporters of the <u>Banque Nationale de l'Investissement</u>. The banks were able to go to the Finance Ministry and point out that at a time when France was in financial difficulties, the international credit rating of the national banks (eg their AAA status on the New York market) was crucial to the economy, and they could only keep this if the state took its hands off them. It did so, and their credit rating stayed high, proof at least that US financial analysts believe that nationalisation did not cause French state-owned banks to make uncommercial loans at the behest of the state.

It would be misleading to write-off the bank

43

nationalisation as a non-event, but the reforms undertaken were long-overdue, and it is very probable that without nationalisation they would have been resisted by the well-entrenched banking establishment. The government probably made more changes to the top management of the banks than to the industrial firms, because the Finance Ministry felt its officials knew how to run banks but not factories. It was also a necessary condition for undermining the cosy 'corporatism' of banking circles.

In retrospect a logic emerges for the nationalisation programme. The state was revitalising capitalism which was in a financial mess. A right-wing government would probably have had to bail out some of the same firms and even some of the weaker banks. In many ways the socialists' operation was a striking success, but they caused considerable confusion by declarations at the start that socialism was being introduced!

Planning. Planning played a major part in Socialist mythology before 1981; radicals saw coordinated state dirigisme as a way of pulling the economy up by its bootstraps, while moderates like Rocard were attracted to the idea of using 'contractual planning' to negotiate and to implement consensual policies. By appointing his rival Michel Rocard as Minister for Planning, Mitterrand signalled his disdain for centralised planning, but he was evidently unwilling to give his erstwhile political rival much liberty to develop the contractual approach. Hitherto the Planning Commissariat had been headed only by a Commissioner who reported directly to the Premier; some saw the appointment of a senior minister as a way of renewing the planning system, while others saw it as a way of keeping Rocard quiet.

In Autumn 1981 Rocard drew up an Interim Plan for 1982-3, which was essentially a restatement of the government's current programme. At the same time he set about redesigning the machinery of planning with three aims in mind. He widened the consultative basis; he tried to create procedures that would give the planning system a continuing role in the implementation and monitoring of the plan during the execution, as well as the elaboration, phase; and he designed a mechanism under which regional authorities would sign planning contracts with the central government as an element in the decentralisation programme. The idea of planning by consultation, negotiation and contract has enormous potential, but Rocard's peripheral political position undermined his influence. Critics have also noted that he spent more effort on the procedures of planning than in systematically analysing what planning could do in a market economy. Rocard seems to have fallen into the trap of supposing that what had gone wrong with planning in the past was that the right mechanism had not been devised; for him this was consultation and contractualisation, while the <u>dirigistes</u> in the Socialist Party would have recommended constraint and regulation. The facts of life in an open economy subject to tremendous uncertainty are that it is very difficult to establish economic strategies that can be adhered to through thick and thin. The Finance Ministry has always argued that uncertainty requires the maximum freedom of manoeuvre. The appropriate use of planning in these circumstances may well be best as a focus for discussion and reflection over the medium term implications of what is being done now and what risks one faces if one's plans go wrong. (2) Contingency planning or strategic planning is valuable: when the socialists found their initial strategy did not work they were forced to operate from day-to-day. In mid-1983, the complex planning procedure designed by Rocard produced a IXth Plan for 1984-88 at the very moment that deflationary policies were replacing the pursuit of growth as the government's strategy. As a result the IXth Plan read very much like Barre's abandoned VIIIth Plan for 1980-85. The central themes were that the government could not control growth, and that inflation had to be reduced and the balance of payments improved before any economic expansion was possible. As a policy for 1983-86, this worked quite well, but as a plan two essential elements were missing: there was no serious attention to ensure that once financial equilibrium had been restored, long-term growth would be resumed, and the planning system did not play any specific role in securing broad popular consent for the strategy adopted. No attempt was made to convince people that the strategy adopted was a 'Plan of the Nation' as opposed to the 'Plan of the Government' as had been the case in the early years; perhaps this was inevitable.

The U-Turn
Many observers see the switch to deflationary policies in 1983 as not so much a reversal of the 1981-83 strategy as its inevitable outcome,

anticipated all along by some members of the government. Another view is that if the franc had been devalued substantially in 1981, and an incomes policy introduced, the expansion might have been sustainable.

The immediate cause of the reversal of apparent direction was in the balance of payments. The rather modest boost to demand of 1981 had occurred when the rest of the world economy was sliding into recession. Two things stand out in economic forecasts published in the summer of 1981. First, as the government later claimed, no-one in mid-1981 anticipated the severity of the world recession in 1982; but secondly, forecasts showed that in 1982, even without the world recession, the French balance of payments was liable to weaken markedly. In any event, France would have had to take measures to cure the deficit or to cover it by borrowing heavily, or both. French inflation had exceeded that in Germany since the start of the EMS so the franc was overvalued; this and the weakness of the French supply side caused by years of low investment, meant that when the government boosted demand, people bought from abroad.

The restrictive measures taken in the summer of 1982 served essentially to contain further increases in the government deficit by moderating expenditure growth. The temporary wage and price freeze also served to dampen inflationary expectations. The deflationary impact was probably slightly less than it looked at the time. There was also a small (6.5 per cent) devaluation within the EMS. The most important measures actually concerned the Social Security system which was to be brought back to balance by higher contributions (from workers) and lower benefits.

The faltering economic recovery, and the accompanying worsening of the balance of payments continued until early 1983. Indeed by late 1982 unemployment had been stabilised and employment had begun to rise again: the original reflation had succeeded in its main aim, but at the price of a major deficit. This occurred as major international financial crisis was brewing due to Mexico's inability to repay its debts. The French government was determined to avoid a French debt crisis but also to keep within the rules of the European Monetary System and to avoid what it saw as the stigma of a third devaluation, or at the very least it wanted to be seen to have resisted a devaluation as long as possible. Government experts argued that technical factors meant that a devaluation would not succeed:

it would worsen the balance of payments by raising the franc cost of oil (whose price was set in dollars), and via indexation it would relaunch inflation. Devaluation, it was argued, would require an intensification of the deflation measures.

But as things got worse in late 1982, Finance Ministry officials recognised that they were doing no more than postponing the evil day of the third devaluation. The long drawn out foreign exchange crisis probably caused the maximum of political embarrassment and economic cost. In particular the decision to defend the exchange rate within the EMS involved borrowing more and more from partner countries, notably West Germany which thus became able to dictate French exchange rate policy. Within the EMS France could not devalue without her partners' consent, but she could not leave the EMS either because she would then have been legally obliged to repay at once the credits obtained from West Germany, which the Finance Ministry maintained was impossible. Mitterrand rejected Industry Minister Chevènement's plan for France to leave the EMS and impose import controls, and in March 1983 the Germans agreed to a substantial, and ultimately successful, devaluation of the franc. Some observers argue that before this date, the public would not have been ready to accept the austerity programme, including an incomes policy imposed on the public sector, that was necessary to make the devaluation work.

After 1983 government policy became quite single-minded. The overwhelming priorities were the rapid curing of the balance of payments deficit, the reduction of inflation and the 'modernisation' of the economy. The latter term meant two things. Public enterprises were told to get back into the black by 1985, at whatever cost to employment, and signals were clearly given that when private industry got into difficulty it should not expect further costly 'restructuring plans'. The mood turned sharply against industrial subsidies. Pre-determined cash-limits or 'capital allocations' were agreed for the state-owned firms, and when Renault failed to respect these, its head was unceremoniously dismissed. On the other hand the government kept up its declared interest in the positive aspects of modernisation. Support for electronics, was maintained, though on a reduced scale.

Monetary policy was tightened, and the government imposed a pay policy on the public sector which also affected the private sector. The

47

government was absolutely insistent on the need to keep the budget deficit to 3% of GDP, and the President personally ordered a cut in taxation to be matched by a cut in spending.

However, the government also put a lot of effort into job-creation schemes and into retraining. The economic policies of Mitterrand after 1983 resembled 'Thatcherism with a human face'. A better way of putting it would be to say that the socialists were implementing Barre's policy of the social market economy. One leading member of the team which drafted the nationalisation law claimed that the rationalisation of state firms was 'dictated by the market', but that nationalisation had permitted the 'necessary social measures'. (3)

The socialists were recognising that much state intervention in the economy was actually converting firms into agencies for collecting subsidies. The 1970s had seen economic activity in France supported by a series of 'Grands Projets', the nuclear programme, the Train Grande Vitesse (High Speed Train), and the modernisation of the telephone network. All these had naturally run their course by the early 1980s, and the socialists saw that, unless they put in place a second wave of such schemes, or opted for a fully planned economy, they would have to be responsible for pushing firms towards the market place and away from the state.

In effect, after its phase of rhetoric, the socialist government came to see itself as the necessary saviour of capitalism. By a quirk of history or sociology, France has a capitalist economy in which capitalists themselves play a minor role. The stock market is small, and despite the wave of mergers in the 1960s and seventies there were relatively few Anglo-American style managerially controlled joint-stock corporations. In the late 1970s the leading firms were predominantly state-owned, family controlled, or multinationals. (4) The capital market exercised very little discipline over them. It fell to the government to act as a kind of 'take-over raider of last resort' to shake up French industry and banking when the private sector failed to do so.

An Evaluation
The argument developed here is that the socialist government was more or less destined by the situation of the French economy and the choices it made at the outset to act as it eventually did. But how well did

it perform its role?

The actual evolution of the economy over the period is quite straightforward. Economic growth was very briefly accelerated in 1981-2, but by rather a modest amount. After deflationary policies were introduced, GDP continued to edge upwards. France never had a drastic fall in GDP as did the UK. Industrial production stayed fairly flat throughout the period. The balance of payments which became so bad in 1982 improved very sharply, being more or less in balance in 1985, so that the falls in oil prices were likely to produce big surpluses in 1986 and 1987. Inflation peaked at 15 per cent in 1982 but subsequently came down steadily, so that in the year to March 1986 it was 3 per cent (against 4 per cent in the UK). The record on unemployment was of course bleak, but at 10 per cent of the workforce France had less unemployed than the UK's 13 per cent and the EEC average of 12 per cent in 1985 (using OECD standardised data).

In order to make a proper evaluation of economic performance, however, one has to compare actual outcomes with something else: with the original hopes or expectations, with past trends, or with performance elsewhere. Even more complex analysis is needed before one may conclude how far a relatively good or bad economic performance was actually due to government policy in the period.

Judged by pre-electoral promises, the socialist record was a disaster. It did not break with capitalism. Nor did it even reduce unemployment, (though it did stabilise the increase in the first two years as promised). However, judged by the more modest standards of comparison with other governments, the socialist record does not look so bad. The French economy achieved a striking reduction in inflation and an improvement in the balance of payments at a low cost in terms of higher unemployment, relative to the past trends of the French economy and to the experience of other countries in the early 1980s.

In particular, the rise in unemployment that occurred in 1981-5 was much less than would have been expected given the fall in growth. Forecasts made for the French Senate in 1980 for the VIIIth Plan predicted a 2.6 per cent per annum growth rate between 1980 and 1985, compared with the actual figure of 1.1 per cent. However, unemployment rose by only a little more than was forecast, up 930,000 against an estimated 755,000; more strikingly, the fall in employment was almost identical to the 1980

Table 2.2: Economic Performance 1981-85 (1)

	France	W Germany	UK
Unemployment % 1981	7.3	4.4	9.9
Unemployment % 1985	10.1	8.6	13.2
Increase over period 1981-85	2.8	3.8	3.3
Inflation average rises in consumer prices 1981-5 % p.a.	8.4	3.0	5.9
GDP/GNP growth (2) 1981-5 % p.a.	1.4	1.7	2.6
Balance of payments current account 1985 $ bn	0.3	13.1	3.8

(1) Source: Federal Reserve Bank of St Louis <u>International Economic Conditions</u> and OECD <u>Economic Outlook</u>.
(2) Figures refer to average rates from 1981 (III) to 1985 (III).

forecasts (down 500,000 against a forecast of 470,000). Thus the economy suffered from growth at half the predicted rate, but experienced relatively little additional unemployment over and above the (admittedly large) increase that had been anticipated on the assumption that growth had been kept up. (5)

If, like most French economic analysts, we take as given that France was condemned to slow growth by the slower growth in the 1980s of the world economy, France seems to have handled the consequential adjustment well. The reduction of inflation to 5% in 1985 was achieved at a much lower cost in terms of unemployment than any similar experience elsewhere, and French GDP never fell in any year. It is true that if 1980 is taken as a base, British economic growth in the 1980s has been faster than French, but this is due to a 'catching up' after a big fall in output in Britain after 1979. Sachs and Wyplosz have estimated a 'sacrifice ratio' for a number of economies in the 1970s. (6) This is the ratio of the 'cumulative percentage increase in unemployment' to the fall in inflation over the period since 1981. This unemployment index is a rather complex figure designed to capture not only how much unemployment rose over the period, but when during the period it rose. On this basis, France has a 'sacrifice ratio' of 2.1 against 4.0 for the UK and 10.9 for West

Germany, which can be read as saying that the cost of reducing inflation in France was half what it was in the UK. More generally, the reduction in inflation in France has been achieved without the total sacrificing of social policy: vital areas of public spending such as education were maintained.

Business confidence has also been maintained. The worst possible outcome for a socialist government is when capitalists are so fearful of the future that they refuse to invest unless given even more favorable business conditions than they would expect from a right-wing government. It is indeed true that private investment rose less than might have been expected from improved business profitability. There was an enormous rise in the Paris Bourse after 1983, and profits also went up sharply, but investment did not. The reason seems to be the very heavy burden of past debt incurred by companies and the high rates of interest they were paying on it. Firms prefer to pay off debt rather than to invest. This was already a problem in the 1970s, and in fact the total amount of private investment in the economy in 1980-85 was actually greater than in the preceding five years. (7) But it was largely devoted to cost reduction and labour-saving, not to increasing capacity for new jobs. Time and again we come back to two central problems, which the socialists did not create, but which they did not solve. If French industry became used to expecting fast growth in 1945-73, it seems that after the faltering recovery of 1976-79, it has come to expect slow growth.

How far can the partial success be attributed to the skilfulness of government policy? There can be little doubt that the socialists made adjustment easier by convincing the population after 1983 that austerity was necessary and undertaking measures to mitigate the worst political, if not economic, damage in hard-hit regions. Muet and Fonteneau argue that the big successes of the Left lay in their labour market policies, of early retirement etc, and they suggest that more imaginative use of reductions in working hours could have been made. Above all, they argue that the ability of the government to achieve a social consensus for an implicit incomes policy following the 1982 freeze was crucial. (8) The willingness of the work-force to give up the automatic link between past inflation and current salary claims was needed to break the wage-price spiral. In essence the socialist government had moved a long way towards securing political acceptance of a genuine 'social market economy', in which the

51

necessary economic changes dictated by market forces are not discouraged, but the losers are given social and financial assistance to adjust.

Table 2.3: Measures of Success of Mitterrand Policies

(a) Sachs and Wyplosz (1): The cost of reducing inflation 1981-85

	France	W Germany	UK
Cumulative extra unemployment	12.1	20.8	27.2
Reduction in inflation	5.8	1.9	6.8
"Sacrifice ratio"	2.1	10.9	4.0

(Sacrifice ratio = cumulative extra unemployment / reduction in inflation)

(b) Muet and Fonteneau (2): the impact of policy 1981-83

Cumulative change with respect to trend by 1983

GNP	1.7%
Retail Prices	1.1%
Unemployment	-171,000
Balance of Trade	-36 bn FF

(c) Senate (3): The French Economy 1980-85

	Average GDP growth % p.a.	Increase in Unemployment	Export/import ratio 1985
1980 Prediction	2.6	755,000	100.0
1980 Prediction adjusted for slower world economic growth	1.2	1,040,000	n.a.
Actual	1.1	930,000	99.1

(1) Source: Sachs and Wyplosz (1986)
(2) Source: Fonteneau and Muet (1985)
(3) Source: Senate (1986)

However even within this frame of reference, there are sound criticisms to be made. The left never seemed to have any kind of long-term vision of where it was going: the headlong rush into expansion did not make allowance for the kinds of problems that could arise; and the later deflation was essentially a short-term operation, for there was no mechanism for ensuring that once industrial profits recovered they would be translated into new investment. (In fact the recovery did occur, but France was still waiting for the new investment at the end of 1986). The socialists had no long-term plan or any other means of righting this deep-seated problem. Nor, despite their U-turn did they manage to tackle the problem of labour costs which comes up so regularly; as in some other EEC countries, the method of financing the social security system in France seems to be a particular discouragement to expansion even when there is a modest growth of demand. The Socialists could not escape the dilemma of how to make the labour market more 'flexible' without undermining long fought-for workers' rights.

One could argue that the very success that the socialists achieved in modifying expectations after 1983 suggests that they could have done more up to that date. It must remain a matter of speculation whether the socialists could have convinced the electorate in 1981 that a big devaluation was needed together with the end of wage indexation. Most government officials say 'no'; the 1981-83 spending spree was needed to teach the population a lesson.

If this analysis is correct it follows that the alternative of even more radical policies at the start was also ruled out. It seems very unlikely that the French working population was ready to accept an intensified degree of state control and regulation of the economy implied by a full-blown socialist experiment, as the low and declining support for the communists indicates. In my view, if policies involving massive import restrictions and forced increases in investment can succeed at all, they can only do so if those already in work are willing to accept considerable economic sacrifices in the short-run to enable jobs to be created for the unemployed. The French balance of payments was in difficulty in 1981: a rapid reduction in imports is inevitably painful, and there were no buoyant export markets. The only alternative was to adjust gradually, borrowing internationally in the meantime. The socialists were always wholly committed to French membership of the EEC and all that implies: policies inconsistent with that were simply not on the agenda.

I would argue that given the political and economic constraints it was under, the government had no option but to engage in what in retrospect can be seen as fairly radical capitalist reforms. In some ways the statist model of economic development that had served France well since 1945 lost its impetus in the early 1980s; there were no more grands projets left to implement. It fell to the Left to create a new consensus in France over the role of market forces and 'modernisation'. However, the socialists might have been able to go further in pursuing social objectives if they had better used the enthusiasm for change in 1981. Their successes came from their ability to muster a sense of social solidarity out of the economic crisis. If the problems of the economy had been announced openly at the outset, the government might have been able to use the leverage created by its initial popularity and legitimacy. What may well have proved fatal for the government was to have adopted the economic policies of Rocard and Delors, whilst gradually marginalising the two ministers who were most admired by public opinion. The combination of austere economic policies and progressive social policies advocated by Delors appeared as an opportunistic manoeuvre when applied under Prime Minister Fabius after 1984. The electorate seemed to accept the inevitability of what the government was doing, but after the earlier commitment to a different rhetoric, they doubted if the socialists were the right people to carry out the policies. Paradoxically, while the socialists were trying to create an image of managerial pragmatism, the right was becoming explicitly ideological and proclaiming its devotion to 'liberalism'. It is not yet clear whether the abandonment of so many dreams that occurred in 1981-86 will lead to the establishment of a new centrist consensus. It may well be that the apparent discrediting of the socialist alternative has actually paved the way for a social transformation by the right. Unless Chirac too is tripped up, as he may well be, by unseemly haste, the permanent legacy of the socialist government could prove to be a hitherto unimaginable wave of privatisation and de-regulation.

Notes
1. This point is made forcefully by R. Fossaert in La Nationalisation des Chrysanthèmes, Seuil, 1985.
2. See. S. Estrin and Holmes, French Planning in Theory and Practice, George Allen and Unwin, 1983.
3. Interview with the author.

4. J-P Gilly and F. Morin, Les Groupes Industriels en France, Documentation Française, 1981.
5. Sénat Français, (Service des Etudes Economiques), 'Retour sur une projection à l'horizon 1985 établie en 1980,' unpublished, March 1986.
6. J. Sachs and C. Wyplosz, 'The economic consequences of President Mitterrand', in Economic Policy, No. 2, 1986.
7. Ibid.
8. A. Fonteneau and P-A Muet La Gauche Face à la Crise, FNSP, 1985.

Further Reading
For an 'official' view of major elements in the government's policy, see Cahiers Francais no. 214, Les Nationalisations Industrielles et Bancaires, 1984, and for a standard reference book, see H. Machin and V. Wright, Economic Policy and Policy-making under the Mitterrand Presidency 1981-1984, Frances Pinter, 1985. This work also contains a chapter by Fonteneau and Muet which summarises their book. For longer term analyses, see S. Estrin and Holmes, French Planning in Theory and Practice, George Allen and Unwin, 1983 and P. Hall Governing the Economy Polity Press, 1986, which also provides an Anglo-French comparative study.

The following partisan sources are also useful. A. Cotta Les Cinq Erreurs, Olivier Orban, 1985 is a 'Barriste' critique of PS policy, while L. Zinsou, Le Fer de Lance, Olivier Orban, 1985 is a thoughtful defence of the nationalisations by a close aid of Fabius. J-P Gilly and F. Morin, Les Groupes Industriels en France, Documentation Française, 1981 is interesting as Morin influenced the strategy of socialist nationalisation, and R. Fossaert, La Nationalisation des Chrysanthèmes, Seuil, 1985 is an acerbic memoir by a PS bank chief. A leftist critique is A. Lipietz L'Audace ou l'Enlisement, La Découverte, 1984.

The following are more technical.
A. Fonteneau and P-A Muet La Gauche Face à la Crise FNSP, 1985; J. Sachs and C. Wyplosz, 'The economic consequences of President Mitterrand', in Economic Policy, No. 2, 1986; and Sénat Français, (Service des Etudes Economiques), 'Retour sur une projection à l'horizon 1985 établie en 1980,' unpublished, March 1986.

Chapter Three

LABOUR AND INDUSTRY: THE DEMISE OF TRADITIONAL UNIONISM?

Martin Rhodes

Although the victory of the French Left in 1981 did not contain the promise of a social and economic revolution, many hoped - and others feared - that significant and radical reform was now at last on the political agenda. Its programme aspired not only to a greater degree of social and economic justice, but to a rationalised and more effective form of state intervention in the economy, nationalisation in industry and banking. It also promised the revival of a planning system which had been increasingly marginalised under the regime of the Right; and the inclusion in decision-making at all levels of those social groups which had previously been considered unimportant.

For workers and their representatives in the trades unions, reform offered significant change: greater participation in decision-making in industry, the creation of new employment in the context of an expansionary economic policy, and measures designed to strengthen union powers and extend workers' rights and protection to marginalised sections of the work force, especially the growing number of part-time, short-term and sub-contract workers. The programme of the Left also promised to constrain the autonomy of employers by expanding the rights of works committees (<u>comités d'entreprise</u>), and by giving them a suspensive veto over dismissals by management. Yet five years later, when the socialist interlude came to a close with the legislative elections of March 1986, not only had deepening recession and a return to economic orthodoxy increased unemployment by 34 per cent (from 1.7 million in 1981 to 2.3 million in 1985), but, industrial relations reform notwithstanding (and, indeed, at least in part, because of it) the many weaknesses of French trade unions had been compounded. French employers had once again seized the initiative to attack socialist labour law reform and to question the entire rationale behind traditional trade unionism and labour market regulation.

The first part of this chapter examines the background to the reforms of the first five years of the Mitterrand <u>septennat</u>. A brief historical detour is required to understand both the objectives of socialist reform and the reasons for the strong element of continuity in industrial relations spanning the Giscardian and Mitterrand eras. The second part studies the impact of socialist reform against the back-cloth of economic recession, technological change and the new <u>projet social</u> of French employers. It is paradoxically the nature of the reforms themselves which, when introduced into a context of diminishing trade union influence and a decentralisation of bargaining to the level of the firm has <u>exacerbated</u> the problems of an already enfeebled labour movement.

The Background: Trade Unions, Employers and the State before 1981

Traditionally, trade unions in France have been highly politicised, ideologically divided, organisationally weak, ignored and excluded from influence by management and government alike and often disavowed by a work-force which, for its greater part (75-80 per cent), remains resistant to trade union affiliation. A strong tradition of individualism and independence among French business has meant that peak employers' associations have also been weak and divided, despite important organisational reform and a high rate of nominal membership among firms. Moreover, a poorly-organised professional basis for industrial relations has been perpetuated by state intervention. This has ranged from the suppression of association (especially among workers) in the nineteenth century, its promotion (among employers) in the twentieth, to the creation of a particular legal framework for collective bargaining and shop floor representation which <u>encourages</u> organisational weakness and a <u>dependence on the state</u> for the resolution of industrial conflict.

Representation and Organisation
The reasons for trade union weakness in France are well known. First, they have the lowest rate of

membership among trade unions in the major industrialised countries - with the possible exception of the United States: around 25 per cent of the work force in the early 1980s. This compares with a high of 50-60 per cent in 1945-1946 and a low of 17-18 per cent in the early 1960s. And, despite the existence of a wider union potential indicated by a higher rate of support (around 67 per cent) in elections for employee representatives (délégués du personnel) and comités d'entreprises the unions have been unable to transform this support into a base of strong, dues-paying, membership. They consequently lack the financial - and thus the organisational - resources available, for example, to their well-endowed West German counterparts. Second, they are divided, and chronically so, along occupational and ideological lines. Periods of unity have been the exception and internecine conflict the rule. The largest union, the Confédération Générale du Travail (CGT), has a membership of some 1.5 millions (according to its own estimates), is closely linked (by political philosophy and overlapping membership) to the French Communist Party (PCF), and while its influence in the service and tertiary sectors is weak, it has traditionally dominated crafts and heavy industries. The Confédération Française Démocratique du Travail (CFDT) with an estimated 800,000 members is close, but not affiliated, to the Socialist Party (PS), is particularly strong in the tertiary sector, in high technology industry and competes with the CGT for support in older sectors such as metallurgy as well. Force Ouvrière (FO) broke away from the CGT in 1947 to create a reformist and anti-communist union, and with its membership of some 600,000, has usually been weak where the CGT and CFDT have been strong, although in recent years it has made important advances. The Confédération Française des Travailleurs Chrétiens (CFTC) with an estimated 260,000 members, split from the old CFTC in 1964 in protest at the new militancy of its majority leadership. Finally, management and administrative personnel are represented by the Confédération Générale des Cadres (CGC) which has some 250,000 members. (1)

The French employers' association, the Conseil National du Patronat Français (CNPF), suffers from similar organisational weaknesses. Created in 1946, the CNPF is a confederation covering industry, commerce and the services, including the nationalised companies of the so-called 'competitive sector' (i.e. all companies apart from state monopolies such as Electricité de France and the

Société Nationale des Chemins de Fer Français (SNCF). In the mid 1970s, this meant representation of over one million firms employing 13 million people, with an affiliation rate in most sectors between 80 and 100 per cent. However, the lines of authority are ambiguous and individual federations such as the Union des Industries Minières et Métallurgiques (UIMM) can be powerful and independent, often pursuing policies at variance with those of their peak organisation. And like the unions, the CNPF has had to function with an irregular fees-paying system, poor quality permanent staff, internal divisions and competition from independent associations such as Entreprise et Progrès (self-consciously reformist and modern), Association des Cadres Dirigeants de l'Industrie (ACADI) - attached to 'Christian ideals' and the aggressive small and medium-sized business group, the Confédération Générale des Petites et Moyennes Entreprises (CGPME) which is poorly organised, lacking in resources and from which a new group, the Syndicat National de la Petite et Moyenne Industrie (SNPMI) broke away in 1977. (2)

Labour Law, Collective Bargaining and the Firm

Organisational cohesion and industrial relations stability are further impeded by an ill-defined legal framework for bargaining. Based on the law of 11 February 1950, labour law in effect restricts works committees to a purely consultative function, and in the case of industrial bargaining, union federations have been restricted to negotiating employment issues only, despite the attempts by the CGT and the CFDT to develop their own expertise in industrial affairs in order to question managerial strategies (contre-propositions).

Following the strikes and disturbances of May 1968, a trade union presence was permitted within firms (sections syndicales), but employers have been constrained more by the fear of strikes - which often escape union control - than by either the law or institutional forms of worker representation. The levels of bargaining, moreover, are the object of conflict themselves (employers preferring tradition-ally to negotiate at those levels where unions are the weakest); agreements signed by one union - even if it is the least representative - can be extended to the workforce as a whole; and by an extension procedure, the state can extend limited agreements to cover an entire region or industrial sector. Company level bargaining, it should be noted, has traditionally been opposed by both employers and trade unions. Before 1971, such bargaining was restricted by law to wage and salary rates, but since that date has been extended to all issues. (3) At the macro-level, bargaining on a cross-industry basis has been actively promoted by the state, as have successful agreements between the peak organisations of capital and labour on such issues as vocational training and the minimum wage (SMIC). But in general, the system of collective bargaining has been condemned from all sides, and the conflict it generates has often severely constrained industrial adjustment. (4)

It should also be noted that before the reforms introduced by the Left after 1982, statutory rights to representation in France were restricted to the larger firms, the vast majority of firms in France thus remaining non-unionised. While workers' representatives were legally entitled to carry out their duties in firms of ten or more workers, union delegates, health and safety committees and works councils were required only in firms of <u>fifty</u> workers or more.

Industrial Relations in the Crisis Years, 1975-1981.
Unity of action between the CGT and the CFDT after 1966 (a year in which 2.5 million working days were lost through strikes), mobilisation in favour of reform of labour law, working time and salaries, and intransigent resistance to these demands by employers subjected the industrial relations system to unprecedented stress. The pressure was relieved by the government which encouraged both sides to negotiate and to extend the 'contractual ethos' of bargaining in the steel sector (where an important agreement on restructuring had been signed in 1966) to the rest of the economy. At the same time, the strategy of the <u>patronat</u> underwent a profound change reflecting the rise of a reformist modernising faction within its ranks led by François Ceyrac, leader of the CNPF after December 1972. With the benefit of internal organisational reform providing the leadership with greater autonomy, the CNPF set out to reconcile the interests of its members with those of the trade unions. There followed a brief but important period of <u>concertation</u> (institutionalised bargaining) during which significant concessions were made on security of employment, paid holidays etc. and in 1975, protection for workers made redundant in sectors such as iron and steel was

extended to the entire work force with the law on redundancies for economic reasons (<u>loi sur les licenciements économiques</u>). (5)

But this period of government-sponsored <u>concertation</u> was short lived. Politically, tensions were being increased by CGT and CFDT sponsorship of the Common Programme of the Socialist and Communist Left which advocated nationalisation and far-reaching social reform: increasingly, the unions became more concerned with long-term political demands than with the immediate interests of the workforce - eventually to their cost. At the same time, the influential Sudreau report on industrial relations recommended radical reform at the level of the firm, including a strengthening of the works committees and the creation of workers' committees at the level of industrial groups along the lines of the West German company councils (<u>Gesamtbetriebsräte</u>). Similar suggestions for reform were being made by labour relations experts and by intellectually influential groups such as <u>Echanges et Projets</u>, a leading member of which was the future Socialist Minister of Finance, Jacques Delors, then a social adviser to Gaullist Prime minister, Jacques Chaban-Delmas. (6) Furthermore, legislative restrictions on dismissals (the laws of 1973 and 1975 subjecting layoffs for economic reasons to administrative approval) and government opposition to redundancies under the then Prime Minister Chirac, hardened the resolve of employers to defend their own interests, especially concerning that citadel of <u>patronat</u> power - the firm itself.

The patronat's response at the level of the CNPF was to campaign vigorously against the reforms recommended by officially-commissioned reports, and at the level of the company or plant it was now a case of everyone for themselves. National agreements on issues affecting labour relations within the firm itself were to be resisted, and French employers began to develop their own company-level social policies. These were to be heavily influenced by American and Japanese techniques of manpower management, and were designed to <u>minimise</u> trade union influence and <u>increase</u> flexibility in the labour market. (7) The disarray of the major trade unions after 1977 and the collapse of the Union of the Left gave employers the opportunity they needed to pre-empt legislation extending workers' participation (extremely likely in the event of a Socialist victory in 1981). In large industrial groups, such as those in steel, textiles, chemicals and electronics, there was an early experimentation with 'Japanisation' - the introduction of new methods of manpower management which bypass union mediation, seek to imbue workers with a 'company' ethos through quality circles, management information systems, productivity bonuses and participation in 'work life improvement schemes'. Labour market flexibility was increased by greater recourse to part-time seasonal, short-term and subcontract labour, forms of employment which increase the autonomy of the employer - especially at a time of economic crisis - and allow certain constraining labour laws to be avoided. (8) Furthermore, it is precisely these sections of the 'marginal' workforce that the unions have been unwilling or unable to recruit and mobilise. (9)

Meanwhile, the government's labour market policy - under Raymond Barre's austerity policy - had become more closely tailored to the needs of employers than to the demands of the labour movement. Trade union victories - such as those achieved by the steel unions in the <u>conventions sociales</u> of 1977 and 1979 - were in reality only thinly veiled defeats initially excluding from employment only the older and immigrant worker, but the wave of redundancies soon began to reach the skilled core of the younger French work force itself. Yet <u>Barrisme</u> did not extend to repealing protective legislation, despite the growing difficulties of French firms faced with recession and an import invasion from low cost foreign producers. (State promotion of industry through subsidies, public purchasing and export credits had become overwhelmingly biased in favour of the largest industrial groups, leaving small and medium-sized firms to sink or swim in competitive markets. Only the large 'lame ducks' benefited from state rescue packages such as that in the steel sector in 1978-1979.) A radical shift of policy fully in favour of employers was prevented during the early years of the recession by the electoral constraint: the presidential election of May 1974 - in which Giscard d'Estaing only narrowly defeated François Mitterrand, opened a campaign which, spanning the March 1976 cantonal elections and the March 1977 municipal elections, came to a close with the defeat of the Left in the legislative elections of March 1978. Nevertheless the number of dismissals 'for economic reasons' continued to rise steadily in the late 1970s, and despite their complaints of growing labour market rigidities, employers seemed able to shed their excess work-force with relative ease. By

Labour and Industry: The Demise of Traditional Unionism?

July 1979 - and despite a series of measures launched by the Government after 1977 to subsidise or support the creation or continuation of jobs (the Pactes pour l'emploi) - unemployment had risen to 5.8 per cent of the labour force - 1,256,623 people - over 250,000 of whom were not in receipt of any form of unemployment benefit. (10)

By 1981 recession, redundancies, new management techniques and the collapse of CGT-CFDT 'unity-in-action' in 1977, had left the labour movement in a state of confusion. While the energies of the major federations had been mobilised behind the electoral programme of the Left, infighting within the Socialist-Communist alliance itself and exploitation by both Left parties of industrial conflict for political gain, had intensified divisions between the CGT and the CFDT. Simultaneously, both of these unions were experiencing a crisis of internal dissension due to a growing gap between leadership strategies (influenced by national political concerns) and the perceptions and demands of an increasingly disoriented militant base. Even attempts to formulate alternative industrial strategies (contre-propositions industrielles) in sectors undergoing radical restructuring, such as steel, had failed to improve leadership credibility in the eyes of an alienated rank-and-file: indeed, the elitist and patronising manner in which such plans were communicated from the union summit to its base may well have had the opposite effect. (11) Management, meanwhile, refused even to consider such alternative strategies, undermining this attempt to enhance the legitimacy of the trade union as a valued economic partner. The crisis of dissension - and disillusionment - translated into a crisis of affiliation, and both major federations experienced a major decline in membership in the late 1970s: while the CGT is estimated to have lost around one-third of its members between 1976 and 1980 (in part because of the job losses in the 'smokestack' industries) the CFDT appears to have lost only a slightly smaller proportion over the same period. (12)

The response to this crisis by the unions was highly equivocal, revealing just how serious the predicament of traditional unionism had become by the late 1970s. For the CFDT - or at least part of it - a strategy of recentrage (re-focusing on traditional union concerns) was required in which attention would be focused once again on shop-floor issues, the (quasi-utopian) goal of autogestion and a new style of bargaining to increase workers' power. But due to the uncertainties contained in this approach (how would it differ from that of the moderate unions such as <u>Force Ouvrière</u>?) it failed to impress either the left of the union (which wanted to remain combative rather than conciliatory) or the rank-and-file which continued to vote with its feet. Furthermore, it assumed - in the face of overwhelming evidence to the contrary - that the patronat would welcome a return to negotiated agreements at this time. A similar assumption lay behind the new strategy of the reformist wing of the CGT which, unlike the PCF hard-liners in the union, wanted to distance itself from the Communist Party, and elaborate 'proposition-force unionism' based on industrial counter-proposals. By developing expertise in industrial affairs, it was thought that the union could modify the restructuring strategies of managers and the government by force of argument linked to traditional forms of rank-and-file action. (13) Unfortunately, the new anti-union trend in labour relations to company and plant-level bargaining (and the new particularism amongst the work force this encouraged) had effectively forestalled the new strategies of both major unions.

The dilemma confronting the unions by the early 1980s was that they would now have to focus their attention less on the sector or industry and increasingly on the firm - a level of labour relations where French trade unions had never been strong. Whether or not they could do so effectively would depend both on labour law reform and their own capacity for change.

"La Fin du Collectif"? Industrial Relations and Industrial Change under the Socialists

The crisis of membership, the problems of organisation (or rather the lack of it) and the strategic dilemmas of French unions in the late 1970s clearly accentuated the imbalance of power which traditionally exists between capital and labour. Capitalist organisations - at both peak and sectoral levels - often experience similar problems, and in France a strong tradition of individualism has weakened the powers of employers' associations. Yet the power of employers at the level of the firm does not necessarily depend on collective organisational strength at higher levels, even though they do frequently associate within cartels, flexible marketing agreements, employers and trade associa tions etc. Their ownership and control of the means of production provides them with a base of power unavailable to workers. (14)

By contrast, the ability of labour to exercise effective countervailing at the level of the company or plant depends crucially on associational strength - on hierarchical control within the union structure and on the union's capacity for mobilisation. Management is more flexible. As industrial unions are weakened by declining membership and organisational fragmentation, management can exploit these difficulties by decentralising its relations with its work-force and by diversifying manpower policies between company and plants, and if possible within the factory itself. A major goal of this strategy is to undermine collective bargaining - which can be costly and time-consuming - and allow maximum freedom for managerial choice. In the process, union representatives are by-passed, union membership is eroded further, and the raison d'être of the industrial union disappears. This trend was already identifiable in France before 1981.

However, the tendency may be resisted or reversed by government legislation, trade union pressure, or even the desire of the patronat itself to retain peak or sectoral level bargaining for certain purposes. The central issue of the socialist reforms in France after 1981 is whether they countered or contributed to this trend in industrial relations.

The "Lois Auroux" and the Labour Market. In March 1982, a report drawn up by the French socialist Minister of Labour, Jean Auroux, was approved by the government and new labour legislation was presented to the National Assembly on 13 May. The content of the five principal laws - modifying some 400 articles (approximately one third) of the Code du Travail - can be summarised as follows:
i) A new law covering collective bargaining (13 November 1982) represented the first major statutory reform since 1950, and while much of the structure created at that time was retained, the new law contained a number of important innovations. First, the old principle whereby any of the five main national unions were recognised as 'most representative' and could sign and validate an agreement opposed by the other unions was modified. Henceforth, an agreement cannot be validated if one or more unions refuse to sign it and if they are

supported by more than fifty per cent of employees registered to vote in works council or employee representative elections. Second, bargaining was to be encouraged at the industry level by an obligation to negotiate pay on an annual basis and job grading once every five years. And third, company-level bargaining (traditionally opposed by employers and unions alike) was to be encouraged by a new obligation to negotiate pay and working time in firms with fifty employees or more.

ii) Two new laws covering <u>workers' representation</u> (29 October 1982 and 23 December 1982) not only strengthened existing <u>comités d'entreprise</u> but also attempted to strengthen union influence at the level of the firm and to extend labour law protection to those categories of the workforce on short-term and part-time contracts or employed on a casual basis. <u>Comités d'entreprises</u> were now to be informed of company strategy and manpower policies and could increase their own expertise on these matters by calling in 'external experts'. Trade union influence was to be enhanced by the unions' new right to appoint trade union delegates in firms with between 11 and 49 workers, as long as these delegates were already elected employee representatives. Also, union delegates were given rights to a <u>comité d'entreprise</u> seat in all companies with between 50 and 300 workers - giving union delegates the same access to the economic and manpower information now available to the works committee as a whole. At the same time an attempt was made to bring previously marginalised workers within the ambit of the firm by including short-term and part-time workers in calculating the threshold at which legal obligations such as those mentioned above come into effect.

Finally, a major innovation was the creation of new group councils (<u>comités de groupe</u>) in an attempt to bring employee representation into line with the evolution of the firm. In the past, works committees had often been unable to discover where decisions affecting workers' interests were made - especially if their company was a subsidiary governed ultimately from the Parisian headquarters of an inaccessible holding company. (15) Now employees in subsidiaries received an automatic right to representation on a <u>comité de groupe</u> consisting of the managing director of the parent company (or his representative), plus two persons of his/her choice, and employee representatives from dependent companies. To meet once annually, representatives were entitled to receive information on a broad range of group activities, including employment and financial trends, consolidated accounts and balance sheets, details of foreign subsidiaries and investment plans. Like comités d'entreprises, comités de groupes were also permitted to enlist the help of an expert in examining this information. (16)

iii) New rights were also given to workers through the law on workers' freedom of expression in the firm (4 August 1982) which responded to demands voiced especially by the CFDT for a movement towards its ill-defined goal of autogestion (self-management). Provision now had to be made for workers' 'self-expression' on work organisation and the implications of new technology in firms of fifty workers or more. In firms of 200 or more workers, special agreements would have to be made on the form and frequency of expression meetings with management. In many ways, these provisions conformed with an already established tradition in many large companies of in-house consultation, one of the techniques of the patronat's new projet social referred to above.

iv) Finally, a new law on workers' democracy in public-sector companies (26 July 1983) aspired to recreate a spirit of tripartism in a sector of the economy where existing statutory rights had failed to provide anything more than a consultative role for representatives. Previously, workers had the right to be represented on the boards of public sector companies with 50 or more staff and were entitled to at least two board seats. Now, public sector companies (previously nationalised companies plus those companies nationalised in 1982 in which the state was the majority shareholder) would be obliged to have tripartite administrative or supervisory boards to which employee representatives would be elected by the work-force.

During the (often stormy) passage of the new legislation, numerous important labour market and employment measures were introduced, aiming to boost employment within the more expansionary climate created by the new government's 'redistributive Keynesianism'. (17) The civil service was to provide a major source of new recruitment and a terrain for experimentation with a four-day week; the policies of the previous government in favour of youth employment (the Pacte National pour l'Emploi) was continued and expanded as the Plan Avenir Jeunes; Marcel Rigout - the PCF Minister for Vocational Training - announced the creation of 40,000 apprenticeships and 15,000 additional training places; the National Employment

Agency (<u>Agence Nationale de l'Emploi</u>) was reformed and its operations decentralised; a decree of March 1982 gave employees the right to retire at the age of 60 on fifty per cent of average earnings during their best ten years of employment; in January 1982 a decree provided for so-called 'solidarity contracts' whereby firms would be subsidised for introducing part-time work or early retirement if they also allowed the creation of new jobs; and most importantly - at least politically if not in terms of job creation - was the negotiation of a 39-hour week by employers and unions in July 1981, considered by the government and trade unions as the first step towards a 35-hour week and as perhaps the most important means of creating new employment. (18) (The CNPF remained highly sceptical as to the job-creating potential of this innovation, and the CGT refused to sign the agreement, demanding the immediate introduction of a 38-hour week.)

Finally, a government decree of March 1982 aimed to provide greater employment security for the growing number of workers on part-time and fixed-term contracts by restricting the circumstances in which employers could use such labour (largely to ensure that permanent employees were not displaced by cheaper and more easily dismissed part-time workers). Henceforth, the law set out to ensure that such workers received the same benefits as full-time workers and trade unions were given statutory rights to institute legal proceedings against employers or temporary work agencies if the provisions of the new law were evaded. (19)

From "Etat de Grace" to "Coup de Grace": The Limits of Reform

The reforms and labour-market measures of 1982 were given a mixed reception. Trade unions were displeased by the extent to which the radical edge of the Common Programme proposals had been blunted by its cautious translation into concrete policies. Mitterrand's 1981 programme had specifically contained a proposal extending works committee rights to include a suspensive veto over dismissals. (20) This had now been discreetly dropped - although employers were still hostile to the limited strengthening of works committee powers - and the CGT and the PCF were suspicious of the emphasis given to 'rights of expression'; rights which did not in practice extend to active participation along co-management lines, thus leaving the CFDT (the long-standing advocate of autogestion) disappointed as well. The main emphasis of the *lois Auroux* was on negotiated reform since the implementation of many of the new provisions at the level of the firm would have to be bargained rather than imposed, and employers were left with considerable freedom of initiative.

Nevertheless, employers were left unappeased by the fact that the extent of reform had been moderated. Many *patrons* - particularly those in the smaller firms - remained hostile to any union presence in their firms, no matter how marginal. They were also unhappy about what they saw as a growing bureaucratic constraint imposed by an increasingly complex system of labour law, especially insofar as it pertained to dismissal procedures. The CNPF and the larger firms were not opposed to workers' rights to expression (indeed, as mentioned above, many had actively encouraged it in the form of quality circles and so on) but they *were* opposed to its being thrust upon them and regulated by law. More generally, it was felt that tightening up labour market regulation - by restricting the use of part-time or short-term workers - would directly contradict the new government's policies in favour of increased employment by making employers more reluctant to bear the costs of recruiting, especially among the growing number of unemployed younger workers.

The unions, in contrast, naturally felt that many of the new reforms should have gone further. Yet they were profoundly divided over the law on expression rights. *Force Ouvrière* had traditionally been the most committed to industrial and national level bargaining and feared that a devolution of bargaining to the company level on working time and work organisation would undermine its role and strengthen the largest unions, the CGT and the CFDT. The other smaller unions - the CGC and the CFTC - were, however, in favour of the new law. The CFDT and the CGT were favourable in principle to workers' rights of expression in the firm, although they differed as to the role such activity should play in the 'wider struggle'. By the early 1980s, the CFDT had pursued its strategy of *recentrage* to its logical conclusion, and had accepted that a level of collective bargaining could exist independently of the trade union federations at the level of the firm. But for the CGT, it was important that company-based *expression* should be linked to higher levels of union policy-making and industrial action. Both of the major unions were unhappy about the fact that the unionisation gap between larger and smaller firms was not effectively closed under the new laws, and that trade union activity was still not fully encouraged in firms of less than fifty workers in the private sector. (21)

But despite discontent on both sides of industry, the Socialist government was able to preserve the so-called état de grace until after mid-1983. Potential conflict with employers was avoided by a series of concessions and a gradual shift by the government to a position of compromise on issues such as the shorter working week. Initially, this issue threatened to generate a major conflict between employers, unions and the government, and the government itself was split on the desirability of reducing the working week rapidly to 35 hours (the initial target was 1985) and on whether shorter working hours should be accompanied by a reduction in wages. Key members of the government (notably the Prime Minister, Pierre Mauroy, the Economy Minister, Jacques Delors, and the Labour Minister, Jean Auroux) felt that this was essential if a shorter working week was to contribute to new employment creation. Edmond Maire, leader of the CFDT, was also sympathetic to this argument. The PCF, CGT and many workers, however, were not, and it was decided that wage levels should be preserved until a threshold of thirty-seven hours was attained. (22) But to appease employers (who had already launched a major offensive against the government, complaining that for every 100 francs paid to a worker, employers had to pay a further 62 francs to cover social security and labour costs) the government agreed in the spring of 1982 not to demand a further reduction in working hours until the end of 1983 and to freeze the level of employers' social security contributions until July of that year. The trade unions and the PCF now began to suspect - correctly as it turned out - that the thirty-five hour week had effectively been shelved.

The social and economic policies of the government had generally been welcomed by the unions. While labour law reform had been more limited than hoped - and the boost it had given to enterprise bargaining rather worrying for the FO and the CGT - the unions' co-operation had been purchased by immediate gains (an increase in the minimum wage, the shorter working week without loss of earnings, much higher pensions and family allowances), and by the promise of greater rewards once the Left had become firmly established in power. The unions (particularly the CFDT) were also encouraged by the greater access to government that they seemed to have secured. Union personnel (especially from the CFDT) gained positions in the Ministry of National Solidarity as well as in other ministerial cabinets. And before the PCF ministers left government in 1984, some CGT personnel were involved in the Communist-led ministries - i.e. Health, Civil Service, Transport and Professional Training. Those unions ideologically more distant from the Socialists - the CGC and the FO - were less enamoured with the new regime in this respect, but although their enthusiasm was certainly not unbridled, tolerance generally prevailed.

The end of the état de grâce began with the Socialist government's major economic U-turn of mid 1982 when, in order to cope with the consequences of 'socialism in one country' - runaway inflation, rising interest rates and a balance of payments crisis - a series of austerity measures were introduced including a statutory prices and pay freeze, linked to a devaluation of the franc against other European currencies. (23) Under these circumstances, the unions - including the CFDT - became actively hostile to the government, although an outright offensive on the part of the Communist CGT was delayed until July 1984 when the Communist Party's ministers withdrew from the government. Free industrial bargaining - most obviously on pay - was now highly restricted by government policies and the tolerance of the first two years of the Socialist-Communist government had largely evaporated by the end of 1983. But it was in early 1984 - when pressures for major restructuring and labour shedding in declining industrial sectors became overwhelming - that socialisme à la française finally received its social, political and economic coup de grâce.

'Flexibilité': Company-level Bargaining and the Crisis of Traditional Trade-unionism.

1984 was the year in which the hopes and aspirations of May 1981 were finally dashed. While the Lois Auroix had strengthened certain institutions and encouraged new forms of bargaining, the traditional problems of French unions remained acute and even accentuated by their equivocal relationship with the socialist regime. The crisis of representation already evident in the 1970s had deepened in the 1980s as workers exchanged their union membership for party cards instead. The patronat had been experiencing similar difficulties. The replacement of François Ceyrac in 1981 by Yvon Gattaz - a representative of the petit patron - confirmed the tendency towards individualism, anti-statism and even the rejection of professional representation within the lower ranks of the CNPF: the aggressively right-wing SNPMI had increased its support among businessmen and a survey conducted in 1982 revealed that over 70 per cent of employers believed that traditional forms of association (ergo the CNPF) were inadequate for exerting pressure on government or for defending their interests. The development of new, individualistic, means of manpower management and communication between employers and workers had flourished: the number of quality circles in operation in France had grown from some 500 in 1981 to 10,000 in 1984, involving more than 200,000 people. (24)

Far from counteracting this trend towards in-house consultation, the lois Auroux seemed to have positively contributed to it. And where new forms of representation had been created - most notably in the public sector - the results were certainly less favourable than the unions had hoped. Elections to the new tripartite management boards in the public sector not only revealed the crisis of support for the CGT and CFDT (as in private sector works committee elections, FO, the CGC and CFTC and non-unionised candidates were increasing their support at the expense of the latter) but managerial staff formed a high proportion of those elected. Once elected, the influence workers' representatives have been able to exert has varied greatly from company to company, reflecting the industrial relations traditions of those private sector groups nationalised in 1982. Early on, important gains were made and in some cases - with the help of government pressure - workers' representatives were able to play a role in the formulation of the new contrats de plan. (25) In theory, these were to help rationalise state-industry relations and bring wider social concerns to bear on company strategies. In reality, the 'democratisation' of the public sector has in many companies created an illusion of participation since the role of administrative or supervisory boards in public sector companies tends to be limited to consultation, and the business secrecy justifies restrictions on the type of information which is made available to them. (26)

In the private sector, a survey of expression rights agreements in 1985 showed that half of the companies required to reach such agreements with their work force had done so (this applies to all companies with more than 200 workers). But of these, only ten per cent had been concluded with works committees, and two-thirds were in companies or plants without trade union representatives. Of these agreements, 62 per cent put senior white-collar staff in charge of the expression groups established – something which pleased the white collar union, the CGC, but which has obviously caused concern in the CGT and the CFDT. (27) In 1985 there was also a sharp increase in company-level bargaining, encouraged by the negotiation of expression agreements and by the obligation of firms with fifty employees or more to negotiate on working time and work conditions annually. Evidence that this decentralisation of bargaining to the level of the firm has been occurring at the expense of the unions is provided by the fact that, of the 4,000 or so expression agreements signed in 1984, 50 per cent were negotiated with works council or employee representatives rather than with union delegates. (28)

Decentralisation in bargaining and a fragmentation of the union base has been encouraged by the ineffectiveness of trade union action and by the divisive consequences of the crisis itself, pitching workers against one another as job security has taken precedence over group solidarity. The shift in orientation of socialist labour market policy – over which the unions were able to exert little influence – equally revealed the consequences of recession on employment. The clashes in steel in April-May 1984 marked the re-ordering of socialist government priorities from redistribution and enhancing the role of the worker in society to preserving as many jobs as possible while also ensuring the profitability of firms. With the arrival of Laurent Fabius as Minister of Industry, a new tone of liberalism began to pervade the official discourse of the government. Public sector firms were now to subordinate all other objectives to one end: a return to profitability in 1985.

At the same time, the manifest failure of the government's employment creation policies gave greater credence to employers' claims that it was the dead weight of the state and regulation that was impeding recruitment and job creation. Public employment schemes (<u>Travaux d'Utilité Collective</u>) and work induction schemes had provided work of a kind for young people and an extension of early retirement and immigrant repatriation schemes introduced originally under Giscard d'Estaing had allowed a large number of people to be eliminated from the labour market. (29) Economic development zones in the crisis regions had created some employment at enormous cost. (30) But the private sector was offering a different remedy: free from regulatory constraint, the CNPF considered employers could create 470,000 new jobs (<u>emplois nouveaux à contraintes allégées</u> - ENCA) over a two year period. Specifically, the following changes would be required: ending restrictions on employers' freedom to make workers redundant: abolishing the thresholds of 10 and 50 employees above which certain obligations are incurred; and reducing social security charges.

Despite the apparently radical nature of these demands, all unions - with the major exception of the CGT - were prepared by 1984 to negotiate a 'flexibility' package with employers. The decline especially of sectoral bargaining and the continuing crisis of the labour movement meant that some of the unions were anxious to restore their image as the key mediating agents of social change. A successful deal with employers on a programme which promised more jobs would enhance their credibility with the government and, most importantly, with their own disaffected rank-and-file. The CGT, meanwhile, remained the intransigent class warrior, and its oppositional role was facilitated greatly by the departure of the PCF ministers from the government of the Left in July 1984. They alone would be able to pursue a consistent strategy of outright opposition to any deregulation of the labour market or any modification to new rules of the game as applied after the reform of the <u>Lois Auroux</u>. In 1986, the benefits accruing to the union from this strategy would become clear when the CGT alone among the major federations markedly improved its scores in <u>comité d'entreprise</u> and delegate elections - after a long period of decline to the advantage of the FO, CFTC and non-unionised representatives.

While the negotiations were ultimately to collapse without agreement in December 1984, the process of bargaining itself provides a number of interesting insights into the state of contemporary industrial relations in France. First, the demands made by the CNPF reflected the growing influence of neo-liberalism among employers and of the rise of the <u>petit patron</u> within the ranks of employers' organisations. Even François Ceyrac - an advocate of <u>la vie contractuelle</u> in the 1970s - now supported a greater devolution of bargaining to the firm, greater freedom for the individual employer in introducing new technology and an end to the constraints imposed by multi-industry national agreements. Secondly, the government itself was now increasingly in favour of the type of labour market deregulation advocated, for example, by employers' groups such as <u>Entreprise et progrès</u>, <u>Ethic</u> and the <u>Institut de l'Entreprise</u>: even the Minister of Labour, M. Delebarre felt that serious problems were being created because 'the complexity of the texts is such that they become, in certain cases, difficult or impossible to apply. (31) Yet, at the same time, the government was as concerned as the unions to ensure that in allowing for greater flexibility in the labour market, the gains made in 1982 were not bargained away. And on this point, the employers were also prepared to make concessions, abandoning their initial demand that prior administrative authorisation for redundancies be abolished. Instead, a reduced role for the Labour Inspectorate would be exchanged for a greater degree of consultation of works committees on dismissals.

Thirdly, the failure to reach an agreement revealed above all the internal weaknesses of the unions themselves, since a draft agreement <u>was</u> reached between the union leaders (the CGT excepted) and employers but it was rejected out of hand by the militant base of the very same unions. (32) The draft agreement reveals how wide the gap between union leaders and their base of activists had become. On matters of important technological change, the most important level of negotiation would be the firm and the role of the works committees would be enhanced. Yet since <u>comités d'entreprises</u> remained creatures of the firm rather than of the union despite the <u>lois Auroux</u>, trade union activists (rather than workers themselves) would not necessarily welcome this because sectoral level agreements would be restricted to broad framework provisions only. Sectoral level bargaining would be encouraged, however, on working hours but the purpose of such bargaining would be to relax and find exemption from legal provisions. If no such agreements were reached, company-level agreements would introduce new forms of flexibility. The draft agreement also accepted that certain categories of workers included in calculating threshold levels on employment obligations should once again be excluded, and that the use of part-time and short-term labour should be deregulated. In May 1985, FO, the CGC, the CFTC and the CFDT successfully negotiated a flexibility package on temporary work which relaxed the protective provision introduced by the socialist government in 1982. The leaders of the reformist unions had accepted that it was better to negotiate such change than to have it eventually imposed by a hostile government of the Right.

Conclusions
By the end of the socialist interlude, technological change, the impact of the recession and a shift of intellectual opinion in favour of economic liberalism, had all begun to affect the nature of the government's labour policies. By the end of 1984, the government was supporting many of the demands for flexibility made by employers and the CNPF, and, in the absence of successful bargaining on these matters, began in March and April 1985 to issue decrees on part-time working, fixed contracts and job creation which aimed to meet some of these demands while also respecting the position of workers. But if flexibility was to create more jobs (and it was by no means clear that it could) then the regulatory direction of the Socialists' earlier reforms would have to be reversed. This much had also been accepted by the more moderate unions.

The very fact that bargaining on these matters had failed - due largely to the fact that French unions are unable to mobilise their base behind bargains which involve trade-offs of this kind - was evidence that the associational basis of French industrial relations was weaker in the 1980s than it had been in the past. But it is the unions which suffer most in these circumstances and the employers who can consciously pursue an alternative form of relationship between capital and labour - one based at the company level where the scope for union influence is at its weakest. And even if sectoral framework bargaining is retained, as French employers seem to desire, the translation of such bargains into concrete form at the company level places similar constraints on union countervailing powers. As a French industrial relations specialist recently remarked, French unions in the 1980s are confronted with a potentially crippling dilemma: '... in order to survive, trade unions in France may well be forced to attempt to return to the firm. But in so doing they are in danger of losing their raison d'être - something of which the employers are already aware. (33)

Notes

1. See J.-D. Reynaud, Les syndicats en France (Paris: Editions du Seuil, 1975).
2. On the patronat, see B. Brizay, Le patronat: histoire, structure, stratégie du CNPF, (Paris: Editions du Seuil 1975).
3. For an overview of the industrial relations system, see J.-D. Reynaud, Les syndicats, les patrons et l'Etat. Tendances de la négociation collective en France (Paris: Les Editions Ouvrières 1978).
4. See, for example, G. Adam 'La négociation collective en France: éléments de diagnostic', Droit Social, (December 1978), pp.420-51.
5. For a full account of these changes and their effects, see J. Rojot, 'France', Bulletin of Comparative Labour Relations, No. 11, (1980), pp.79-102.
6. P. Sudreau (Chairman) Rapport du comité d'étude pour la réforme de l'entreprise, (Paris: La Documentation Française, 1975); Echange et projets, 'La négociation salariale. Pourquoi? Comment?" Droit Social, (November 1978), pp.392-98.
7. There is a growing literature on this subject. For an overview, see P. Morville Les nouvelles politiques sociales du patronat. (Editions la Découverte 1985) and J. Freyssinet, 'La déstabilisation des formes d'emploi: stratégies patronales et stratégies syndicales', Critique de l'Economie Politique, Nos. 23/24, (April-September 1983), pp.111-24.
8. On the strategies of these large companies, see J. Freyssinet, Politique d'emploi des grands groupes français (Paris: Presses Universitaires de Grenoble 1982).
9. See F. Sellier 'Du mouvement ouvrier au syndicalisme réel", Esprit, 90, (June 1984), pp.29-41 and T. Baudouin and M. Colin Le contournement des forteresses ouvrières: précarité et syndicalisme, (Paris: Librairie des Meridiens 1983).
10. Rojot, 'France', p.79.
11. For an analysis of industrial counterproposals, see P. Zarifian, 'La culture syndicale face à la nécessité de propositions industrielles: défis, mouvements, portée", Critique de l'Economie Politique, No. 23/4, (1983). pp.263-84.
12. See G. Ross 'French Trade Unions Face the 1980s: the CGT and the CFDT in the Strategic Conflicts and Economic Crisis of Contemporary France' in M. Zeitlin, (ed), Political Power and Social Theory, vol. 3 (1982), pp.53-75.

13. Zarifian 'La culture syndicale' and P. Lange, G. Ross and M. Vannicelli, <u>Unions, Change and Crisis: French and Italian Trade Union Strategy and the Political Economy 1945-1980</u>, (London: George Allen and Unwin, 1982).

14. See M. Rhodes 'Organised Interests and Industrial Crisis Management: Restructuring the Steel Industry in West Germany, Italy and France' in Alan Cawson, (ed), <u>Organised Interests and the State</u>, (London: Sage 1985), pp.192-220.

15. G. Lyon-Caen 'Plasticité du capital et nouvelles formes d'emploi', <u>Droit Social</u>, Nos. 9-10, (September-October 1980), pp.8-15.

16. For further details, see <u>European Industrial Relations Review</u>, no. 107, (December 1982).

17. See P. Hall in P.G. Cerny and M.A. Schain (Eds.), <u>Socialism, the State and Public Policy in France</u>, (London: Frances Pinter, 1985).

18. For a useful summary of these measures, see V. Lauber, <u>The Political Economy of France: From Pompidou to Mitterrand</u>, (New York: Praeger, 1983), Ch. 13.

19. <u>European Industrial Relations Review</u>, no. 98, (March 1982).

20. Lauber, <u>The Political Economy of France</u>, pp.196-7.

21. See. A. Roudil 'Flexibilité de l'emploi et droit du travail: "La beauté du diablé", <u>Droit Social</u>, No. 2, (February 1985), pp.85-94.

22. Lauber, <u>The Political Economy of France</u>, pp.189-96.

23. For details of socialist economic policy see Chapter Two.

24. See <u>European Industrial Relations Review</u>, No. 126 (July 1984) and No. 128 (September 1984).

25. This was the case, for example, in steel and textiles. See L. Zinsou, <u>Le fer de lance: essai sur les nationalisations industrielles</u>, (Paris: Olivier Orban, 1985) and G. LeMaitre and M. Vervaeke, 'Evoluzione delle strategie padronali e del movimento sindacale in un gruppo nazionalizzato', <u>Economia e Lavoro</u>, vol. 18 (1986), pp.119-25.

26. The experience of 'expression' in the electronics company Thomson indicated the limits to genuine participation. See D. Martin 'L'expression des salariés: technique de management ou nouvelle instititution?', <u>Sociologie du Travail</u>, vol. 28, (1986), pp.173-92. The more general nature of the problem was confirmed by the major report on the public sector published in 1984: Haut Conseil du

Secteur Public, Rapport 1984, Volumes I and II. (Paris: La Documentation Française, 1984).
27. European Industrial Relations Review no. 143, (December 1985).
28. Ibid.
29. On the use of these various policies - and their success rates - see D. Boissard et al., 'Les rescapés du chômage', Liaisons sociales - mensuel, (February 1986). Between 1981 and 1986 there had been 800,000 early retirements, just over 800,000 young people placed on special work schemes, 200,000 enterprise allowance successes, 50,000 repatriated immigrants and 30,000 retrained workers from declining industrial sectors.
30. F. Grosrichard, 'Un bilan de France malade', Le Monde, 5-6 October 1986.
31. See D. Boissard, 'Faut-il brûler le Code de Travail?' Intersocial, (May 1985).
32. For a concise analysis of the flexibility negotiations, see R. Soubie, 'Après les négociations sur la flexibilité', Droit Social no. 2, (February 1985); no. 3 (March 1985); and no. 4, (April 1985). On the wider context and implications, see J.-F. Amadieu, 'Les tendances au syndicalism d'entreprise en France: quelques hypothèses', Droit Social, No. 6, (June 1986), pp.495-500.
33. P. Zarifian, 'Le syndicalisme face à l'entreprise industrielle', Sociologie du Travail, vol. 27, (1985), p.343.

Further Reading
The following books provide the best introduction to French trade unions and industrial relations: J.-D. Reynaud, Les syndicats, les patrons et l'Etat: Tendances de la négociation collective (Paris: Les Editions Ouvrières 1978); J.-D. Reynaud, Les syndicats en France, Vols. One and Two (Paris: Editions du Seuil 1975); R. Mouriaux, Les syndicats dans la société francaise (Paris: Presses de la Fondation Nationale de Science Politique); G. Adam Le Pouvoir Syndical (Paris: Dunod 1983); A. Touraine, M. Wieviorka, F. Dubet Le mouvement ouvrier (Paris: Fayard 1984). In English, there are few detailed studies of the industrial relations system as such, although the work of George Ross on the CGT in particular has been an exception. His study of French unions in P. Lange, G. Ross and M. Vannicelli, Unions, Change and Crisis: French and Italian Union Strategy and the Political Economy 1945-1980, (London: George Allen and Unwin 1982) provides a

useful introduction, and his Workers and Communists in France (Berkeley: University of California Press 1982) a more detailed study of the relationship between the PCF and the CGT. There is also a recent collection of articles - mostly by French authors - edited by Mark Kesselman under the title The French Workers' Movement, (London: George Allen and Unwin 1984).

For more specialised reading on shop floor issues, collective bargaining and labour law, Sociologie du Travail and Droit Social provide an enormous range of high-quality material. For a Marxist perspective, see the journal Critique de l'Economie Politique. Useful articles on France can also be found in English in journals such as Labour and Society and the British Journal of Industrial Relations. The following are a sample of some of the most recent journal literature on issues discussed in this chapter: G. Caire, "Les tendances récentes de la négociation collective en France", Revue Internationale du Travail, (November-December 1984); W. Rand Smith, "Dynamics of Plural Unionism in France: the CGT, CFDT and Industrial Conflict", British Journal of Industrial Relations, Vol. 22, No. 1, (March 1984) pp.15-33; J. Rojot, "The Development of French Employers' Policy towards Trade Unions", Labour and Society, Vol. 11 no. 1, (January 1986) pp.1-16; J.F. Amadieu and N. Mercier, "Le débat sur la 'flexibilité'", Sociologie du Travail Vol. 28, No. 2, (1986) p.193-201; F. Eyraud and R. Tchobanian, "The Auroux Reforms and Company Level Industrial Relations in France" British Journal of Industrial Relations, Vol. 23 No. 2, (July 1985) pp.241-259; J. Pelissier "La fonction syndicale dans l'entreprise après les lois Auroux", Droit Social, no. 1, (January 1984) pp.41-8; J.-P. Bonafé-Schmitt, "L'expression des salariés et l'action syndicale", Droit Social, no. 2, (February 1986), pp.111-17.

Chapter Four

A MORE EQUAL SOCIETY? SOCIAL POLICY UNDER THE SOCIALISTS

Doreen Collins

Introduction
Prior to achieving office, French Socialists had made no secret of their belief that it was time to modernise social policy in order to make it more appropriate for the needs of an up-to-date, industrial society. Social welfare had for long been promoted by a number of ill-co-ordinated institutions which, within a framework of national responsibility, gave expression to sectional needs. The Socialists believed this structure had two limitations: firstly, it no longer functioned well; and secondly, it left many modern problems unmet. A new look for social policy, therefore, required not only reform of the social security system, but of many other social institutions as well so that the notion of a caring society would permeate more widely. In order to appreciate the task the Socialists set themselves, some understanding of this background may be helpful.

New Needs
With the ending of the Second World War France, in common with other states in Western Europe, established a new social consensus in which social policy, spear-headed by government, was to play a significant part. The importance of including the whole nation, of appealing to the traditions of the working class, and to a strong sense of mutual aid, was summed up in the concept of 'national solidarity' which became the underlying theme of significant reform and rationalisation. (1) The reforms did not mean, however, a complete recasting of social provision on a basic principle of uniformity but the adapting of existing institutions so that they might progressively implement the notion of social

protection for all whilst retaining many of their own individualist features. The subsequent rapid economic and social change created new needs and brought fresh ideas about their handling. The traditional view of social progress was to concentrate upon winning improved conditions of work and cash benefits as a result of negotiation between the social partners. The newer view meant starting from the human needs of the citizen body and placing a greater stress on the role of public authorities in meeting them. A broader approach to social policy seemed necessary as a means of bringing coherence into many public activities. No longer could social progress be thought of solely in terms of improving the social security system but would have to consider such varied problems as the legal basis of family ties, the effectiveness of the educational system, the role of the modern hospital and the problems of the inner cities. Above all, a problem of social marginalisation had developed. Social costs were being borne disproportionately by particular groups rather than by the community as a whole. These groups included the migrants, the elderly, large families and, more recently, the unemployed and whole communities in older, industrial areas. One result was that inequalities of income had been found by OECD to be particularly wide in France. (2) It was for such reasons that the arguments for a broader social policy to protect the needy, to tackle the problems of urban infrastructure and, more generally, for economic and social redevelopment had come to be seen by many reformers as the true way forward.

A necessary, but not sufficient, aim in this analysis was reform of the social security system. This had expanded rapidly to cover virtually the whole population and a wide range of needs but could, nevertheless, be criticised on several counts. It had not originally incorporated the principle of a basic minimum for all. To get round this, it had used the notion of a 'minimum guarantee' which was applied to particular groups of beneficiaries held to be in most urgent need. The mechanism had been used for the elderly, the disabled and for some family allowances, but was still far from serving as a principle of universal national protection.

A second big problem for social security stemmed from the changing position of women whose social protection could no longer be seen as a function of marital status. Thirdly, the growth in part-time and short-term work and high unemployment levels were producing situations in which members of the labour force could fall outside the social security system whilst the exclusion of older workers from the labour force was creating a class whose long-term prospects were of a minimal retirement pension only. More variable family patterns required a re-thinking of the purposes of family allowances while young people increasingly found it more difficult to build up an entitlement because of their inability to get jobs. Thus, long before the advent of the Socialist government, France had been experiencing problems in maintaining and developing her social security system as it tried to deal with the rising volume of social problems. Arrangements were complex, overlapping and confusing for the administrator and user alike, partly because of the multiplicity of schemes which had been allowed to continue. The most intractable problem was the escalating cost of social security as schemes for retirement reached their full maturity and as the coverage of the population and the range of needs was extended. Some of the heaviest increases were the result of developments in health care. For twenty years before the achievement of power by the Socialists, the share of GDP devoted to social expenditure had been increasing and had outstripped the rate of economic growth, not only in comparison with the past but also in comparison with other European countries. By the second half of the 1970s, France was finding it particularly hard to brake the cost increases despite the exhortations of the VIIIth Plan and the austerity measures of Raymond Barre. (3)

The onset of high unemployment, and its persistence, imposed a further burden and highlighted the fact that relatively little attention had been given to the social protection of the unemployed in comparison with the needs of the elderly, the sick and young children. But over-riding such specific issues, there existed a general dissatisfaction with the achievements of post-war welfare. It had created bureaucracies which were often insensitive to the needs of potential clients, were not flexible enough to adapt to emerging problems and neither abolished need nor appeared to allow room for the expression of public views on welfare functions. This change of mood was captured by the policy intentions of the French Left.

Social Policy. Socialist Aims
The policy statements from the Common Programme to

the 110 Propositions contained a major emphasis upon the need for change in order that French society might incorporate more fully the themes of social justice, social equality and openness with the aim of establishing a new balance in relationships between public authorities, public authorities and individuals and between individuals themselves. It is clear, therefore, that a broad brush was necessary to paint the main outlines of a re-furbished social policy and from this point of view many of the policies described in other chapters must be considered in the light of their social contribution. The aim of the Socialists was to develop in French social welfare an approach more akin to that of the social democracies of Scandinavia. This did not just imply a coherent, all-embracing view of social policy but required a shift in the terms of debate as well as an alteration in accustomed methods of handling social problems.

The theme of producing a more open society assumed major importance on the Left after 1968 with a crystallisation of the belief that, although many changes would be necessary to pursue the aim of social justice, they would need to be in tune with French institutions and customs. Concrete proposals in the Common Programme of 1972 included the raising of the minimum wage, the reduction of the working week, the lowering of the retirement age, equal pay for women, the decentralisation of state power and greater devolution to the regions. Later thinking began to push the aims away from a preoccupation with traditional labour goals through the addition of autogestion (which has a clear relevance to the administration of social welfare) and a discussion of the needs of disadvantaged groups such as women and migrants. In this way, it began to reflect a view of individual welfare as deriving from the rights of citizenship rather than as primarily vested in working status. By the time of the 110 Propositions, the social programme included a firm commitment to improving the standard of living of the least well-off through raising both the minimum wage and certain social benefits as a matter of social justice. More decisions relating to the quality of life were to be taken locally and support given to local groups and to minority cultures and special attention given to methods of improving the position of women in society. Parental leave for both parents, with the protected rights to re-entry to the labour market, changes in family allowances and more nursery places would all help the family and, in particular, the working woman. Better rights for young people and improved protection for migrants were promised, although curbs on the entry of foreign workers were also agreed.

The proposals on a unified society perhaps expressed the most fundamental theme of social policy for it accepted the long-term aim of providing universal national protection. In the meantime, the elderly and handicapped were to receive special help and their full social participation ensured through improved housing, leisure and cultural facilities. They were to have the right to contribute to the formulation of social security policy and further reductions in the retirement age for men and women were envisaged. The provisions concerning health care are of considerable interest for they foreshadowed the development of health centres, a renewed importance for preventive medicine and referred to a clearer role for hospitals and better rules for the use of medical equipment. An improved housing policy (including better communal facilities), a more open educational system and a two year sabbatical leave policy all found their place. Whilst space does not permit a discussion of all these issues, the range of interest is significant as an indication of the scope intended for social policy and the importance attached to finding a place for all within French society.

The achievement of these goals was dependent upon the adaptation of existing institutions, particularly the social security and health care delivery systems. To a degree, such changes can be considered as a continuation of a long-term aim to modernise and increase the efficiency of those structures in order to obtain an improved return for beneficiaries. Nevertheless, for the Left, social reform entailed a second, more fundamental, line of attack: the incorporation of new needs and groups; and the adoption of a more egalitarian philosophy which would emphasise the claims of the least well-off. These two approaches to social reform are often conflictual rather than re-inforcing for they stem from very different views about the functions of social policy. In fact, the main crisis for the Socialists arose from the finances of social security and the decision to give priority to their restoration meant that neither aim was wholeheartedly pursued.

Social Security

The opportunity for a fundamental re-casting of the social security system had briefly seemed a possibility in the late 1940s but, in the event, sectional interests had proved too strong to allow a really new beginning. Thus, existing structures and methods continued to be used. As a result, social security consists of a complex of funds representing both the general class of employed workers and different sectional groups. These funds are grouped together into three branches covering old age, sickness and family allowances, each of which should, in principle, be self-financing from membership contributions supplemented by government payments for specific purposes. The funds are run jointly by employer and union representatives, or representatives from the appropriate groups, but their committees are strengthened with representatives from government and relevant professional organisations. The funds must operate within the legislative framework determined by government. Locally, sickness and family allowance funds deal with the administration of cash benefits and are also responsible for a network of health and social services. Although these are part of the country's national system of health and social care, each fund has a degree of discretion which allows services to adapt to local needs.

The creation of a Ministry of National Solidarity (which included responsibility for social security) under Mme Nicole Questiaux, of the left-wing CERES group, at first gave prominence to those elements in the Socialist party which favoured the use of the social security system to develop the universalist view of reform. This meant a refusal to consider social security as a burden on the productive process but rather as a necessary part of it and of the promotion of a modern society. According to this view, reform had to be seen in the context of the fragmentation of the labour market and the heavy demands made by the elderly and sick. An absolute priority had to be given to full employment and, since funds were limited, a redirection of the social security budget towards priority groups. Better treatment for those currently penalised economically required a broadening of the financial base, and a questioning of both the continued use of a ceiling on contributions and of the privileges won in the past by the special schemes and occupational pensions. It implied that true reform would incorporate the whole nation on more standardised terms within which differentiation according to need might occur. At the same time, the social security system needed to find ways to insist upon greater individual responsibility and to make more knowledge of its working available through increased powers at local level. Solidarity thus implied a curtailment of the benefits of some in order to deal with the new needs and the limited benefits of the many. A radical new approach was, therefore, required. (4)

The immediate action of the new government was to take measures to help the least well-off. The minimum wage was increased by 10 per cent - significantly more than was necessary to compensate for inflation - whilst retirement pensions, family allowances and allowances for the handicapped were also improved. These increases were to be paid for by a mixture of measures including higher contributions, (with temporary relief for firms employing workers at the lower wage levels), an increase in petrol tax, greater efficiency in collecting dues and a broadening of the wage-base for contributions. It was not long, however, before the social security system was subordinated to the government's austerity programme. The replacement of Mme Questiaux by M. Bérégovoy in June 1982 marked the introduction of a new phase in which priority was to be given to restoring financial balance within two years. After this, the promise was of relief in contributions rather than of radical reform of benefit targetting. During this period of austerity, the government's aim was limited to that of protecting the position of beneficiaries as far as possible and of giving special consideration to the poorest amongst them. And, while further increases in benefits for the handicapped, the elderly and in some family allowances later became possible, extra costs were also imposed. The duration of unemployment benefits was reduced, a basic hospital charge, with exemptions, was introduced and contributions from the early retired and unemployed towards health care were demanded although, once again, the worst off were exempt. The limits on income assessed for social insurance contributions were increased and the income base upon which employers and the self-employed were assessed for contributions changed. The cost of support for handicapped adults was transferred to the national government but some taxation on alcohol and tobacco was also ear-marked for this purpose. A 1 per cent tax on personal incomes was imposed (excluding the poorest one-third of taxpayers) and a 1 per cent 'solidarity' contribution levied on civil servants towards the cost of unemployment insurance. Nevertheless, despite austerity, the real value of social protection made modest increases. Within the total, the greatest benefit was reserved for the poorest whilst income was raised in ways which made a modest shift towards general community financing and away from traditional insurance methods.

Table 4.1: Total Social Protection as a % of gdp

1981	1982	1983
27.4	28.5	28.8

Table 4.2: Benefits per inhabitant at 1980 prices and purchasing power parities (EC standardisation)

1980	1982	1983
2160	2380	2430

Table 4.3: Source of Receipts

	1970	1983
Employers	59.2	52.8
Protected persons	18.9	23.6
Public Funds	18.6	20.5
Other	3.3	3.1

Source: Commission of the European Communities, *Report on Social Developments*, 1985, Statistical Appendix VIII.

Until 1967, the local committees for social security had been elected bodies and one of the changes brought by the socialist government was to restore those elections. This fitted well with the idea of a more responsible society, but no indication was given as to how significant this change was intended to be. The work of the funds had become steadily more confined in order to ensure that it conformed to the wider goals of national policy, whilst the standardisation of monetary benefits which had occurred left no room for discretion over this part of the work. To be effective as a reform, therefore, elections needed to be combined with a clear view of the functions of the local committees. Since both the sickness and family allowance funds provided a variety of social service functions there was a case for considering their amalgamation, but this possibility seems to have been disregarded. The first elections took place in October 1983 and were widely regarded not simply as a test of overall government policy, but also of the degree of support held by the unions themselves. The striking feature of the result was the extent to which the CGT and CFDT lost ground to the more right-wing and independent unions compared with similar elections in the 1960s when the CGT had won over 40 per cent of the vote. The elections were seen in political terms, were divisive between the unions and, given the high degree of non-unionisation amongst French workers, many of whom were thus disenfranchised, it is difficult to see these elections in terms of a contribution to social policy or to new forms of government.

Family Allowances
Since the early 1970s, family allowance policy had been shifting its emphasis away from blanket allowances for all to more help for specific groups including low income families, single parents and families with very young children. Attempts were being made to couple them with an increase in the scale and quality of child care services. This greater selectivity had not, however, been matched by corresponding changes in the taxation system where the use of the family quotient principle notoriously favoured the wealthy families. (5) A socialist family policy dedicated to greater equality and to the belief that every child should be a wanted child and that potential parents should not be deprived of children for economic or, indeed, unnecessary medical, reasons therefore required further action. The 1981 election was rapidly followed by a significant increase of 25 per cent in family allowances and a 50 per cent rise in housing allowance for less well-off families as well as by improvements in allowances for low income families. These changes were followed by rules to limit tax concessions for the better-off and, in 1983, by the extension of the right to deduct the cost of child care for all children under the age of three years, not just vulnerable ones. This right was later extended to include all children under five years old in some cases. The removal of the concept of the head of the household from the tax code was intended to help women obtain these benefits. On the other hand, austerity measures led to efforts to restrain family costs whilst again trying to protect priority groups. In February 1982 there had been a further 25 per cent

increase in allowances for families containing two eligible children, but some benefits were abandoned and the starting and finishing dates for eligibility altered. Later, cash increases were less than the amounts necessary to maintain the real value of family benefits except for the poorest groups.

Meanwhile, support for a policy of providing an environment favourable to family well-being was expressed in the IXth Plan. This aim was reflected both in wider recognition that child-minding facilities were inadequate to meet demand (6) and in the attempt to develop local social improvement programmes intended to encourage the formation of support groups to protect families and enable them to use services more effectively. These schemes had the needs of larger families particularly in mind.

By 1985, a considerable rationalisation of allowances had occurred. A young child's allowance became payable to all pregnant women, continuing until the child was three months old and subject to medical surveillance. This was extended until the age of three years on a means-tested basis. Other types of supplementary, means-tested family benefits remained for both one and two parent households where there were at least three children over three years of age. Although the income limit for allowances varied according to the position of the child in the family and the number of dependent children, these ceilings were made more favourable where both parents were working or where a single parent was in charge and were linked to changes in wage levels. Those taking parental leave to care for three or more children, provided they fulfilled the eligibility rules, also received certain benefits in kind, such as priority on vocational training courses as well as a non-taxable, non-means-tested benefit. Finally, a new boost was given to research into family problems including an interest in the effects of changing family structures, of women's employment and the impact of local social policies on family life.

These changes express a particular interest in the needs of young children, large families, families where the mother is working and the least well-off families. At the same time, the government tried to create an enabling environment so that effective choices about parenthood were possible. Large increases in standard family allowances for the third and subsequent children were avoided.

Health Care

The provision of personal health care in France is the responsibility of a large number of institutions and is dependent on a subtle mix of public and private provision. The stress laid on the doctrine of 'liberal medicine' and the careful protection of the position of the non-hospital doctor as a private practitioner must not obscure the importance of the functions of central and local government and the sickness funds whereby great efforts are made to ensure access to health care and direct overall provision towards socially acceptable goals. This is seen in the trend towards the socialisation of the cost of health care. Whereas 60 per cent of the cost of personal health care was carried by the community in 1960, by 1981 this figure had risen to 75 per cent. (7) This increase reflected, in part, the steady incorporation of the population into membership of the sickness funds. Members, and their dependants, thereby obtain access to a GP or consultant, a supply of necessary drugs and appropriate hospital care, and can freely consult a doctor of choice, including those offering specialist services. Great importance has always been attached to the principles of direct payment for medical services and the obligation of the patient to retain some financial responsibility for health care. The justification given for this is twofold: first, that it reinforces the individualistic nature of the doctor-patient relationship and its essentially private nature; and secondly, that the cost of medical care is thereby made more obvious to the public. This form of provision requires agreement between the main providers of health care on the appropriate medical services to be offered, the scale of charges and any exemptions from payment, e.g. for the disabled or for very expensive drugs. The small proportion of the population without fund membership, or unable to pay its share, can have recourse to local assistance services for financial support. Whilst payment for hospital care is based on the same principle, the sickness fund pays the hospital directly instead of via the patient and many of the more significant costs are entirely borne by the funds. A common way of introducing a health care reform is to include a new service on the list of approved medical acts as was done in December 1982 with the agreement to re-imburse 70 per cent of the cost of an abortion in order to fulfil an election pledge.

Liberal Medicine. Developments in the provision of health care rest on negotiations between government, sickness funds and the medical profession. These relations have been characterised by periods of great tension. The system leaves considerable power in the hands of the doctors whilst their political influence has ensured that the hospital structure has grown in a way well suited to the interests of the medical profession. The basis of the arrangements between the community and doctors has been the acceptance of the doctrine of liberal medicine by successive governments. This sets out the right of doctor and patient to choose each other and to agree a fee, the principle of direct payment of doctor by patient, the freedom of the doctor to diagnose and prescribe and the right to confidentiality. If, then, the public is to receive the right to health care, a major question has to be that of establishing a scale of fees for approved medical acts and prescribable drugs and related services, which is broadly acceptable to both the profession and the sickness funds. The scale has to try to keep up to date with changes in medical practice and, simultaneously, be confined within acceptable cost. Agreement on a scale has proved a major source of friction and the Socialists inherited an already difficult situation in that the 1980 convention, which attempted to establish tighter norms of medical practice and offered inducements to doctors willing to keep within the terms of the agreement, was unacceptable to many doctors. The new government soon began negotiations for its revision and appeared willing to accept traditional forms of payment provided costs could be curbed.

The Hospital Sector. The hospital sector also presented the Socialist government with immediate problems of which the lack of coherence between public and private provision, the widespread use of certain hospitals for private practice, the difficulty of keeping running costs under control and the need to change the pattern of provision towards care in the community rather than in hospital were some of the more obvious. It can be argued that the French health care system is one which finds it particularly hard to adapt both to outside financial control and to the establishment of coherent care patterns since it is geared to the individual practitioner, locks doctor and patient into a situation of upward consultation costs and distributes decision-making over a number of authorities used to acting independently from each other. The preparations for the IXth Plan recognised these issues and argued the need to establish sensible priorities, financial controls and more open decision-making. (8)

M. Ralite, of the Communist Party, became Minister of Health in June 1981 and developed an active hospital policy. The <u>Charte de la Santé</u> of June 1982 accepted the reality of a public and private sector but marked the intention to improve the standards in the general hospitals as opposed to the big teaching centres which had hitherto been favoured, to introduce reform in the employment contracts of full-time hospital doctors and to improve evaluation of hospital performance. A further element was the intention to phase out the use of the public hospital for private consultation and practice; a move which was bound to be interpreted as a direct attack on the traditional attitudes of the medical profession and the position of some of its more eminent members. (9) However, the new policy was introduced from 1986 and the salaried doctors in hospital received improved working conditions as compensation. (10) Hospital staffing structures also needed changing for the independence of specialities from each other had become notorious as each one developed under the control of its 'grand patron'. The introduction of new hospital management arrangements was thus highly significant, particularly when associated with an attempt to set up specialist teams working in groups under an elected chairman in which not only younger doctors but non-medical staff might serve. It was not until 1985 that this change began to operate.

The financial squeeze made such steps harder to take than they might otherwise have been. There had, originally, been some relaxation of hospital budgets and of recruitment as part of the job creation programme. However, this could not be sustained and the charges payable through social security had to be increased. In the spring of 1983, after M. Ralite's departure from the Ministry, his successor was subordinated to the overall control of the Ministry of Social Affairs and National Solidarity and cost control became increasingly important. The minimum charge for hospital patients was enforced and hospital budgets tightened. The regional sickness funds and hospital administrators were henceforth to agree a total annual budget with strict, detailed control whilst limits were imposed upon the permitted increase in staff consequent upon the reduction in the standard working week. Thus, the new arrangements of moving budgetary control to the level of the individual hospital and of providing hospitals with a more open system of decision-making could hardly have been tried at a less favourable moment. However, the subsequent fall in inflation and the slackening of the austerity measures as social security costs were curbed began to relieve some of the pressures in the service.

Broader Reforms. Ever since the Common Programme, it had been thought desirable to encourage health centres and forms of group practice. These would be able to supply a range of auxiliary and social services and operate on a salaried basis. The argument rested on the need to shift the balance of care away from the hospital and on the boost it would give to the erosion of the fee-for-service principle in favour of health financing by sickness funds, central and local government. An experimental pilot scheme was established in St. Nazaire in 1983, but lack of funds prevented any further development along these lines. Although for many Socialists these changes were at the heart of desirable reforms in health care provision, particularly the attack on the fee-for-service method of payment, there was less chance of their succeeding once the restoration of social security finances had been achieved and the elections for the funds had failed to give control to the more radical unions. Many of the other issues of relevance to a socialist approach to health care provision are long-term and depend upon a better use of existing services, improved linkages between the payers, the providers and the community together with the ability to strengthen long-term planning techniques. Health care management only rated eleventh place out of the twelve priority programmes in the IXth Plan for which the preliminary work accepted that a change in attitudes and a willingness to work in a new way were more important factors than technical changes for the improvement of health care and these take time to show themselves. (11) A tentative conclusion might be that traditional medicine has been put on the defensive but that a more socialised framework has not yet emerged.

Unemployment Benefit
Social security has always been primarily concerned with the twin problems of old age and health care,

but a major question for the Socialists was that of income maintenance for the unemployed. This issue diverted attention and resources away from the longer-term issues of reform necessary for a new style social policy. Once high unemployment rates had become endemic the weaknesses in the cash benefit system became apparent. The Socialists found it necessary to tighten up the benefit schemes as part of their austerity curbs, but also continued with a tidying-up process. A decree of 24 November 1982 introduced changes to remedy financial deficits and these were to continue until the social partners had time to agree similar measures. The result was to lengthen the contribution period, to link benefit duration more closely to the time spent in insurable employment, lengthen the waiting period for those leaving work without just cause and to introduce a waiting period for those receiving more than the minimum of redundancy pay. Longer-term benefits were to be variable in amount according to whether the beneficiary was under or over 50 years of age, some lump sum benefits were curtailed and the special daily allowance payable to those deemed redundant or unemployed on 'economic grounds' was curbed. In 1984, the administrative arrangements were clarified and the contribution/benefit equation further restricted. Two types of benefit were put into the same scheme for administration by the social partners. The contributory insurance scheme continued and benefits were to last for 30 months (60 months for the over 55s). Benefit level was to differentiate between those under and over 50 years subject to a maximum benefit of 75 per cent of previous earnings. Backing this up was a solidarity scheme, or system of non-contributory allowances, paid for by central government and intended for certain categories such as young people, single parents for a limited period of payment and the long-term unemployed. This benefit would be payable for six-monthly renewable terms. In October 1985 a further agreement became essential for financial reasons and contributions were again increased.

It seems clear that unemployment insurance cover declined substantially. (12) Those who had no benefit had to fall back on local assistance and local charity, thus bringing another section of the population into the ranks of the new poor and creating adverse publicity for the socialist government as some supermarkets began to provide free food parcels for the unemployed. In 1985, the Cabinet increased the wealth tax in order to provide subsidies for organisations providing basic services such as hot meals, agreed to make surplus food stocks and empty housing available and decided to provide a basic allowance of 40 francs per day for some of the unemployed over the age of 50 who had been left out of the benefit scheme. Thus, support for the unemployed remained patchy whilst the increases in public spending (intended to stimulate the economy) were insufficient to absorb the unemployed. For the longer term, the Socialists remained committed to the belief that the more positive role for government was to ensure a fairer division of available work amongst the total working population. (13)

Migrants
The Socialist Party had promised to improve the position of migrants as part of its programme for better protection of civil liberties. Problems of racial tension, particularly in inner city areas, had been compounded, with the rise in unemployment, by a backlash against the presence of migrants resulting in calls for repatriation and a curb on further immigration. In consequence, initiatives were limited and must be seen against a background of stricter entry controls. A number of illegal immigrants had their position regularised and the conditions pertaining to residence and work permits eased. In 1983, France ratified the Council of Europe's Convention on the Legal Status of Migrant Workers.

Many migrants work in casual and irregular employment which escapes statutory employment controls, but it was hoped that the above changes would at least mean there would be no formal barriers to their chances of moving out of this twilight world. Other measures were aimed at more effective social integration through providing migrants and their children with educational and training skills. A new drive began in 1981 to encourage local authorities to establish programmes including housing schemes, literacy programmes and the setting up of young people's and women's groups. A deeper issue, never solved, was whether the role of the school was to encourage assimilation or to maintain the language and culture of the country of origin, particularly if migrants might subsequently be returning home. The socialist government tried to give a lead in many of these issues by opening talks with the authorities in some of the main countries of origin, easing nationality rules in the public sector, associating representatives of migrant groups with public authority work and, in 1984, the creation of an Immigrants Council. For the first time ever in France, migrants were permitted to vote in a municipal election. In May 1985 in the Lille suburb of Mons en Baroeul, all foreigners aged 18 and over who were legally resident before 1 January 1985 and who were local taxpayers were allowed to participate in the local poll. It should be stressed, however, that this was an isolated experiment and Mitterrand's promise to give all migrants voting rights in local elections was not implemented. (14)

Women in Society
The Socialist Party came to power with a clear commitment to improve the position of women in society. The political lead inherited from the previous government was continued with the appointment of Mme Y Roudy as Minister for Women's Rights, attached to the Prime Minister. A number of other women received government posts.
    Employment policy for women aimed to encourage their spread throughout the occupational structure, including into more responsible positions. In 1982, legislation was passed to ensure their full, legal eligibility for all civil service posts and an active policy to encourage them to come forward for promotion was adopted. The civil service also introduced a scheme of parental leave to help with the care of sick children. 1983 saw legislation to encourage greater equality in the private sector. Firms must now make an annual report on the employment conditions and training opportunities for women and present a statistical analysis of their position in the firm, whilst the comité d'entreprise (works committee) must ensure equality promoting measures are taken. Government contracts with individual firms were envisaged as another means to encourage wider employment chances for women although by 1985 only a handful had been negotiated. (15) Rules for parental leave in the private sector were adopted in January 1984. And in 1985, the appointment of equal opportunity counsellors at the regional level of the educational service was announced. The intention was to ensure that girls had full access to courses in science and technology and were given vocational guidance to encourage them to try out new fields of employment.

The Elderly

Retirement at 60 had been a long-standing union demand and in 1983 all members of the general scheme obtained the right to a full pension at 60 years payable at a rate of half the reference wage in return for 37½ years contribution. The government agreed, at the same time, to increase the real level of the minimum pension and to improve the pension position of some public sector employees. Rules concerning work after retirement were also tightened. Later negotiations brought retirement at the age of 60 into the occupational schemes although the financial terms for so doing could only be agreed for a seven year period. How far these arrangements are largely a formalisation of existing patterns of retirement, whether they give individuals a greater choice or force them into retiring earlier than they would wish is hard to say. Modern thinking is more interested in the possibility of introducing flexible retirement ages than in a simple reduction which may well be a response to pressures which have little to do with the needs of the elderly.

Both the VIth and VIIth Plans had recognised the need to promote the social integration of the elderly. The IXth Plan contained a priority implementation programme which stressed the importance of locally based services, the need to take local factors into account in developing policy and to encourage co-operation between different providing services. Thus, once again, new policy drives were concerned as much with the way things were done as with the allocation of more resources. Such a move fitted well with the belief in strengthening the local community, both evoking its own resources and creating social services which are appropriate to it. In this connection, many would like to see a changing role for social workers and their more flexible use, not just in connection with services for the elderly but for the general community.

To mark the importance of the problems of the elderly, the government appointed a Secretary of State, attached to the Ministry of Social Affairs and National Solidarity, to carry special responsibility for them. Furthermore, in order to try to relate policy to the felt needs of the elderly, it set up a central advisory committee to examine social policy from their point of view and carry out special studies and enquiries. This body became especially concerned with monitoring the attempts at co-ordination and encouraging policies aimed to help the elderly stay at home rather than enter residential care. To do this meant continuing to divert resources towards the provision of domiciliary and community services, including home help and meals services, health care in the home, leisure and visiting services. It also implied experimenting with more adaptable, open and relaxed forms of residential care. Later policy concentrated on enlarging the scale of support services, notably the availability of home helps.

Conclusion
The record of this period of Socialist government is mixed. From an historical perspective, which would see the changes of the 1980s as an effort to complete the reforms only partially achieved in the late 1940s, there is still some way to go. The main structure of social security remains intact. Although the improvements - and there were many detailed changes - do not add up to a sea-change in social policy they were steps compatible with the aim of moving in the direction of the Northern European approach to welfare. It was unrealistic to expect more. The severe economic problems meant that there were few resources available to soften the costs and that some groups would have to pay for social reform. The imposition of the austerity programme was a significant move in that it meant that the goal of financial probity was to take precedence over the aims deriving from greater social justice and equality in social security. The replacement of Mme Questiaux by M. Bérégovoy in 1982, together with the subsequent subordination of the Minister of Health to the Minister of Social Affairs and National Solidarity, were the political signs of the turning away from radical social reform. Whilst this implied that social policy was to be subordinated to other governmental aims, it is feasible to argue that only high social discipline enabled the socialist government, and the French population, to give priority to restoring the finances of the social security system and that this achievement was the most valuable service that could be given to French social welfare at the time.

One should not, however, take refuge in the argument that external, economic factors brought down Socialist social policy. A major weakness of the Socialists was to enter office seemingly oblivious to the long-standing deficits in the social security funds. Thus, the changes brought in to re-establish the finances give the appearance of ad hoc reactions rather than of carefully thought out moves in a long-term plan of reform.

Since the social policy aims were very far-reaching, a definite plan of priorities amongst them, detailed costing plans, a determination to strengthen the position of the Ministry of National Solidarity within the central civil service and the development of social service work at departmental level were all necessary pre-conditions of success. The type of welfare state the Socialists wanted grew up on strong public welfare administration, high-grade social investigation and social statistics and on a corps of professional workers with good career structures. The problems of helping the marginalised groups, of managing the delivery of health care, of ensuring individuals get their entitlement are problems where solution depends as much on the way services are run as on the amount of money made available to them. Some years of major effort would have been necessary to strengthen French provision in these fields.

Finally, it may be questioned whether the socialist government was imprisoned in a view of social policy which was already out of date. The Common Programme had, after all, been established in 1972. It, therefore, reflected the aspirations of the late 1960s when the climate of opinion about the role of social policy was very different. The rapid development of social policy, based on growing prosperity, disguised the problems appearing on the horizon. A more cautious approach was necessary for the 1980s. This was not just because of the change in economic fortune but because the short-comings of the post-war welfare state were becoming apparent. It was to these newer problems of administrative patterns, detailed planning and involvement of the general public that governmental policy needed to turn. Many countries now see the reform of social security finances in terms of amalgamation of a contribution/benefit scheme with the taxation system, while the needs of women workers have to be considered in different terms from those available in a traditional insurance scheme. Equally, the social isolation of the elderly is a well-known phenomenon: this problem is not to be solved by retirement at the age of 60 - indeed, this may exacerbate it.

Nevertheless, the picture is not a negative one. Within the constraints, the government made serious attempts to fulfil its election pledges. The changes which occurred may in themselves have been detailed and sometimes relatively small-scale but together they add up to an active programme of social reform. The attempt to incorporate migrant groups more fully, to help women overcome disadvantages at work, to use selective increases in social security benefits and in family allowances to improve the position of the worst-off, to involve the elderly in social policy and to introduce improvements in hospital administration were all steps towards the just and unified society of which the Socialists had spoken. These changes also show a strong continuity with previous reforms. There is little in this list which does not follow, and build on, the work of previous governments. They demonstrate a traditional picture of incremental change.

Notes

1. A. Getting, La Sécurité Sociale, Que sais-je?, (Paris: Presses Universitaires de France, 1976), p.16.
2. See esp. M. Sawyer, Income Distribution in OECD countries, (Paris: Economic Outlook, Occasional Studies, OECD, 1976).
3. OECD, Social Expenditure 1960-1990, (Paris: OECD, 1985), p.21.
4. N. Questiaux, 'Social Protection and the Crisis'" International Social Security Review, (1982), pp.383-90.
5. For an explanation of the family quotient see J. Bradshaw and D. Piachaud, Child Support in the European Community, Occasional Papers on Social Administration No. 66, (London: Bedford Square Press, 1980), pp.61-2.
6. Commission of the European Communities, Report on Social Developments, (European Communities, Commission, 1981), p.123.
7. J. Barrot, 'Quelle politique sociale dans une économie en mutation?', Droit Social, Paris, (Jan. 1981), p.12.
8. M. Wurmer, C. Pigement, J-P. Weiss, 'La santé choisie', Droit Social, Paris, (May 1983), pp.345-55.
9. One estimate suggests that rather under 4,000 out of 15,000 full-time hospital physicians treated private patients; P. Godt, 'Doctors and Deficits: Regulating the Medical Profession in France', Public Administration, vol. 63, (Summer 1985), p.164.
10. Victor G. Rodwin, 'Management without objectives: The French health policy gamble', in A.

McLachlan and A. Maynard (eds), The Public/Private Mix for Health, (London: Nuffield Provincial Hospitals Trust, 1982), p.276.
11. Droit Social, Paris, (May 1983), p.346.
12. OECD, Economic Surveys, France, 1984/5, p.47.
13. M. Fabius, Le Monde, 8 January 1986.
14. For details of voting in the municipal election at Mons en Baroeul see Keesings Archives, vol. XXXII, p.34307. On Mitterrand's views and government initiatives see Commission of the European Communities, Report on Social Developments, (European Communities, Commission, 1985), pp.1-14.
15. E. Vogel-Polsky, 'Positive Action Programmes for Women', International Labour Review, (1985), pp.385-99 is the source for this paragraph.

Further Reading
1. For a comprehensive account of the formal structure of French social institutions see P. Laroque (ed.), The Social Institutions of France, (New York, Gordon and Breach, 1983). For details of the law, development and structure of the social security system see J-J Dupeyroux, Droit de la Sécurité Sociale, (Paris: Dalloz, regularly revised).
2. Information on the financial costs of French social policy can be found in Commission of the European Communities, Cost Containment in Health Care. The Experience of Twelve European Countries 1977-83, (European Communities, Commission, 1984) which discusses French attempts to curb health care costs in relation to other European experiences. A comparative analysis of the trends in social expenditure of OECD countries and their underlying causes is also available in OECD, Social Expenditure 1960-1990, (Paris: OECD, 1985).
3. For a broader, sociological discussion of modern social problems in France see J. Fournier and N. Questiaux, Traité du Social: Situations, Luttes Politiques, Institutions, Paris: Dalloz, 1978). A. Lion and P. Maclouf, L'Insécurité Social, (Paris: Editions Ouvrières, 1982) take a similar approach in their analysis of contemporary social problems (notably poverty) and the inability of existing welfare systems to deal adequately with them.
4. B. Jobert, Le Social en Plan, (Paris: Editions Ouvrières, 1981) discusses the use of the planning mechanism to achieve social objectives.

Chapter Five

DECENTRALISATION: LA GRANDE AFFAIRE DU SEPTENNAT?

Sonia Mazey

Shortly after his election in May 1981 President Mitterrand declared that political and administrative decentralisation would be la grande affaire du septennat - the major achievement of his presidency. The announcement came as no surprise. The centralised 'one and indivisible' Republic established initially by the Jacobins and consolidated by Napoleon I had attracted widespread criticism in the 1960s and 1970s. It had been argued, particularly within opposition circles, that France had become excessively centralised. Since 1972 the Socialist and Communist Parties had repeatedly promised that a future left-wing government would implement a radical programme of decentralisation. This pledge had been maintained throughout the 1970s and reiterated in 1981 in both the Socialist Party's manifesto, the Projet Socialiste and Mitterrand's personal manifesto, les 110 Propositions.

The first step in the socialist decentralisation programme was taken on 2 March 1982 when Parliament passed the necessary enabling legislation. Subsequent laws and decrees between 1982 and 1986 systematically transformed the traditional relationship between Paris and the provinces. A priori legal, financial and technical control by the central administration over local government decisions was suppressed and the prefects - the local agents of the central administration - replaced by Commissaires de la République who lack the local executive powers of their predecessors. The traditional local authorities - the communes and departments - received increased powers and resources, 26 regional governments were established and Corsica accorded a special status. In this policy area the Mitterrand administration accomplished - in formal terms at least - most of what it set out to do in 1981. While it is too early to assess the long-term impact of these reforms there is no doubt that important changes have taken place in the formal organisation of central-local government relations in France. Less clear, however, is the extent to which these changes have produced a decentralised political system or brought about the Socialists' declared objective of greater local democracy and political participation.

French Local Government: an Introduction

The Constitution of the Fifth Republic left untouched the traditional system of local government based upon the 37,708 communes and 96 departments created after the Revolution. This arrangement had evolved out of the Napoleonic prefectoral system of provincial control and by 1958 was a curious combination of administrative control and political power. It was this system - modified somewhat by earlier governments of the Fifth Republic - which the Socialists inherited in 1981.

In each of the 96 metropolitan departments a directly elected general council, with 'general powers' of intervention was responsible for the building and maintenance of main roads, gendarmeries, public housing and schools, and for administering government policies. Although each council elected its own president the departmental executive remained the prefect, appointed by and directly accountable to the Minister of the Interior. The prefect, assisted by sub-prefects, was a formidable figure of authority within the department. He was simultaneously the executive officer of the general council and the representative of the state, the government and the Minister of the Interior. As the local executive he determined the council's agenda, timetable and budget. As the representative of the state he presided at all official functions and ceremonies. On behalf of the government he liaised with the local field services of the Paris ministries and made sure that government directives were implemented. Finally, as the local agent of the Minister of the Interior he took action against local authorities guilty of illegality, technical or financial irregularity and undertook responsibility for the maintenance of law and order in the department. In addition to <u>a priori</u> prefectoral control, departmental (and communal) council decisions were subject also to <u>a priori</u> financial and technical control from other central

Decentralisation: La Grande Affaire du Septennat?

government ministries.

Each of the 37,708 communes also elected its own municipal council which in turn elected its executive, the mayor. In addition to providing basic services such as sanitation and rubbish collection, municipal councils (which also enjoyed 'general powers') were expected to maintain local roads and provide public amenities such housing, parks, libraries, etc. As head of the municipal council the mayor was responsible for ensuring the safety, security and sanitation of the commune. But he was also the official representative of the state and, as such, directly accountable to the departmental prefect. In this capacity, he was the official registrar of births, marriages and deaths and responsible for the promulgation and implementation of laws, regulations and circulars emanating from Paris.

Yet, while the formal relationship between the government and the local authorities prior to 1981 was a straightforward one of administrative control, the reality was more complex. In particular, local politicians - particularly mayors - were often more powerful and their relationships with local administrative officials less antagonistic than implied above. Most French local politicians hold office for a considerable length of time. Indeed, some of the principal towns in France have elected the same mayor since the war: Chaban-Delmas in Bordeaux, Gaston Defferre (until his death in 1986) in Marseilles and Pierre Pflimlin in Strasbourg are notable examples. Such stability undoubtedly strengthened the position of <u>notables</u> in their dealings with administrative officials who rarely remained long in one place. And, while relationships between local politicians and prefects obviously varied from place to place, they were rarely overtly hostile. Indeed, prefects and mayors frequently joined forces in defending the interests of 'their' department at the national level. The basic reasons for such co-operation were quite straightforward ones of self-interest. An ambitious prefect anxious to prevent local conflict, for instance, might use his influence within the administration to secure extra resources for the locality or exercise discretion when applying central government directives to the community. Such actions increased the electoral popularity of the mayor who, in return, offered his support to the prefect on other sensitive issues.

Many local politicians could also influence

government policy by more direct means. Contrary to their British counterparts, most national politicians in France hold at least one local elective office: in 1980 42 per cent of senators held two local offices; 246 of the 491 Deputies elected to the National Assembly in June 1981 were mayors, 249 were general councillors and nineteen were members of the Paris city council. The Mauroy government formed that month contained no fewer than twenty-four mayors. (1) Cumul des mandats - the accumulation of elective offices - is publicly deplored and widely practised by politicians of all parties in France. President Mitterrand, for instance, was Deputy-Mayor of Chateau-Chinon and President of Nièvre general council while the present Gaullist Prime Minister, Jacques Chirac has since 1978 been Mayor of Paris. Gaston Defferre, author of the socialist decentralisation reforms was himself a government minister, member (and former President) of the Provence-Alpes-Côte-d'Azur regional council, president of the Bouches-du-Rhône general council and Mayor of Marseilles.

The origins of cumul des mandats lie in the localized nature of nineteenth century French parliamentary politics, but the practice has been sustained by the electoral benefits to be gained by national politicians from maintaining a local power base. The presence of local politicians at the national political level (both in Parliament and in government) is a central feature of French politics. It means that local interests cannot easily be overridden by national governments. This fact is crucial to an understanding of French local government reform and decentralisation: the parliamentary weight of local notables has been a key factor in shaping and setting the pace of local government reforms in the Fifth Republic - both before and after 1981.

Local Government Reform 1958-1981. Gaullist governments of the 1960s and 1970s, while opposed to political decentralisation, were nonetheless painfully aware of the need to rationalise French local administration. The system had been designed for a rural nation and was patently unable to meet the administrative and planning needs of a modern industrialised economy. The departments were simply too small to be viable units for the purposes of economic planning while demographic change had rendered the communal structure functionally

Decentralisation: La Grande Affaire du Septennat?

obsolete: by 1968, 95 per cent of the 37,708 communes had fewer than 5,000 inhabitants, 10 per cent contained fewer than one hundred people and some had no population at all. Most communes lacked the financial resources to build or maintain even the most basic of amenities and were thus totally dependent upon state financial and technical aid.

Despite their constitutional and parliamentary strength these governments nevertheless found local government reform a difficult and delicate task. Given the national political strength of the - generally conservative - local notables, comprehensive modernisation of the system - such as that undertaken by the Conservative government in Britain in 1972 - was out of the question. Equally, the growing strength of left-wing opposition parties at local government levels in the 1960s and 1970s precluded the introduction of political decentralisation by these right-wing regimes. Finally, many Gaullists, who shared General de Gaulle's views on the need for a strong state, were convinced that such measures constituted a serious threat to national unity. The major developments during this period were, therefore, piecemeal adjustment of existing structures and the introduction of an additional regional level of administration.

Attempts to rationalise the vast mosaic of communes made by successive gaullist governments met with only limited success. Few mayors welcomed the new opportunities for inter-communal co-operation provided by the Multi-Purpose Intercommunal Syndicates and Districts created by decree in 1959 and the Urban Communities established by law in 1966. (2) The 1971 Marcellin Act providing for voluntary mergers between communes was also greeted unenthusiastically by local élus: by the end of 1975 just 1,957 communes had merged and the total number of communes had been reduced by a mere 800.

On becoming President in 1974, the reformist Valéry Giscard d'Estaing - at that time an advocate of further decentralisation - declared local government reform to be an urgent priority. Between 1974 and 1981 the subject was rarely absent from the national political agenda: two major government reports were published and Parliament spent two years debating government proposals. But opposition to these initiatives from local politicians within the parliamentary ruling coalition impeded the reformers; the principal results of their work were the 1979 and 1980 Bonnet laws which grouped together the numerous government subsidies to communes under a single block grant (<u>Dotation globale de Fonctionnement</u>) and introduced an element of progression into local taxes. These changes were, not surprisingly, supported by the notables. Thus, when the Socialists came to power little had changed: France with 36,034 communes boasted more units of local government in 1981 than the rest of her EEC partners put together.

The regional authorities inherited by the Socialist government in 1981 were those established in 1972 by the Gaullist government of President Pompidou. Earlier administrative reforms in 1960-1 and 1964 had created regional prefects and planning agencies. These early regional reforms had been designed primarily to co-ordinate local administration and improve national economic planning, but they had sparked off a much bigger - and confused - public debate in the 1960s on political decentralisation and regionalisation.

Continuing public support for regional decentralisation after the 1969 referendum on regional reform together with pressure from the planning agency, DATAR, (Delegation for Regional Planning) eventually forced a reluctant government to further develop the regional structures. The 1972 Frey Act granted the 22 planning regions (established in 1959) the legal status of territorial public establishments - corporate bodies with legal authority within a functionally defined area. Their official role was the promotion of regional economic and social development. In each region a new regional council was established comprising all national politicians within the region - who were *ex officio* members - together with an equal number of local politicians from local councils in the region. The regional executive remained the regional prefect. The regional council and prefect were assisted by a consultative economic and social committee composed of representatives from socio-economic and professional organisations within the region who were appointed by the prefect.

The timidity of the reform was widely deplored. Government suspicion of the region and the influence of the notables were evident in the pivotal role accorded to the regional prefect and the composition of the regional council. Similar considerations were reflected in the limited powers and meagre resources granted to the new authorities. The regional assemblies were told by the regional prefect of state investment in the region and consulted over the formulation of the regional section of the national economic Plan. They were also responsible for the raising and spending of their own budget, the size of which was strictly limited by law. Compared with those of local authorities, the regional budgets were derisory: in 1975 the budget of the single department, the Nord, slightly exceeded the sum total of regional budgets for that year. But, the budget was essentially an investment budget, since the regional authorities were prohibited from establishing any independent technical or administrative services. Regions could contribute financially to projects 'of direct regional interest' which none the less had to be authorised and carried out by either the state or the constituent local authorities. Initially opposed to the reform, local notables soon began to seek seats in the new regional councils in the hope of securing extra funds for their constituencies.

Yet, despite this inauspicious beginning, between 1974 and 1981 the regional public establishments gradually assumed an institutional identity and a more coherent economic role. Although President Giscard d'Estaing in 1975 abandoned his earlier promise to establish directly elected regional authorities he did extend the budgetary and policy-making powers of the regions after 1977. In particular, the regions were given new powers to help new and ailing industries and more influence over the allocation of some state investments in the region. Regional budgets steadily increased in size and several regions - particularly those controlled by left-wing opposition parties - had by 1981 developed ambitious regional investment strategies. And although they were specifically prohibited by the 1972 reform, several regions had also established independent administrative and technical services. Most significant of all perhaps, by the time the socialists came to power, the region was no longer regarded as simply an administrative unit, but as an important level of political activity.

Between 1958 and 1981 French local government reform was a slow and piecemeal process. None the less, important changes were initiated during this period. Government commitment to economic planning and administrative rationalisation prompted the introduction of some inter-communal co-operation as well as the creation of regional administrative structures and representative assemblies. When the socialists came to power in 1981, the ground had thus already been prepared for further decentralisation: the regional framework existed; financial rationalisation was already under way; local notables were more positive about the prospect; and local government reform was already on the political agenda.

The Parti Socialiste and Decentralisation

In 1945 left-wing parties were united in their support for a centralised administrative state which they regarded as the principal guarantee of democratic equality and essential for socialist economic planning. While committed to the republican local government structures - the communes and departments - these parties were at this time opposed to regional decentralisation which they associated with reaction and the Vichy regime. Although several figures on the left such as Pierre Mendès-France in the 1950s advocated functional regionalism - the use of regions for economic planning purposes - socialists were generally opposed to regional political decentralisation. During the 1960s, however, several left-wing intellectuals, many of whom were later to join the new Socialist Party became vocal supporters of regional decentralisation - notably the Breton regionalist, Michel Phlipponneau and Michel Rocard, leader of the PSU and author of the provocative Décoloniser la Province. (3) The Communist Party, prompted into action by these initiatives, in 1971 publicly declared its commitment to greater democratic participation at the communal, departmental and regional levels of government (though it was least specific on the regional role).

The shift towards the region on the part of the left was prompted partly by the need to be seen to respond to - and present a democratic alternative to - the gaullist regional reforms. It was also a response to widespread public concern that the centralized state had become 'overloaded'. Growing economic disparities between regions - notably between Paris and other regions - which were exacerbated by the economic crisis of the 1970s, convinced many on the left of the need for decentralised economic planning. Added to these pressures was the fact that the 1960s were in France characterised by the revival of regionalist movements which tended to equate regionalism with socialism. Meanwhile, economic and industrial disputes also began to assume the character of regional protests against a capitalist, centralised state. Party political considerations were also involved. Though the left had been out of power at the national level since 1958, local electoral agreements during the 1970s between the Socialist and Communist parties had produced impressive results: after the 1977 municipal elections left-wing parties controlled 153 of the 221 largest towns and many left-wing councillors - particularly younger ones - were eager to increase local political autonomy.

As a broad coalition movement, the rejuvenated and modernised Parti Socialiste attracted the support of regionalists, environmentalists and autogestionnaires in favour of greater citizen participation. The presence of these groups served to revive the ideological debate within the Party on decentralisation. Yet while a consensus quickly emerged within the Socialist Party in favour of decentralisation, this was variously interpreted. As Michael Keating indicated:

> There were regionalists, wanting a break with the traditional system: these in turn divided into technocrats who saw the region as an ideal planning unit; supporters of 'micro-nationalism' in Brittany, Occitania and elsewhere; and a few exponents of the 'internal colonization' thesis brought in from the Parti-socialiste Unifié (PSU). There were supporters of the commune as the traditional basis of French local democracy; these included the big city bosses and socialist notables who wanted more power for the cities. Some supported the departments; others were autogestionnaires wanting more citizen participation in local government. Finally, there was a strong remaining 'jacobin' element which believed that implementation of the Socialist programme required a strong centralized State. (4)

The need to reconcile such diverse attitudes towards decentralisation meant that the policy eventually adopted by the Socialist Party was an ambiguous compromise. While the proposals were in no sense federalist, they did include special provisions for Corsica and the Basque region together with a commitment to promote regional cultures and languages. But the weight of local notables in both the Socialist and Communist parties precluded any reduction in the powers of the communes and departments. The new regional authorities were, therefore, to be grafted onto the existing structures.

The Socialist Party's proposals for decentralisation were first published in its 1971 programme of government, *Changer la Vie* and subsequently endorsed by the Communist Party in the 1972 *Programme Commun de Gouvernement*. This committed a future left-wing government to the introduction of regional government, the abolition of the prefectoral system and all forms of *a priori* control over local authorities by the central administration. After extensive debate within the Socialist Party during the 1970s these proposals were further elaborated upon in the *110 Propositions* and the *Projet Socialiste* which described decentralisation as:

> one of the most powerful levers of the break with capitalism, which will enable citizens to take the most direct part in the immense enterprise of social transformation which will be undertaken when the power of the State has been conquered by the Left. (5)

The reforms thus constituted an essential element of the socialist programme of *le changement*, the aim of which was to establish a participatory democracy characterised by a new kind of citizenship and pluralism. Henceforth, people at all levels of government would be responsible for running their own lives instead of relying upon the paternalistic state. Regional decentralisation was linked to socialist proposals to democratise and decentralise economic planning: regional authorities were to be the privileged partners of the state in the formulation and implementation of the national economic Plan. *Concertation* would thus render local democracy compatible with national planning objectives.

The Loi Defferre

In June 1981 Gaston Defferre, Mayor of Marseilles and Socialist Deputy for 45 years was appointed Minister of the Interior and Decentralisation and given a *carte blanche* by Mitterrand to prepare legislation for comprehensive administrative and political decentralisation. Defferre lost little time: the Law on the Rights and Liberties for Communes, Departments and Regions was presented to the National Assembly at the opening session of the new Parliament in July 1981. The bill, which was essentially an enabling one, was debated in the National Assembly and the Senate for over 170 hours over an eight month period; 1,500 amendments were discussed and a further 39 articles added to the initial draft. But given the overwhelming Socialist majority in the National Assembly, the outcome was never really in doubt and the bill was finally promulgated on 2 March 1982. Over the next four years a further 22 laws and 170 government decrees completed the decentralisation programme.

Within weeks of the initial legislation having been passed, executive power at the departmental and regional levels was transferred from the prefects to the elected presidents, and the prefects abolished. In each case a convention signed by the prefect and president specified the number of official cars, buildings and state civil servants to be placed at the disposal of the latter. To supplement those officials transferred to them from the prefecture, presidents could appoint additional political administrative and technical advisers to the regional administration. The prefects were replaced by *Commissaires de la République* who are now the official representatives of the Prime Minister. While these officials lack the local executive powers of their predecessors, they nonetheless enjoy considerable authority. In addition to inheriting the prefects' powers relating to law and order, they have been granted new powers concerning economic planning and greater control over all the ministerial field services. All forms of *a priori* control over local authority decisions disappeared along with the prefects. Local government activity is now subject only to *a posteriori* legal and financial control by the regional administrative tribunals and newly created regional *cours des comptes* (courts of accounts), which audit local authority budgets. It is up to the commissaire to report any action which he believes to be illegal or financially irregular to these authorities within 15 days of its promulgation.

The major concession made to regionalists and autonomists was the 'Special Statute' granted to Corsica in March 1982, which set the territory apart legally from other regions. This provided the region with additional state subsidies and greater autonomy over educational, economic, social, and cultural policies. Government hopes that the 'Special Statute' would solve the 'Corsican problem' were, however, fairly shortlived. The first elections to the Corsican Assembly in August 1982 failed to produce a stable majority in favour of the reforms and the ensuing deadlock within the Assembly prompted further elections in 1984 (four years early). Meanwhile, the Corsican National Liberation Movement

Table 5.1: Results of the March 1986 Regional Elections

% Seats won by parties Region	PCF	PS	MRG & other Left	Reg	Ecol	RPR+ UDF	CNIP & other Right	FN	Total no. of seats	President
Alsace	–	21	2	–	4	57	–	15	47	Marcel Rudloff (CDS-UDF)
Aquitaine	10	36	2	–	–	42	5	5	83	J. Chaban–Delmas (RPR)
Auvergne	9	32	–	–	–	53	2	4	47	V. Giscard d'Estaing (UDF-PR)
Bourgogne	9	31	2	–	–	42	9	5	55	Marcel Lucotte (UDF-PR)
Bretagne	5	37	–	–	–	46	10	2	81	Yvon Bourges (RPR)
Centre	11	31	4	–	–	37	13	4	75	Marcel Dousset (UDF-PR)
Champagne-Ardenne	9	32	–	–	–	43	6	11	47	Bernard Stasi (UDF-CDS)
Corse	11	10	20	10	–	30	16	3	61	J-P de Rocca Serra (RPR)
Franche-Comte	5	37	5	–	–	44	–	9	43	Edgar Faure (UDF-Rad)
Ile-de-France	10	31	2	–	–	41	5	12	197	Michel Giraud (RPR)
Languedoc-Roussillon	14	32	2	–	–	31	9	12	65	Jacques Blanc (UDF-PR)
Limousin	20	37	–	–	–	41	2	–	41	Robert Savy (PS)
Lorraine	5	33	–	–	–	48	4	10	73	Jean-Marie Rausch (UDF-CDS)
Midi-Pyrenees	6	30	11	–	–	37	11	5	87	Dominique Baudis (app. UDF)
Nord-pas-de-Calais	17	32	3	–	–	34	4	11	113	Noel Joseph (PS)
Basse-Normandie	2	22	11	–	2	44	13	4	45	Rene Garrec (UDF)
Haute-Normandie	11	36	2	–	–	40	6	6	53	Roger Fosse (RPR)
Pays-de-la-Loire	5	32	4é	–	–	42	13	3	93	Olivier Guichard (RPR)
Picardie	15	33	–	–	–	38	7	7	55	Charles Baur (UDF-PSD)
Poitou-Charentes	6	36	4	–	–	43	9	2	53	Louis Fruchard (UDF-CDS)
Provence-Alpes-Cote-D'Azur	12	26	1	–	–	34	6	21	117	Jean-Claude Gaudin (UDF-PR)
Rhone-Alpes	9	30	1	–	–	38	13	9	151	Charles Béraudier (UDF)

Table 5.1: continued

% Seats won by parties Region	PCF	PS	MRG & other Left	Reg	Ecol	RPR+ UDF	CNIP & other Right	FN	Total no. of seats	President
Gaudelopue	24	29	–	–	–	46	–	–	41	Felix Proto (PS)
Martinique	–	51	–	–	–	49	–	–	41	Aimé Césaire (PS)
Guyane	–	–	61	–	–	29	10	–	31	Georges Othily (PS app.)
Reunion	29	13	–	–	–	40	18	–	45	Pierre Lagourgue (Ind. Right)

é Includes two PSU representatives. Table compiled from 'La France des Regions', Le Monde – Dossiers et Documents, April 1986

(FLNC) resumed its violent activities. (6)
According to the loi Defferre the 21 metropolitan regional public establishments and the four overseas territories (Guyane, Réunion, Guadaloupe and Martinique) were to become fully-fledged local authorities with directly elected regional councils (until the regional elections they remained public establishments). The first regional elections in the four overseas territories were held in February 1983. Elections to the 21 metropolitan regional councils were also scheduled for 1983, but were repeatedly postponed by Defferre. The official explanation for this delay centred upon the amount of time required to complete the legislative programme relating to the regions. Other reasons, however, included the Corsican experience and the waning electoral popularity of the Socialist Party after 1982. These elections were eventually held alongside the National Assembly elections on 16 March 1986 under the same electoral system - a single ballot in which electors voted for departmental party lists and seats were allocated to lists on the basis of the 'highest averaging' system. The results of the regional poll closely mirrored those of the legislative contest: the right-wing coalition parties won control of 20 of the 21 metropolitan regions (the Socialists maintained control of Limousin and Nord-Pas-de-Calais). (7)

While the reforms left intact the 'general powers' of intervention enjoyed by French local authorities they attempted to give each tier of government a specific role. The raison d'être of the regions remains economic planning and socio-economic development. To carry out this role, regional authorities were given more extensive powers of intervention. They may grant loans, give subsidies, offer tax exemptions and provide financial and technical advice to public and private industries in the region. In addition, regions were made responsible for the provision of all forms of industrial and professional training and for the maintenance of lycées.

In order to ensure the compatibility of local authority investment with national economic planning priorities, the regions were given a bigger role than ever before in the formulation and implementation of the IX national economic Plan (1984-88). Each regional council, in consultation with the commissaire prepared a five year regional Plan outlining medium-term regional investment priorities. This document formed the basis of a contractual

Decentralisation: La Grande Affaire du Septennat?

agreement (Contrat de Plan) between the region and the state. The agreement committed the signatories to the financing of regional programmes (often in conjunction with other local authorities or nationalised industries) which were officially designated as being compatible with national planning priorities. By April 1985 all regions including Corsica had signed such an agreement and the total amount of money allocated to over one thousand projects for the duration of the IX Plan totalled nearly 63,000 million francs (37,000 million francs on the part of the government and 25,581 million francs on the part of the regions). (8) Primary among the projects currently being financed in this manner are industrial, technical and professional training, industrial development, information technology and communications development and agricultural modernisation.

Departments were given special responsibility for solidarité which means they are now responsible for the provision of socio-medical care and the organisation of most social security schemes (amounting to 75 per cent of social security expenditure). While such schemes must conform to certain national minimum standards, general councils freely organise their own services and may, if they wish, increase benefit levels. Responsibility for the provision of school transport in rural areas and the maintenance of secondary school buildings was also devolved to the departments.

The reform defined the primary task of communes as town planning and urban development. 'Land Use Plans' (Plans d'occupation des sols) drawn up by one or more communes are submitted to the central government (via the commissaire) for approval. Once this has been given, mayors may grant planning permission (permis de construire) for specific projects without further recourse to the Minister for Urban Development - something which they have for many years demanded the right to do. By 1 January 1985, 6,075 such Plans had been approved affecting 7,007 communes. (9) In addition, communes were made responsible for the provision of urban public transport (including school transport) and the maintenance of primary schools.

A general principle of the reforms was that any transfer of function would be accompanied by a corresponding financial transfer from the state. Compensation for new functions takes the form of specific fiscal transfers and index-linked block grant subsidies. Tax revenue from vehicle registration, for instance, has been transferred to the regions (to finance the cost of industrial training), while a percentage of the revenue accruing from various property taxes now goes to the department (towards the cost of welfare provision). Fiscal transfers are supplemented by subsidies from a new general block grant for decentralisation (<u>Dotation Générale de Décentralisation</u>). Communes also receive revenue from this source for the implementation of their local urban plans. Fiscal transfers to local authorities to finance new responsibilities totalled 23,000 million francs in 1984. (10)

Apart from compensation for new functions, the complex system of French local government finance, based upon local taxes, central government grants and loans was left virtually untouched. The only significant change was the creation of a new block grant for investment (<u>Dotation Globale d'Equipement</u>) which between 1983 and 1986 gradually replaced the various grants previously given to departments and communes by different government ministries for specific programmes. This complements the block grant for revenue spending <u>Dotation globale de Fonctionnement</u> introduced in 1979. State subsidies to local authorities from revenue and capital block grants totalled 66,000 million francs in 1984 and 70,000 million francs in 1985. (11)

The Socialists insisted that effective political decentralisation necessitated administrative decentralisation. The 1984 administrative reforms were thus designed to ensure parity between local government officials and state civil servants within a unified administrative system and career structure. Officials may now be recruited either at the regional or national level and move between the two levels without loss of salary or career prospects. The formerly low status of local officials was further boosted by the creation of a new <u>corps</u> of territorial administrators comprising local government officials and any officials transferred to local authorities from the prefecture who wish to join.

The reforms outlined above transferred powers and resources downwards from the central government to local authorities and horizontally at each level from state administrators to elected politicians (assisted by appointed <u>cabinets</u>). Three further measures - local electoral reform, extra powers for the <u>conseils d'arrondissement</u> (electoral constituency councils) in Paris, Lyons and Marseilles and limitations upon <u>cumul des mandats</u> - were also introduced in an attempt to increase the democratic and representative nature of local politics.

Prior to 1981, the winning list in municipal elections had taken all the municipal council seats. Socialist electoral reform for municipal elections in communes of more than 3,500 inhabitants means opposition lists are (since the 1983 municipal elections) now represented in these councils. According to the new system, the list which wins an absolute majority on the first ballot or a relative majority on the second ballot obtains half the council seats and the remainder are distributed proportionately among all the lists (including the winning one).

In 1982 Gaston Defferre announced that the conseils d'arrondissement in Paris which, since 1975 had enjoyed advisory powers, should be given increased powers. The ostensible purpose of this reform was to increase local democracy, but few doubted that the real aim was to weaken the local power base of Jacques Chirac, mayor of Paris and national leader of the gaullist RPR opposition party. (At this time, the Conservative government in Britain was espousing similar arguments to justify its decision to abolish the Labour controlled Greater London Council and metropolitan councils). Protests from opposition parties forced Defferre to make two concessions: the proposed increase in the powers of the conseils d'arrondissements were reduced (they are now essentially directly elected administrative agencies with responsibility for the provision of some public amenities); and the scheme was extended to include two other cities, Lyons and Defferre's own fiefdom, Marseilles.

In an attempt to increase political participation the government increased the financial allowances of local politicians, who are now also entitled to paid leave from their jobs to attend courses in public administration. While local politicians welcomed these developments they were less enthusiastic about the limitations imposed upon the number of elective offices an individual may hold. To ignore the practice of cumul des mandats would have made a mockery of the whole decentralisation programme, but it was, for obvious reasons, an extremely sensitive issue. The Debarge report on the subject, presented to the government in 1982 formed the basis of a government bill put before Parliament in November 1985. Since this legislation had to be passed in the same form by both the National Assembly and the Senate (which is composed solely of local politicians) concessions to local notables were inevitable. The law, which was eventually passed in December 1985 restricts the number of 'significant' elective offices an individual may hold to two. 'Significant' mandates include those of Deputy, Senator, MEP and mayor of large towns (more than 20,000 inhabitants). The reform will be introduced progressively: from 1987, as elections take place, politicians holding more than two 'significant' offices will gradually have to give up mandates in order to reduce the total number they hold to two. (12)

The Reforms in Practice - 1982-86

Presidents of the regional and general councils welcomed their new powers. A few, anxious to display their authority over the commissaire, took up residence in the former prefecture, while others signalled their superiority by ordering several official cars. (In Nice, Jacques Médecin, president of the Alpes-Maritimes general council, ordered the commissaire to change his twelve CV car for a seven CV one). Political differences sometimes led to frosty relations - in the Meuse department, the Communist official had his entertainments allowance stopped by the centrist president in the name of good housekeeping. Elsewhere, however, relations were more cordial and in some places such as the Nord department, the commissaire was a close political ally of the president. For their part, most commissaires - many of whom had formerly been the prefect of the locality - accepted their new role gracefully - though several complained that presidents bypassed them and negotiated directly with government ministers. (13)

In general, left-wing presidents appointed more administrators and policy advisers than their right-wing counterparts, who continued to rely more heavily on the central administrative agencies. In total, some 5,000 new jobs were created in the departmental and regional administrations. Former prefects and sub-prefects figured prominently and by autumn 1982, 35 departmental presidents - anxious to conquer the complexities of local administration - had appointed a member of the prefectoral corps as head of their administrative services. These were often right-wing prefects who had been unhappy working for a socialist regime and who welcomed the opportunity to move to a politically sympathetic environment without jeopardising their career prospects.

Decentralisation: La Grande Affaire du Septennat?

Responsibility for medical care, child care facilities, family allowances and care of the elderly was transferred to departmental presidents in January 1984. This transfer produced little <u>immediate</u> change in formal benefit regulations. There were two major reasons for this continuity: most departments were at first overwhelmed by the complexity of the task; and all local politicians were worried about the financial consequences of the reform. Fearful of rapidly rising costs, many departmental presidents introduced more stringent monitoring of benefit allocation and reduced discretionary payments. Politicians from all parties complained that annual increases in financial compensation from the state failed to cover the spiralling costs of welfare provision in a period of economic crisis. Meanwhile, the government and departments argued incessantly about who should bear the financial burden of certain groups of people - notably homeless people temporarily resident in a department and young people placed in detention by magistrates. (14)

In general, the decentralisation of urban planning to the communes in 1983 caused little disruption, partly because mayors of large towns had already, in practice, been closely involved in urban planning prior to the reforms. Stability was further ensured by the prominent role government agencies continued to play in the formulation and financing of urban plans. All mayors, anxious not to infringe the law, exercised their new powers to grant planning permission with extreme caution: mayors of small communes, who lacked their own technical services, often continued to refer all applications for planning permission to the central government technical agencies. Predictably, although there was a proliferation of applications to the government for approval of <u>Plans d'Occupation de Sol</u> from rural areas, the reforms did little to foster closer inter-communal co-operation - as always, mayors were loathe to see their autonomy reduced.

Decentralisation was linked to Socialist economic strategy: the government hoped that greater local authority intervention would stimulate economic and industrial development. In practice, the extent to which local authorities exploited their new powers of intervention during this period varied considerably. Broadly speaking, right-wing authorities (at all levels of local government) were less interventionist and more reluctant to increase local taxes and borrow money than their left-wing counterparts. Local councillors from these authorities argued that such actions were not the proper responsibility of local government. Departments and communes were particularly cautious in this respect. Political objections apart, many local politicians argued that they simply could not afford to take on such commitments. There was often some truth in this claim. Local authorities were adversely affected after 1982 by rising unemployment (which stretched local welfare services and reduced local fiscal income) and government austerity measures which made loans more expensive and state subsidies more difficult to obtain. Indeed, many local politicians claimed that they received less from the new block grant for investment (Dotation Générale d'Equipement) than under the old system of specific ministerial grants.

Given their official role, it was hardly surprising that the regions played the major role in initiating, undertaking and co-ordinating local authority intervention often within the framework of the Contrat de Plan. Although the official report on the IX Plan was critical of the often inadequate and hurried nature of negotiations between the regions and the government, it concluded that the decentralised planning exercise had, on balance, been fairly successful in coordinating regional and national investment. (In 1984, 36 per cent of regional investment was allocated to programmes covered by Contrats de Plan). (15) The contractual agreements were, however, criticized by right-wing local authorities which claimed that they constituted a form of central government control since higher levels of state subsidies were often dependent upon co-operation in such schemes (an argument frequently heard from left-wing authorities prior to 1981).

Despite the regions' new powers, the size of their budgets remains (until 1987) limited by law and, as illustrated in Table 5.2, are but a fraction of those of the departments and communes. It is true that in contrast to those of other local authorities, regional budgets are principally investment budgets. But as the administrative costs of the regions have risen (with the proliferation of independent services), so the proportion of the budget available for investment has fallen. Regional initiatives thus suffered from lack of funds. Moreover, rising unemployment and government economic policy after 1982 placed heavy demands on these modest resources and ambitious regional investment strategies increasingly gave way to 'fire-fighting' exercises – particularly in industrial areas with high unemployment levels. In an attempt to avoid an ineffectual dispersal of investment most regions channelled support towards traditional local subsidies – the Limousin region established a centre for the development of the ceramics industry, the Nord-Pas-de-Calais region concentrated on developing the cross-channel ferry ports, while agricultural modernisation was given priority in Brittany. Most regions also set up Economic Development Institutes to coordinate local authority investment and provide research support for industries. With regard to industrial and professional training, some regions created their own training schemes while others, such as the Auvergne and the Aquitaine regions established links with large private employers in the region (respectively Michelin and Elf).

Table 5.2: Public Authority Budgets in France 1985

Authority	Budget+
Communes	320
Departments	120
Regions	17
Total of local authority budgets	457
State	1018
Gross National Product	4418

+ Amounts expressed in milliards (1000 millions) of francs.

Source: J.P. Muret, D. Fournier, S. Peyre, F. Pian, Le Conseil Régional, (Paris: Syros, 1986), p.197.

Encouraged by the Energy Minister, Edmond Hervé, many regions drew up energy development and conservation schemes. The Provence-Alpes-Côte-d'Azur region, for instance, financed a solar energy scheme, while the Midi-Pyrenées region signed a controversial agreement with the nationalised industry, Electricité de France. This permitted the latter to build a nuclear power station at Golfech in return for financial compensation to the region and a guarantee of jobs at the plant for local people. The more ambitious authorities even began to engage in foreign trade: the Haute-Normandie regional council entered into negotiations to export Normandy cattle to Ecuador; Giscard d'Estaing, president of the Auvergne regional council, visited American chemicals firms in an attempt to persuade them to invest in the Auvergne; and several frontier regions established trading and cultural links with neighbouring European countries.

Evaluation
Assessment of the Defferre reforms involves three related questions: to what extent and why did the government succeed in implementing its election programme in formal terms? Did the reforms constitute a radical departure from the past? And what contribution did these reforms make to the Socialists' declared goal of a more egalitarian, pluralistic society.

Judged simply in terms of the volume of legislation passed, decentralisation was certainly a grande affaire du septennat. Several factors contributed to Defferre's success in this respect. Unlike previous regimes the Socialists came to power with a longstanding commitment to decentralisation and a fairly clear notion of what they intended to do. And key ministers, in addition to Defferre, supported the proposals - notably Nicole Questiaux, Minister for Solidarité, Marcel Rigout, responsible for professional training and Michel Rocard, Minister for Planning. Moreover, in contrast to previous right-wing regimes, the Mitterrand government was not dependent at the parliamentary level upon the support of those conservative local notables who had in the past regularly blocked any major changes. Besides, as indicated above, by 1981 many local councillors (particularly those on the Left) were in any case in favour of further decentralisation.

The pragmatic manner in which Gaston Defferre sought to implement the reforms was also important. Above all, he was aware of the need to act quickly before opposition to the proposals from other ministries - notably the Finance Ministry - became effective. Once the initial framework legislation had been passed, the detailed measures were easier to implement, not least because they could be introduced by government decree. Symbolic and popular changes such as the abolition of the prefects and the 'Special Statute' for Corsica were among the first changes to take place and created a favourable impression. The more difficult and controversial were prudently left until the end, by which time decentralisation was 'irreversible'.

Defferre was also careful to avoid antagonising key groups. The winners in the reforms were the grands notables, who had for many years demanded the replacement of individual subsidies with block grants to be spent freely, the right to issue permis de construire and the abolition of a priori control. No attempt was made to reduce the number of communes and the once discussed possibility of abolishing the departments in favour of the regions was never mentioned. Comprehensive financial reform of local government was avoided and Mitterrand's promise to create a new department for the Basque Provinces (Proposition 54) was quietly abandoned. Concessions were also made along the way to obstructive government ministers. Thus, Roger Quilliot, Minister of Housing and Urban Development, maintained control of the housing budget on the grounds that housing was a national priority, while the Education Minister, Alain Savary, successfully resisted proposals to decentralise responsibility for teachers' salaries to the departments. And, despite the government's commitment to the promotion of cultural diversity, the Minister for Culture, Jack Lang, resolutely refused to relinquish control over that part of the budget allocated to regional projects and gained support from President Mitterrand for his assertion that culture was 'un sort à part'. (16) All such omissions and concessions limited the impact of the reforms, but they undoubtedly eased the passage of legislation.

The introduction of the reforms was further helped by the fact that while they were far-reaching, these reforms did not constitute a dramatic break with the past. They were in many respects the culmination of a long piecemeal process of local government reform reluctantly initiated by previous right-wing regimes. Essentially, the loi Defferre legitimised and extended practices that had already emerged by 1981. Mayors of big cities, for instance, had for several years been virtually immune from prefectoral control, while the 1972 regional reform had prepared the way for the introduction of regional government. Whereas Socialist policy in other areas involved overturning established practices, the decentralisation reforms accelerated existing trends.

As indicated above, this continuity with the past was further reinforced by the practice of the reforms. Those authorities which had been interventionist before 1981 became more so and many of those which had previously been less assertive often chose not to exploit their new powers of intervention. Financial constraints further limited the impact of the reforms. Indeed, for mayors of small, rural communes, who lacked financial resources, the changes were often more formal than real. Unable to employ independent advisers many continued to rely upon the informal advice of the commissaire rather than risk having to appear before the regional administrative tribunal or Court of Accounts. Others turned to the president of the general council for advice and financial support - a trend which prompted fears of a new form of political control over communes by departmental presidents. The abolition of the prefects and a priori control was also in many respects a symbolic rather than a significant change: as one commentator wryly observed, the prefects were abolished only to reappear as commissaires. And within a brief space of time, the commissaire once again became known as Monsieur le Préfet. The diverse impact of the reforms confirms the simple but often ignored fact that apparently radical reforms may, in practice, be less than dramatic. More fundamentally, these local variations highlight the tension - and possible contradiction - between the Socialists' commitment to political decentralisation on the one hand and to the establishment of a more egalitarian society on the other. (The considerable variations in local fiscal revenue and the decentralisation of responsibility for welfare provision are particularly pertinent in this respect.)

These reforms have undoubtedly prompted potentially significant shifts in the balance of power within the politico-administrative system. Local politicians who have traditionally sheltered behind the prefect are now directly accountable for their actions. The introduction of directly elected regional assemblies endowed with considerable policy-making powers is also a potentially important development: grands notables such as Olivier Guichard, regional president of Pays-de-la-Loire have lost little time in exercising their new powers not simply over constituent local authorities, but also in relation to the national government. This assertiveness has not been welcomed by the Gaullist Prime Minister, Jacques Chirac who has publicly deplored the politicisation of the regional assemblies. (17)

Yet, while important changes have occurred within the politico-administrative system, the system itself has not been transformed. Essentially, the reforms gave local authorities more legal autonomy and encouraged them to intervene in the market economy. Indeed, just as they had been throughout the 1970s, the regions were once again exhorted to establish closer links with the <u>forces vives</u> of the community - local industrialists, chambers of commerce and industry, universities and professional associations. This was hardly likely to bring about a rupture with capitalism. Equally, the measures designed to enhance local democracy focused upon increasing opportunities for participation within existing structures (i.e. regional councils, municipal councils and <u>conseils d'arrondissements</u>) rather than creating new forms of citizen participation. While these changes should not be dismissed as insignificant, they fell some way short of socialist promises in 1981 to create a participatory, pluralist democracy. The Corsican experience curbed the government's enthusiasm for regionalism and while the Socialists emphasised their commitment to bringing women into government at the national level, they remained on the periphery of local government and administration. (18) No new forms of citizen participation were established and Mitterrand's promise to give migrants voting rights in local elections was subsequently abandoned on the grounds that the French people were not yet ready for such a step. Thus, while the French local government system was definitely changed by the Mitterrand administration, it was not radically transformed.

Acknowledgement
I am most grateful to the Nuffield Foundation for financing research undertaken in France for this chapter.

Notes
1. V. Wright, <u>The Government and Politics of France</u>, 2nd Edition, (London: Hutchinson, 1983), p.278.
2. <u>Multi-Purpose Intercommunal Syndicates</u> enable communes to enter voluntarily into a contractual agreement with each other to provide specific services. <u>Districts</u> are public establishments composed of several communes which have planning and development responsibilities. <u>Urban communities</u> are administrative public establishments comprising a number of communes. They have financial

and planning responsibilities for housing, land zoning and land-use planning. In 1966 four Urban Communities were created by law centred on Bordeaux, Lille, Lyons and Strasbourg. Since then five others have been established in Dunkerque, Cherbourg, Le Mans, Brest and Le Creusot-Monceau-les-Mines.

3. M. Rocard, Décoloniser la Province, (Paris, 1967); M. Phlipponneau, Debout Bretagne, (St Brieuc, 1970).

4. M. Keating, 'Decentralization in Mitterrand's France', Public Administration, Vol. 61, 1983, p.241.

5. Le Projet Socialiste, (1980).

6. On the reforms in Corsica see M. Keating and P. Hainsworth, Decentralisation and Change in Contemporary France, (London: Gower, 1986); J. Loughlin, 'The elections to the Corsican Regional Assembly', Government and Opposition, vol. 20, (1985); J. Loughlin, 'A new deal for France's regions and linguistic minorities', West European Politics, vol. 8, (1985).

7. See S. Mazey, 'The French regional elections of March 16th 1986', Electoral Studies, vol. 5 (1986); 'La France des Régions', Le Monde - Dossiers et Documents, April 1986.

8. J.P. Muret, D Fournier, S. Peyré, F. Pian, Le Conseil Régional (Paris: Syros, 1986).

9. P. Delage, 'Les Tranferts de Compétences' in 'La Décentralisation en Marche', Cahiers Français, No. 220, (Paris: Documentation Française, 1985), p.37.

10. M. Chatot, 'La compensation Financière' in 'La Décentralisation en Marche' Cahiers Français, No. 220, (Paris: Documentation Française, 1985), p.51.

11. Ibid, pp.58-9.

12. Le Monde, 21 December 1985.

13. 'La guerre des pouvoirs a commencé', L'Express, 8 March 1985, pp.22-35; 'Les nouveaux seigneurs de l'an II', Le Point, 11 March 1985, pp.65-9.

14. Commissariat Général du Plan, Compétences transférées aux Collectivités Territoriales, (Paris: Documentation Française, 1985); Commisariat Général du Plan, Interventions Economiques des Collectivités Locales, (Paris: Documentation Françaises, 1985).

15. Commissariat Général du Plan, Evaluation de la Planification Décentralisée (Paris: Documentation Française, 1985).

16. For details on regional cultural policies see Chapter 6 on cultural policy by Jill Forbes.

Decentralisation: La Grande Affaire du Septennat?

17. Jacques Chirac, in a speech to the 57th Congress of Presidents of General Councils, quoted in Libération, 21 October 1986.

18. Figures from the Ministry of the Interior show that in 1985 there was only one female departmental préfet - commissaire in Orne (out of a total of 102) and nine women sous préfets - commissaires (out of a total of 235). In 1985, only four per cent of French mayors and general councillors were women. Of the 1,840 regional councillors elected in 1986 only eight per cent were women. The proposed restrictions on cumul des mandats may increase the political representation of women.

Further Reading

1. On French local government organisation before 1981 see H. Machin, 'Traditional Patterns of French Local Government', in J. Lagroye and V. Wright (eds.), Local Government in Britain and France, (London: George, Allen and Unwin, 1979); H. Machin, The Prefect in French Public Administration, (London, Croom Helm, 1977).

2. For details of informal collaboration between local politicians and prefects see P. Grémion, Le Pouvoir Périphérique, (Paris: Editions de Seuil, 1976).

3. For details of French local government reform before 1981 see 'Decentralisation', Cahiers Français, No. 204, 1982 (Paris: La Documentation Française, 1982); D. Ashford, British Dogmatism and French Pragmatism, (London, George, Allen and Unwin, 1982) and Y. Mény, 'Central Control and Local Resistance', in V. Wright, (ed.), Continuity and Change in France, (London: George, Allen and Unwin, 1984).

3. Specifically on the subject of regional reform after 1958 see J-J Dayries and M. Dayries, La Régionalisation (Que sais-je?, Paris: Presses Universitaires de France, 1978); P. Gourevitch, Paris and the Provinces, (London: George, Allen and Unwin, 1980); V. Wright, 'Regionalisation under the Fifth Republic', in L.J. Sharpe, (ed.), Decentralist Trends in Western Democracies, (London: Sage, 1979).

4. On the attitude of the Socialist Party towards decentralisation after 1969 see M. Phlipponneau, La Grande Affaire: Décentralisation et Régionalisation, (Paris: Calmann-Levy, 1981); M. Rocard, 'La Région, une idée neuve pour la Gauche', Pouvoirs, No. 19, 1981; 'La Décentralisation', Nouvelle Revue Socialiste, No. 54, (1981) (special

issue).

5. For details of the Socialist decentralisation reforms and their impact in practice see A. Mabileau (ed.), <u>Les Pouvoirs Locaux à l'Epreuve de la Décentralisation</u>, (Paris: Pedone 1983); 'La Décentralisation en marche', <u>Cahiers Français</u>, No. 220, (Paris: Documentation Française, 1985); M. Keating and P. Hainsworth, <u>Decentralisation and Change in Contemporary France</u>, (London: Gower, 1986); 'Décentralisation: le sacré de la région', <u>Régards sur l'Actualité</u>, No. 120, (Paris: Documentation Française, 1986); J.P. Muret, D. Fournier, S. Peyré, F. Pian, <u>Le Conseil Régional</u>, (Paris: Syros, 1986).

Chapter Six

CULTURAL POLICY: THE SOUL OF MAN UNDER SOCIALISM

Jill Forbes

This chapter attempts to discuss the cultural policy pursued by the Socialists between 1981 and 1986. It looks at what the Socialists inherited from their predecessors, examines the constraints imposed on them as well as the opportunities available to them, and puts forward an assessment of the activities of the five year period. What is the justification for paying particular attention to culture which, though it is an item of expenditure like any other in the national budget, is smaller than most? François Mitterrand frequently remarked that Socialism is a 'cultural project', and the Socialists in general attached a significance to cultural policy out of all proportion to the amount they spent on it in the belief that socialism is not merely realised through economic or social reforms but also has a specifically ideological dimension. (1)

Cultural Policy in the Fifth Republic

Everything that may be described as 'culture' is not necessarily amenable to a government cultural policy. For example, culture is sometimes defined as all that is not nature, so that all artefacts may in some sense be considered cultural forms. On other occasions culture is defined by an opposition between the cultural and the functional which means that an object such as a motor car, though the product of design, is not a work of art because it has a use. Both these definitions are much too widely drawn to be of much help in considering cultural policy.

However two further definitions are of particular relevance to cultural policy in the Fifth Republic. The first is one that might prove most spontaneously acceptable and it encompasses all that is designated in English by the term 'the arts'. This covers the national heritage (le patrimoine) (i.e. paintings, drawings, sculpture, architecture; the contents of museums, libraries, stately homes, churches) and the live or performing arts (i.e. theatre, opera, dance, music and sometimes the cinema). Under this definition cultural policy is essentially an arts policy and includes such activities as acquisition, conservation and exhibition, subsidy to capital programmes, production and performance. After the French Revolution, the state inherited from the church and the monarchy responsibility for administering the national heritage, and a sub-section of the Ministry of Education known as the Direction des Beaux-Arts was later created to take care of conservation and acquisition. Subsidy to the performing arts, however, traditionally came from municipal authorities except for a few major institutions such as the Comédie Française and the Opéra which were supported from central funds.

The second definition sees culture as a set of shared values and assumptions. Under this definition cultural policy is essentially a process of direct or indirect acculturation carried out through different institutions. Historically the agents of cultural policy have been the church, the army and the education system which have been joined, since the Second World War, by the mass media, particularly television. The modern state therefore pursues its cultural policy through the control of education and broadcasting which it uses to obtain a degree of cultural consensus. (2)

Cultural policy in the Fifth Republic may be seen as a series of attempts to reconcile a policy for the arts and the processes of acculturation through the recognition of a specific field of activity called 'culture'. A Ministry of Culture was created in 1959 with the following objectives:

> Le ministère chargé des affaires culturelles a pour mission de rendre accessibles les oeuvres capitales de l'humanité, et d'abord la France, au plus grand nombre possible de Français; d'assurer la plus vaste audience à notre patrimoine culturel, et de favoriser la création des oeuvres de l'art et de l'esprit qui l'enrichissent. (3)

The first Minister was André Malraux and his term of office is well known for having initiated an ambitious programme of architectural restoration, the listing of sites and monuments, the stimulation of the theatre in the provinces, the <u>avance sur recettes</u> subsidies for the cinema, and the inception of a programme of large art exhibitions. But perhaps it is most famous for having created the <u>Maisons de la culture</u>, dubbed 'cathedrals of modern times' by Malraux. The origins of the <u>Maisons de la culture</u> are to be sought in the popular education movements which had been so active in the Resistance and at the Liberation and which made an important contribution to Gaullist policies. These institutions fulfilled two essential functions: on the one hand they had a role to play in the restoration of national pride and grandeur and the forging of a national consensus. On the other hand, as Malraux constantly emphasised, they were a necessary response to the machine age, since culture was to be the means by which man recognises his humanity and, ultimately, overcomes his mortality. (4)

Cultural policy then, offered ideological support for the regime and served as a repository of moral values. But it also responded to socio-economic trends. Just as the creation of paid holidays had launched the popular tourism and leisure industries in the 1930s, so now, on the threshold of the 1960s, with a measure of economic prosperity, greater spending power and more free time, leisure began to be a significant element in personal expenditure and the national economy. (5) The Fourth Plan (1962-65) was the first to have a separate <u>Commission de l'Equipement Culturel et du Patrimoine Artistique</u> and its creation was described as the logical follow-up to that of a ministry of culture. The Commission roundly dismissed the hitherto dominant but in its view outdated nineteenth century view of culture and defended state intervention and technocratic organisation on the grounds that culture had become a social as well as an individual need. The 1960s, therefore, confirmed the transition from tastes to needs and from the superfluous to the essential in all approaches to cultural policy. (6)

However, the 'crisis of civilisation' in May 1968 demonstrated the failure of the first decade of the Fifth Republic's cultural policy - at least in its ideological dimension: 'C'est le principe même de la démocratisation culturelle qui est contesté: les professionnels dénoncent ... les fausses unanimités d'une culture oecuménique et conciliatrice et les vertus illusoires d'une émotion née du seul contact individuel avec les oeuvres'. (7) Cultural policy in the 1970s, therefore, could no longer rely on the self-evidence on which it had previously been based and there were successive attempts to find it a raison d'être. Decentralisation was one solution. Under Jacques Duhamel, Minister in 1971 and 1972, a system of cultural charters - or contracts - was developed in participation with local councils and a Fonds d'Intervention Culturelle (FIC) was created to provide assistance on a one-off basis. Many of the individuals who were later to join the socialist Ministry in Paris became active in the regions at this time and the government was content to let the initiative pass increasingly to the local authorities. Another solution was to stress the socio-economic rationale for cultural policy by linking the Ministry of Culture first with that of the Environment (1974-77) and later with that of Communications at a time when a degree of rationalisation was taking place in various communications industries. President Giscard's book Démocratie Française, however, devoted little space to culture, and for a period between 1974 and 1977 the Ministry was demoted to a Secrétariat d'Etat. Overall spending on culture rose in the 1970s but remained low as a proportion of the national budget (0.45 per cent in 1972, 0.55 per cent between 1973 and 1978, 0.47 per cent in 1981) and there continued to be a marked imbalance between Paris and the provinces with three Paris based institutions - the Comédie Française, the Opéra and the Pompidou Centre - together absorbing more than 60 per cent of the Ministry of Culture's revenue spending. (8)

The Socialists' Proposals

In its review of government policies of the preceding 25 years, La France en Mai 1981 concluded that despite Malraux's good intentions 'The main characteristics of the Ministry of Culture's management remained very similar to those of the Secrétariat d'Etat aux Beaux-Arts that it succeeded'. (9) When the municipal elections of 1977 brought many socialist majorities to power in French cities they found that though infrastructural improvement had been considerable, little sense of mission or enthusiasm inspired cultural activities in the regions, and that two decades of regional policies had, if anything, reinforced the traditional division between a well-provided eastern half of the country and a poorly served western half (see Figure 6.1).

Even so, the proposals concerning cultural

Cultural Policy: The Soul of Man under Socialism

Figure 6.1: Map of Institutional Decentralisation

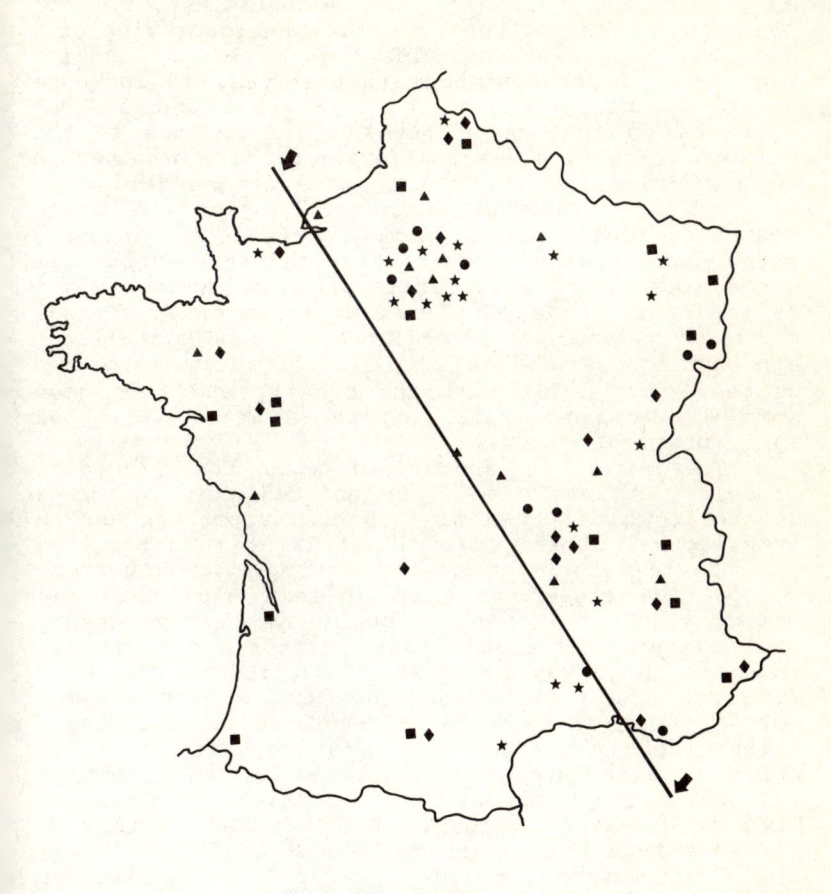

▲ Maison de la culture
♦ Centres dramatiques nationaux (national drama centres)
■ Orchestras
★ Companies subsidised on a regular basis
● Centres d'action culturelle (cultural action centres)

Source: La France en Mai 1981, Tome III, p.321.

135

policy contained in the Programme Commun and the 110 Propositions are surprisingly cautious. Whilst stating that 'la renaissance culturelle du pays (est) au premier rang des ambitions socialistes', they do not suggest that culture is to be the locomotive of a socialist revolution. They promise to assist regional and international initiatives, to increase aid to the performing arts and to art education. But there is no mention of how culture relates to the culture industries (except in the promise of a return to a fixed price for books), and in particular no view taken of the cultural impact of mass communications. Indeed radio, television and the press are treated separately and the proposals concerning these media relate principally to freedom of expression. (10) In fact, at least three strands of thought may be identified in the Socialists' approach to cultural policy, each of which is to some degree incompatible with the others, and this goes some way towards explaining the limited nature of their proposals.

The first is associated with the President himself. As has often been pointed out, he is a generation older than many of his supporters and an intellectual whose professional literary activities and belle-lettriste tastes bring his cultural perspective closer to that of Léon Blum than any postwar technocrat. Any adept of symbolic geography will have understood that Mitterrand's public investiture in May 1981, which shifted the ceremony from the Arc de Triomphe, the tomb of the unknown soldier and the Champs Elysées, with all their militaristic associations, into the Latin Quarter which is associated with intellectual and counter-cultural activities, was an expression of the break with right-wing values. But as an interview Mitterrand gave to Catherine Clément confirms, it was also an expression of his personal cultural preferences which tend towards the fine arts traditionally conceived, and the nineteenth century view of the artist. For Mitterrand, at least, it is inconceivable that art should be mobilised in the service of a political cause. (11)

A second strand of thinking is that of the 1968 generation incarnated in the socialist Minister of Culture, Jack Lang.

> Pour les hommes de ma génération, cet endroit (la Sorbonne) où nous sommes est un endroit qui, voici un peu moins de vingt ans, a annoncé, a préfiguré, les changements dont nous sommes

> aujourd'hui au gouvernement chargés d'assurer l'inscription dans la vie de chaque jour ... Nous étions ici nombreux ... à espérer construire vite un monde nouveau. (12)

Although some of the post-1968 utopianism had been tempered by 1981, certain habits of thought, interests and commitments remained: distrust of old-fashioned populism (whether Gaullist or Communist); willingness to entertain new forms and styles, whether belonging to those traditionally excluded from cultural consideration or to countries or areas traditionally regarded as unimportant; a commitment to internationalism rather than nationalism; and a belief in the revolutionary power of cultural movements and the relative autonomy of the cultural sphere. The socialist electorate is profoundly marked by the legacy of May 1968 and in the years following the signing of the Programme Commun in 1972 some socialist intellectuals began to discuss in groups such as L'Atelier or Mélusine how the lessons of May 1968 might be incorporated into the cultural policy of the Left in power. (13)

A third strand, which might be termed autogestionnaire, first found expression in municipal socialism rather than any central government policies. Instead of emphasising that cultural policy is a locus of ideological struggle, this group of thinkers argued that cultural policy was a means by which individuals might take control of their own lives. They therefore shifted their attention to the practices of everyday life and the individual or collective choices made in it. The Rencontres Internationales de la Culture in January 1975 declared that it 'would be pointless to distinguish a specific cultural sector' and defined culture as the 'totality of collective representations made explicit by knowledge, justified and shaped by ideology and experienced through daily practices'. (14) The aim was to reject esotericism, open up institutions, deprofessionalise cultural practice and to refrain from imposing choices of any kind. Certain cities such as Grenoble had practised such an approach since the early 1970s; others, such as Lille, had deliberately increased their spending on culture; many more adopted this approach after 1977 but found themselves frustrated by lack of sympathy or incomprehension at the centre. (15) After the socialist election victory of 1981, the Direction du Développement Culturel under Dominique Wallon was created to respond to these needs.

The Socialists in Office

'Is it sensible to double spending on culture at a time of economic crisis?' This was how Jack Lang, newly appointed socialist Minister of Culture opened his first budget speech to the National Assembly in November 1981. The answer was that economic recovery and cultural revival go hand in hand and that a nation which did not pay as much attention to the art of living as to its standard of living was doomed. (16) In their first year of office the Socialists increased spending on culture from 0.45 per cent of the national budget to 0.75 per cent and spending continued to grow in real terms, though less spectacularly, throughout their period in office (see Figure 6.2). The increase did not quite match the much vaunted 1 per cent target, but was nevertheless sufficiently large to allow some action on all fronts - international, national and local. All the different approaches to culture identified above were satisfied in some way and the limitation usually placed on subsidy-giving bodies, namely that such a large proportion of revenue is committed in advance that there is little margin for change, was avoided in this case. The Socialists were indeed able to take new initiatives in their programmes and these have been set out, for the sake of clarity, under a series of headings.

The President's 'Grands Chantiers'

Every President of the Fifth Republic to date has followed the tradition of French kings and emperors in attempting to leave a mark on the capital city. François Mitterrand is no exception. As President his destiny is intimately bound up with that of Paris whose geography, as has been seen, is charged with symbolic significance. As a man of letters, too, he has inherited the Romantic view of Paris and has exploited it for his own ends. The most radical transformation of Paris remains that undertaken under Napoleon III. Georges Pompidou runs a close second with the Seine Expressway, the destruction of the Halles and the creation of the Pompidou Centre, but by the time Mitterrand reaches the end of his term of office his constructions may well rival Pompidou's since they are extremely ambitious in scale and range.

The major projects approved, initiated or continued by the socialist administration are the Musée d'Orsay, the development of La Villette (with the construction of a museum of science and

Cultural Policy: The Soul of Man under Socialism

Figure 6.2: Growth of the Budget of the Ministry of Culture since 1975

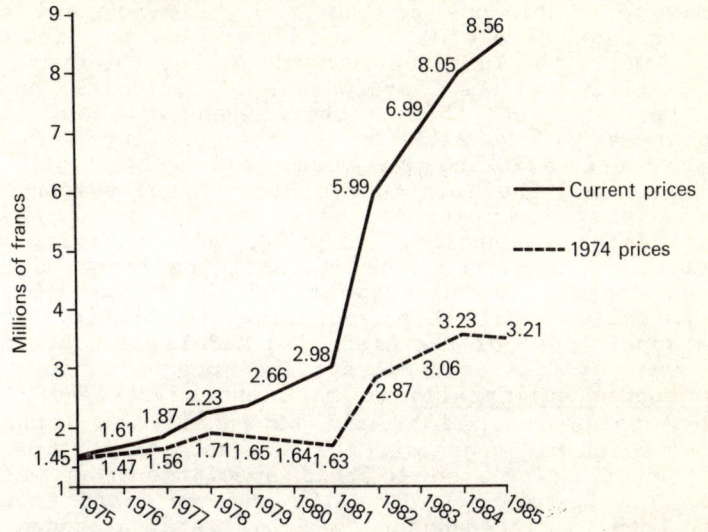

Budget of Ministry of Culture as a percentage of total state budget

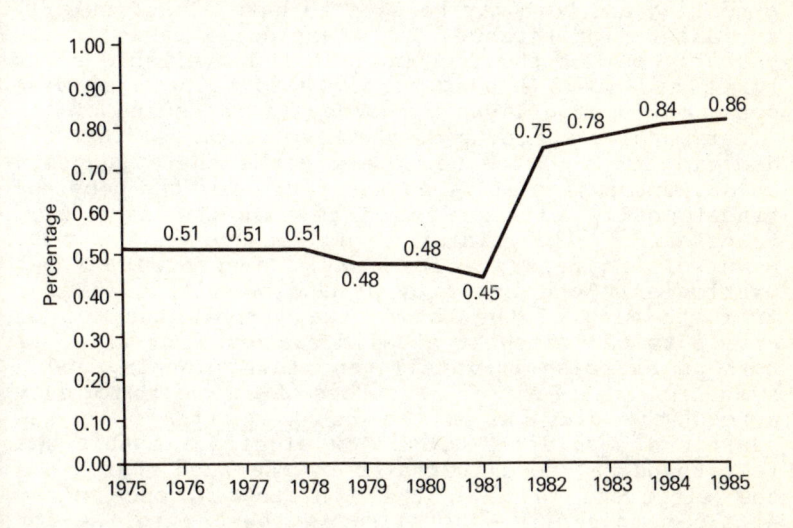

Source: <u>Ministère de la Culture: La lettre d'information June 1986</u>

technology and several concert halls), the Grand Louvre project, the accompanying removal of the Ministry of Finance to the Quai de Bercy and the consequent development of that part of the embankment, the Institut du Monde Arabe, the Opéra de la Bastille and the Carrefour de la Communication at La Défense. Of these, the Musée d'Orsay, the development of La Villette and the Institut du Monde Arabe were existing projects, and while both La Villette and the Institut du Monde Arabe respond to socialist preoccupations - the one by its emphasis that design, technology and practical creativity are part of culture, the other in its commitment to the Third World - the development of the Musée d'Orsay temporarily acquired a socialist orientation with the appointment of the historian Madeleine Rebérioux as one of its directors. The proposal for an exposition universelle to mark the bi-centenary of the Revolution in 1989 and to recall the Popular Front which had organised the last such exhibition in 1937 must be related to this appointment as well. (17) The Opéra de la Bastille and the Grand Louvre were both initiated under the Socialists, although in the case of the former all parties agreed on the inadequacy of the existing opera house. Both projects were said to have commanded Mitterrand's special attention and both may be seen to have a particularly socialist significance. The Place de la Bastille was probably one of the few possible and available sites for a new opera house, but it also holds a special position in republican mythology as the scene of the first popular uprising of the Revolution, so that the decision to site the new opera house there suggests an attempt to, as it were, recapture for the people a traditionally elitist art form. In the same way, transferring the Ministry of Finance - the most powerful ministry in any government, but particularly one beset by financial difficulties - from the wing of the Louvre that fronts the rue de Rivoli to the somewhat squalid eastern dock area, is both an exercise in intelligent town planning and a symbolic transfer of resources from west to east across the city, from the beaux quartiers to the quartiers populaires. Just how significant this was felt to be may be illustrated by the fact that since the elections of 1986 the Ministry is once more, albeit temporarily, installed in the Louvre. As for the Carrefour de la Communication, which was a socialist inspired idea, and whose construction has been halted since 1986, this may be viewed as a cultural complement to an industrial policy which sought to combat the influence of American multinational corporations and to create indigenous centres of media activity and production powerful enough to offer a counter force and a counterweight.

Thus the <u>grands chantiers du Président</u> do lend a partially socialist veneer to the traditional prerogatives of the rulers of France. But they also represent the opposite of the commitment to decentralisation or to the local, smaller initiatives which some Socialists had been demanding. They result from centralised planning decisions, they are concentrated in the capital and they are projects which are intended to have an international as much as a national impact. In his budget speech of November 1982, Jack Lang made much of the Ministry's regional investment:

> Alors que dans le projet de budget de 1983, nous vous demandons 300 millions de francs d'autorisations de programme pour les grands équipements situés à Paris, c'est 1,5 milliards de francs qui vous est demandé pour l'ensemble des réalisations hors Paris. Il y a là une véritable inversion par rapport au passé: l'effort consenti pour Paris est largement compensé par un effort considérable au bénéfice de chacune des régions de France. (18)

However his claim is misleading. For although it is true that capital projects in the regions increased considerably, the proportion of the ministry's budget spent on regional initiatives remained low, and although there was a switch of resources from the Pompidou Centre and from music in 1982 this was the only major alteration in the overall structure of the budget (see Figure 6.3).

An International Cultural Policy. André Malraux had travelled the globe when Minister of Culture and acted as an ambassador for France and for Gaullism, his presence at many of the important archeological and architectural sites of the period (Brasilia, Egypt, Athens) underlining the fact that France represented an alternative set of values. Under his direction, culture was conceived as an agent of prestige and reputation, an ideological weapon and an export. Its geopolitical impact was particularly noticeable in Africa where co-operation agreements, scholarships for students and the maintenance of the French language (<u>francophonie</u>) accompanied a foreign

Cultural Policy: The Soul of Man under Socialism

Figure 6.3: Percentage Distribution of Ministry of Culture's Budget

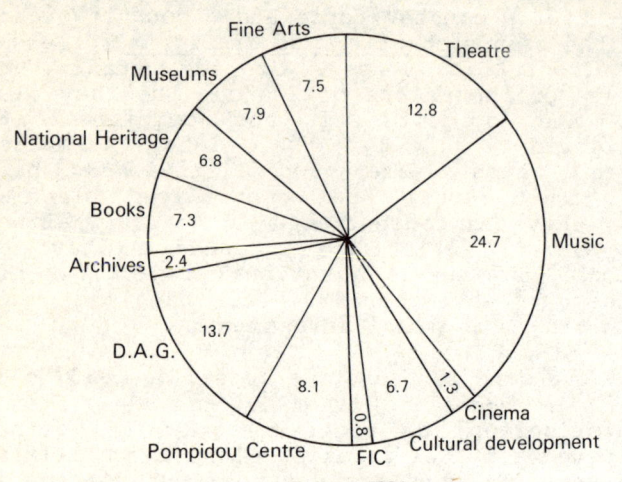

Budget 1981
Total: 2,159 million francs

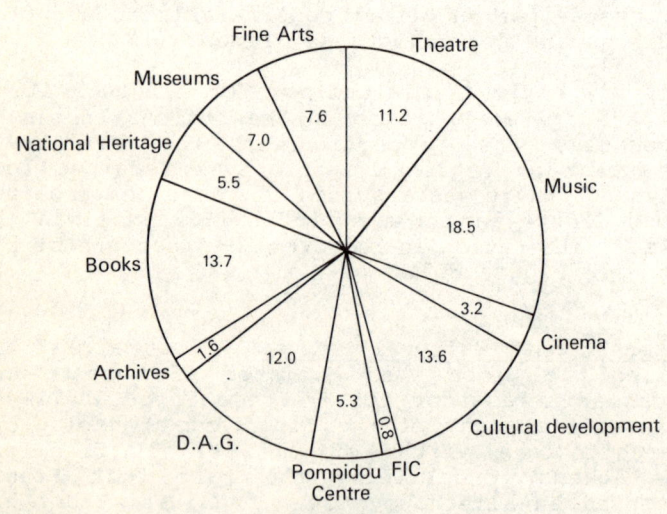

- Fine Arts: 7.5
- Museums: 7.9
- National Heritage: 6.8
- Books: 7.3
- Archives: 2.4
- D.A.G.: 13.7
- Pompidou Centre: 8.1
- FIC: 0.8
- Cultural development: 6.7
- Cinema: 1.3
- Music: 24.7
- Theatre: 12.8

Budget 1982
Total: 4,488 million francs

- Fine Arts: 7.6
- Museums: 7.0
- National Heritage: 5.5
- Books: 13.7
- Archives: 1.6
- D.A.G.: 12.0
- Pompidou Centre: 5.3
- FIC: 0.8
- Cultural development: 13.6
- Cinema: 3.2
- Music: 18.5
- Theatre: 11.2

Source: Ministère de la Culture: La lettre d'information (1 February 1982)

policy which sought to preserve and extend French influence in the region. These preoccupations have been a continuing feature of French international cultural relations, sometimes providing a justification and sometimes a camouflage for foreign and industrial relations in general. As Sean MacBride once put it: 'France is the only country which has realised how important moral and cultural values are at a time of economic crisis but she is also ... the third largest arms exporter in the world'. (19) The other target of French cultural policy was the United States. Gaullism contrived to bring together an anti-Americanism based on national pride which grew up in opposition to the post-war dominance of the United States, and an anti-Americanism based on anti-capitalism, most powerfully articulated by the Communist Party. (20) The role of culture in this configuration was to articulate an ideological opposition which, on occasions, was imperfectly translated into political action, and therefore, perhaps, to allow a greater pragmatism and a higher degree of self-interest to prevail in foreign policy than might otherwise have been the case.

In the Fifth Republic, cultural policy has continued to have a significant international and geopolitical dimension, but Jack Lang was no doubt the first minister of culture since Malraux to attempt to update policy in this respect. Two changes had supervened. Expansion had been replaced by recession which, according to Lang, made an active cultural policy more not less necessary: 'Our predecessors' economic failure was first and foremost a cultural failure'. (21) In addition, the expansion of media technology and the information industries since 1958 had transformed the terms in which American influence and capitalist domination might be discussed.

In a series of speeches in 1982 and 1983 Jack Lang set out a new programme of international cultural relations emphasising, in particular, the 'European dimension' and the 'North-South dimension'. The European dimension was clearly inspired by a period when France was both ideologically and politically pre-eminent on the world stage: 'We are building a movement which affirms the European conscience that was so strong in the 18th century'. (22) As for the North-South dimension, this was most clearly presented in Lang's speech to the UNESCO Conference in Mexico City in July 1982. This speech was reported all over the world and was taken to signal a new departure in French cultural policy:

> La culture est universelle, oui, mais nous veillons à ne pas mettre tout sur le même plan ... Nous savons bien aujourd'hui que la culture du monde n'est pas une ... Le premier des droits à la culture c'est le droit des peuples de disposer d'eux-mêmes ... Tous nos pays acceptent passivement, trop passivement, une certaine invasion, une certaine submersion d'images fabriquées à l'extérieur et de musiques standardisées, stéréotypées qui, naturellement, rabotent les cultures nationales et véhiculent un mode uniformisé de vie que l'on voudrait imposer à la planète entière. Au fond, il s'agit là d'une modalité d'intervention dans les affaires intérieures des états, ou plus exactement d'une modalité d'intervention plus grave encore, dans les consciences des citoyens des états (...) Notre destin est-il de devenir les vassaux de l'immense empire du profit? (23)

In his Mexico City speech, Lang appeared to believe that cultural self-determination is an inalienable right. In practice, however, it would appear that with the creation of the Institut du Monde Arabe, the expansion of the activities of the Maison d'Amérique Latine, and the creation of the Association Dialogue entre les Cultures, socialist policy was concentrated in those areas, such as Latin America or the Arab States, where some counter-American impact might be felt. At home, as will be seen, self-determination for different groups within France was to prove more problematic, and Lang was criticised in many quarters for a rhetoric which seemed purely demagogic.

As regards Europe, however, it is clear that France was bidding to become the cultural leader of the continent and attempting to establish a cultural order as a counterweight to an economic order. The key interface between the cultural and the economic is to be found in the media and information industries and most of the Ministry's European proposals concerned this field: creation of an espace audio-visuel européen, encouragement of European co-productions, establishment of a European cultural foundation in Paris. Moreover, a States General of World Culture, bringing together more than four hundred intellectuals from all over the world, was convened in Paris in February 1983, and addressed by Mitterrand in terms which apparently made clear that technological creativity and independence were the central issues of the future:

> Après les saisons du dogme et de la répétition revient le temps de l'invention; là réside l'ambition du projet français: investir dans la formation technologique et investir dans la création artistique et intellectuelle (...) Ce projet résulte d'une conviction: les industries de la culture sont les industries de l'avenir, investir dans la culture c'est investir dans l'économie. (24)

In Mexico City and in Paris, therefore, international cultural policy was defined as relating essentially to mass communications and the new technologies. Indeed, media technologies interestingly illustrate the socialist approach to nationalisations which took key industries, including the electronics group Thomson, into public ownership less to 'democratise' them than in order to prevent them becoming 'internationalised' - i.e. part of American-owned multi-national corporations. The Socialists' international achievements in culture must therefore be judged by their degree of success in the communications field. This was not immediately clear, however, and Jack Lang's speeches betray an interesting evolution as he ceased to refer to cultural self-determination from 1983 onwards, and as the difficulties of maintaining a European presence in the culture industries became more apparent.

The Performing Arts. There are two reasons why it might have been supposed that Jack Lang would pay particular attention to the theatre. One was that he had himself been the director of the Festival de Nancy and was familiar with the needs of theatre, in the provinces in particular. The other was that the national theatres had not fully recovered from the events of May 1968 and the apparently anti-governmental stance adopted by some directors such as Jean-Louis Barrault at that time. However, the aftermath of May 1968 together with the influence of American companies such as the Living Theatre and the rediscovery of Brecht had meant that the late 1960s and early 1970s had been an extraordinarily creative period for theatre in France with new forms, new subject matter and a desire to take the theatre out onto the streets. By 1975, the Minister of Culture, Michel Guy institutionalised this movement with the appointment of Jean-Pierre Vincent to Strasbourg, Patrice Chéreau to the TNP (Théâtre Nationale

Populaire) in Lyon, Gildas Bourdet to Tourcoing and Georges Lavaudant to Grenoble.

Socialist theatre policies continued and reinforced this process. Jean-Pierre Vincent went to the Comédie Française and Patrice Chéreau to the Théâtre des Amandiers in Nanterre whilst Giorgio Strehler was invited to lead the Théâtre de l'Europe housed at the Odéon. The structure of subsidy to the theatre did not alter substantially (cf. Figure 6.3) with the only significant readjustments to be found in some transfer of resources from the subsidy of the national theatres to the support for theatre companies which did not necessarily have an institutional home. (25)

The Socialists' music policy was much more original and it succeeded a period which had already been one of extensive innovation and of increased spending with the creation of the IRCAM (Institut de Recherche et de Coordination Acoustique-Musique) and the return of Boulez to France. (26) A considerable investment was made in music education with the establishment of five new music schools in the <u>départements</u> and the revamping of the Conservatoire National de la Musique at Lyon. In addition, the range and capacity of performance facilities in Paris was enormously increased: the Opéra de la Bastille and the Cité Musicale de la Villette allow for specialist performance in a way that was sadly lacking in Paris before (it had no auditorium comparable to the Albert Hall or the Festival Hall in London), and a 2000 seat concert hall, le Zénith, primarily designed for rock music concerts but adapted for all uses, was also constructed. Furthermore, when the Opéra leaves the Palais Garnier this will also create a venue for the exclusive use of the national ballet company to which Jack Lang appointed Rudolf Nureyev as director.

<u>Museums, Libraries and the National Heritage: une politique de la mémoire.</u> If, as some historians suggest, a 'politique de la mémoire' is the third and most recent stage of cultural policy, then the approach to archives of all kinds and to the national heritage will be areas of particular political and ideological sensitivity. (27) The Socialists' approach to memory does indeed have some interesting features. There has been a veritable explosion of new museums in the last twenty years in France - the Pompidou Centre and the Musée d'Orsay being the two best known examples. The Socialists continued their predecessors' policies with the Grand Louvre project and the opening of the Picasso Museum at the Hôtel Salé. The museum budget quadrupled and particular sums were set aside, for the first time, for large regional projects including the creation of a number of new museums in the provinces such as the Museum of Prehistory at Carnac and the Ecomuseum at Chartres. A Fonds Régional des Acquisitions was created to assist provincial museums in the purchase of works of art and the state actively continued the existing policy of encouraging bequests in lieu of death duties. But it remained the case that by far the greater proportion of resources for acquisition and current spending still went to Paris and the museum budget remained skewed in favour of the Pompidou Centre. This distribution was not seriously challenged.

Libraries and publishing benefited from new thinking and an injection of funds. Aid to publishers and authors was restructured and book prices were fixed once again - the object being to assist smaller publishing houses and specialist bookshops. Financial assistance was provided for the export of French books and the network of regional lending libraries was considerably reinforced. On the other hand, the Socialists notably failed to resolve the problems of the Bibliothèque Nationale which remains chronically under-resourced and ill-equipped not simply to offer reading facilities but also to preserve printed material.

An inability to establish a clear role for the Bibliothèque Nationale may be taken as symptomatic of the Socialists' lack of coherent thinking with regard to the national heritage in general. Archaeology, ethnography and historic buildings and monuments - generally grouped under the rubric patrimoine - all benefited from the general increase in resources but without reconsideration of the policies of conservation and, above all, access. The audio-visual archive is a case in point. Its conservation is split between three institutions - the Bibliothèque Nationale which operates the dépôt légal; the Cinémathèque Nationale and the Institut National de la Communication Audiovisuelle (INA). The two former institutions simply do not have the resources to catalogue their holdings, still less allow access to them. INA, on the other hand, has an effective catalogue because its archive is used for commercial purposes, but access to it is prohibitively expensive for private individuals. It has always been a tenet of republican belief that the archive is the foundation of the nation state and the repository of the revolutionary tradition; more recently historiography has been rediscovered by thinkers who have attempted to use memory – especially the popular memory – as a form of counter cultural practice. One might therefore have expected archives to receive privileged attention. (28) But whereas access to paper archives is relatively well-established and well-resourced, the newer media (sound and vision) have presented problems which have received little attention. Indeed, one of the most disappointing aspects of Lang's period in office was the failure to update heritage policies and the failure to address questions of access.

On the other hand, the Socialists clearly did pursue a museum and heritage policy which may be considered national, and in so doing broke with some of the traditional assumptions as to what does and does not constitute culture. The creation of museums of fashion and the culinary arts, together with support for the chanson, betray a desire to protect and encourage what is perceived as typically 'French', so that culture in this sense is national rather than universal, just as Lang had said in Mexico City. Similarly, with the creation of the Musée de la bande dessinée at Angoûleme and the Circus School at Chalons, the conventional borders of 'art' were considerably stretched, so that although the Socialists did not arrive at a completely new definition of culture their intermittently nationalist policies contrived to render old definitions too narrow.

Le Développement Culturel

Cultural development was perhaps the most dynamic and certainly the most interesting aspect of socialist cultural policy between 1981 and 1986. Cultural development is a notion created by analogy with economic development. It was first seriously discussed in the period of postwar reconstruction and it combines a commitment to democratisation, a commitment to popular education and a particular interpretation of socio-economic conditions. (29) The first products of the theory of cultural development were the Maisons de la Culture, but by 1968 this national cultural development policy was seen to have failed. The idea of cultural development was then suspended, along with regional cultural policies, until the Ministry of Culture created the Mission du Développement Culturel in 1979. After the socialist victory of 1981 the Mission was absorbed into the Direction du Développement Culturel headed by Dominique Wallon. This appointment was obviously crucial to the success of cultural development policies for Wallon was a former Inspecteur des Finances, who had been closely involved with the Maison de la Culture in Grenoble for many years, and who was described by Jack Lang as 'a militant who has sacrificed his career to his beliefs'. (30) Even more significant, perhaps, was the fact that a major part of the increased culture budget went to this department since of all the departmental budgets within the Ministry only this one was more than doubled in percentage terms (see Figure 6.4). There was thus real scope for innovation enabling cultural development to become the channel through which the Ministry of Culture implemented some of the Socialists' general commitment to decentralisation.

At a press conference in November 1982 Dominique Wallon set out the plans for his department. These consisted in helping existing arts and cultural establishments in the regions to redefine their policies and to seek central funds for mutually agreed projects or policy lines; in funding the creation of new centres; in creating a Fonds Spécial de Développement Culturel to which all regions could apply for specific projects; in seeking out new audiences, whether young people, the inhabitants of rural communities, or those who traditionally did not frequent cultural establishments; in recognising and assisting regional and community cultures; and in collaborating with new partners, such as industry, in the development of cultural activities. The sums which the Direction du Développement Culturel had at its disposal were also to be used to attract funds from other sources, notably other government departments, local authorities and the private sector. (31)

Thus decentralisation and pluralism were to be the watchwords of cultural development, but both were problematic. According to Wallon and his collaborators, the failure of previous policies was to be ascribed to a failure to ensure that popular education and local initiatives went hand in hand with artistic merit: 'The very idea of cultural action is in crisis because cultural action has often been exclusively assimilated to community activity and has, wrongly, been separated from artistic creation'. (32) The Department had to negotiate a difficult path between those in the Ministry – including at times the Minister – who felt that money was being spent on insufficiently meritorious

Cultural Policy: The Soul of Man under Socialism

Figure 6.4:

Budget of the Direction du développement culturel

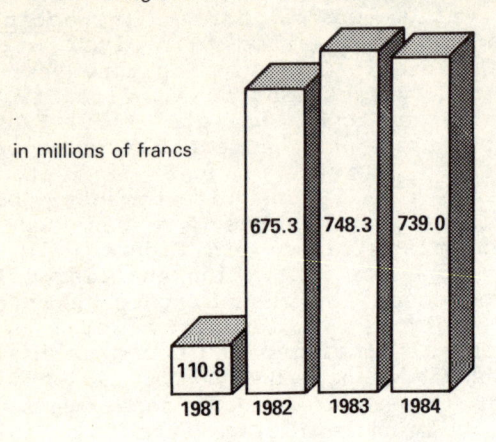

in millions of francs

1981	1982	1983	1984
110.8	675.3	748.3	739.0

Départments which received a cultural development agreement in 1982 and 1983

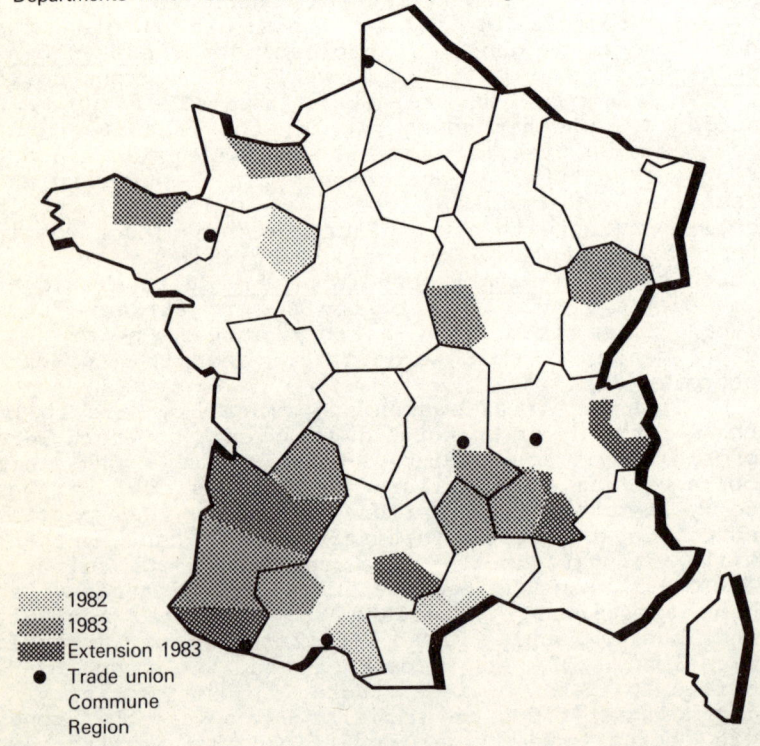

- 1982
- 1983
- Extension 1983
- ● Trade union
- Commune
- Region

Cultural Policy: The Soul of Man under Socialism

Towns which received a cultural development agreement in 1982 and 1983

▼ Agreement 1982
■ Agreement 1983
● Extension 1983

Ile-de-France
● Meaux
▼ Milly
● Mitry
● Mantes
■ Etampes
■ Juvisy
  Corbeil
▼ Antony
● Chatenay
▼ Chatillon
■ Gennevilliers
▼ Sarcelles
▼ Athis-Mons
▼ Le Blanc-Mesnil
● Villiers-le-Bel

Guadeloupe
Les Abymes
Point-à-Pitre
La Réunion
Le Port
Saint-André

Source: Ministère de la Culture. La Politique Culturelle 1981-5, Bilan de la législative

projects in which national standards were not maintained and those outside who believed that cultural development was little more than an instrument of Socialist propaganda and a means of buying local votes.

A mechanism of support known as the Convention de Développement Culturel was devised to steer a course between these twin pitfalls. A convention could be drawn up between the Ministry and a department, a region, a town, a company or any other voluntary or commercial organisation, and it theoretically provided the regional body with the chance to set out what it wished to do whilst allowing the Ministry to support the projects it approved of. The Ministry in all cases, however, retained the right to authorise the project and, at least in the first stages, seems to have actively gone in search of partners. Nevertheless, the volume of conventions signed in 1982-3 (the first year of operation) suggests that the initiative was extremely welcome and necessary at regional level with 162 bodies receiving ministerial approval. Where this policy of cultural development differed from a conventional regional cultural policy was in its willingness to enlarge the scope of its activities. Thus many of the conventions were with the traditional local authority partners, but many more included trade unions and popular education organsations, prisons, hospitals, the army and the comités d'entreprises (works committees). The Ministry of Culture signed conventions with the Ministry of Health and the Ministry of Defence relating to cultural activities in hospitals and among the armed forces with the twin objective of providing resources for traditionally excluded groups and a means for penetrating traditionally closed institutions. The approach to the comités d'entreprises is perhaps even more significant of the general thrust of socialist policies. Following the report by Pierre Belleville Pour la Culture dans l'entreprise and the enactment of the lois Auroux, the comités d'entreprises, which in the case of large employers had at their disposal considerable sums of money, were empowered to become involved in cultural activities, and by 1985 the Ministry was spending 6 million francs on programmes agreed with such bodies. (33)

The Direction du Développement Culturel was extremely successful in putting large sums of money into the regions and, to that extent, carrying through decentralisation policies. However, it was less successful in achieving a shift in decision-making away from the centre and it is not altogether certain that it attempted or indeed wished to do so. There naturally continued to be large areas of cultural activity funded by local authorities to a degree which was locally determined and which varied from region to region, over which the Ministry exercised no central control. But as far as its own budgets were concerned, it retained a degree of influence which is startling in the light of international comparisons. In Great Britain, for example, sums of money are effectively made over to regional bodies to spend as they see fit and the notion of piecemeal agreements would be considered an unwarranted interference in local freedom. The control retained by the French Ministry partly reflects a desire to avoid repetition of past failures which were seen to result from a lack of selectiveness and rigour. But if one considers the areas chosen for particular action, whether industrial companies, prisons, hospitals or the army, they are all those where cultural activity might be held to act as a counterweight to forms of oppression (and this includes hospitals, following Michel Foucault), particularly state oppression, and therefore to be particularly amenable to socialist intervention. The vehemence of some right-wing criticism of cultural development suggests that these initiatives had some measure of success.

On the other hand, the policy came to grief in its approach to regional and community cultures. The Ministry commissioned a report from Henri Giordan <u>Démocratie Culturelle et Droit à la Différence</u> (Paris: Documentation française, 1982) which set out policies for community support and which resulted in the establishment of the <u>Conseil National des Langues et Cultures Régionales</u>. However, the Direction culturelle encountered the insurmountable difficulty that many regional and linguistic movements were neither democratic nor progressive and were often a home for extremists and anti-republicans. Generations of centralisation have made it difficult to view such movements as authentic or in any way providing an outlet for genuine popular sentiment, and Socialists therefore find particular difficulty in supporting them. Ethnic minority groups, however, posed a rather different problem since they challenged the notion of nationhood or <u>francité</u> which was powerfully articulated by Jack Lang in his early years at the Ministry, especially in his Mexico City speech, and while it is true that most European countries with large immigrant communities share problems of separatism and integration, the question may be particularly acutely posed in France because of its nationalist and centralising traditions. Certainly, Dominique Wallon and his team did not make significant advances in this area, which, like everything else to do with ethnic minorities under the Socialists, increasingly became determined by forces outside the government. (34)

An interesting comparison might therefore be developed between the policies of cultural development under Wallon and the policies of Labour controlled local authorities in Britain in the 1980s, particularly those of the GLC (Greater London Council). For the British Left, the fragmentation of the electorate was a given and mechanisms were created to channel funds to identifiable 'minority' groups - women, children, gays and lesbians, the handicapped and so on. This approach was justified in democratic terms but the political rationale was that election success would henceforth be based on aggregative alliances. The contrast with the French Ministry is striking. For Wallon and his team all community activity existed within the perspective of making the totality of cultural experience ultimately available to all. Whereas elements of the British Left therefore set out to break up cultural consensus, the French Left attempted to broaden it in order to maintain it.

The Socialists' Achievements

What was the impact of six years' socialist administration on cultural policy in France? The continuation and extension of a <u>politique de grandeur</u>, particularly in Paris; the incorporation of a variety of different art forms into the range of the Ministry of Culture's activities; a relatively shortlived attempt to claim that France headed the progressive states of the world in a crusade against cultural imperialism; the intermittent pursuit of a nationalist cultural policy; a 100 per cent increase in spending which created jobs, allowed for a huge injection of resources into the regions and was maintained even in the face of growing economic difficulties and austerity budgets; and a degree of decentralisation in decision-making.

These are substantial achievements, but they are unlikely to prove lasting. They have been particularly badly affected by the 1986 election of a government dedicated to privatisation and cutting public expenditure. Thus the Chirac government allowed the future of the Opéra de la Bastille to remain in doubt for several months, before confirming its continuation and cancelling the Carrefour de la Communication. Similarly, a major casualty has been the cultural development budget which was cut by more than half, provoking the resignation of Dominique Wallon. Even had there not been budget reductions, it is difficult to see how the interventionism of the Direction du Développement Culturel could have been reconciled with the laissez-faire liberalism pursued by the new Minister of Culture François Léotard. (35)

However, the question that must be asked is to what extent any of these policies - socialist or otherwise - influence the cultural habits and practices of the French. Surveys carried out by the Ministry of Culture since its creation indicate a much slower rhythm of cultural change than is implied by the five-year term of office of a government, and the relation between economic conditions and cultural consumption seems to be a more significant factor in the face of change. (36) The Socialists were extremely good at increasing the facilities available but they did not substantially effect a shift in the allocation of resources from the culturally rich to the culturally poor, while a comparison of audiences and levels of subsidy shows no change in the traditional inverse proportions, with opera, with the smallest percentage audience, still receiving the greatest level of subsidy (see Figure 6.5). Further democratisation or the extension of culture to greater numbers of people remained impossible, no doubt because cultural policy under the Socialists remained a policy for the arts, while many of the most popular forms were not traditionally considered to be arts at all. As has been seen, both the President and the Minister were acutely aware of the way in which the leisure industries and the mass media influenced culture and cultural habits but their perceptions were not translated into policy. Nowhere was this more apparent than in the Socialists' approach to television.

Both the Programme Commun and the 110 Propositions had emphasised the need for freedom of expression on television and had promised to create a watchdog body to ensure its preservation. After the Moinot Commission had reported on the future of broadcasting, an Haute Autorité was duly created. (37) Partly as a result of the contention that had

Cultural Policy: The Soul of Man under Socialism

Figure 6.5: Pyramid of Subsidies (1)

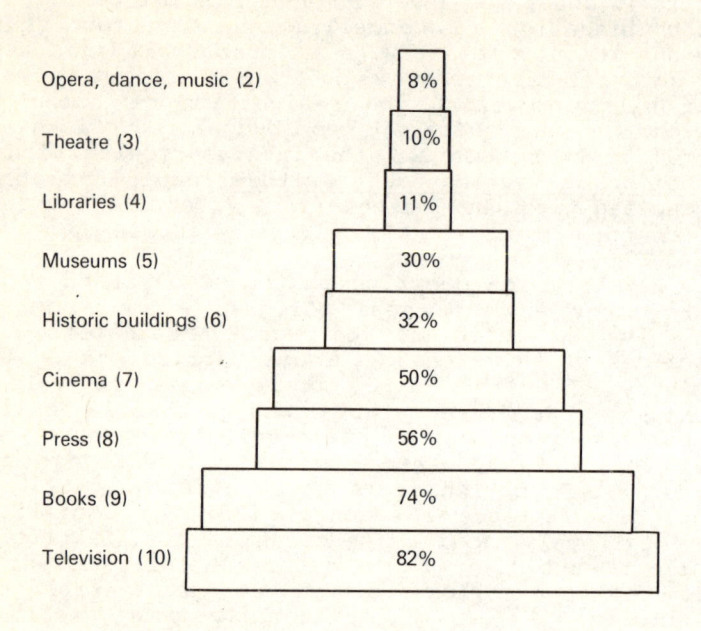

Sector	%
Opera, dance, music (2)	8%
Theatre (3)	10%
Libraries (4)	11%
Museums (5)	30%
Historic buildings (6)	32%
Cinema (7)	50%
Press (8)	56%
Books (9)	74%
Television (10)	82%

(1) Includes current expenditure by all ministries (not just the ministry of culture) but excludes non-repeatable capital spending.
(2) These three sectors are treated as one because the opera budget clearly includes, to some extent, dance and music.
(3) This figure represents only direct aid to the press.
(4) Excluding the Fonds culturel du livre which concerns exports.
(5) Direct state financing of television is negligible. The licence fee provides the main source of revenue for state radio and television (and the proportion deriving from advertising is limited to about 25%).

Source: L'Impératif culturel (Documentation Française, 1983), pp.112-113.

Cultural Policy: The Soul of Man under Socialism

Figure 6.5: Pyramid of audiences (1)

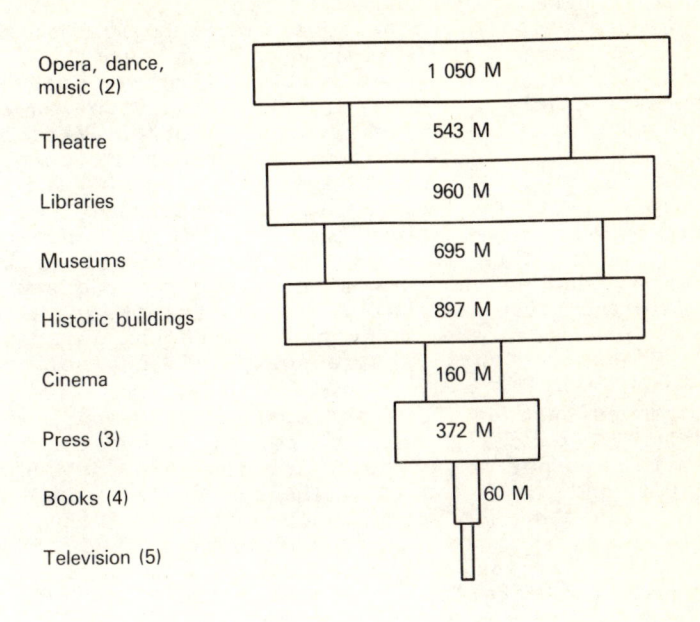

Category	Value
Opera, dance, music (2)	1 050 M
Theatre	543 M
Libraries	960 M
Museums	695 M
Historic buildings	897 M
Cinema	160 M
Press (3)	372 M
Books (4)	60 M
Television (5)	

(1) Figures are expressed as a percentage of the French population of more than 15 years of age (1% represents approximately 400,000 people).
(2) These three sectors are distinct but are not treated separately in terms of financing.
(3) Calculated as people who go to the theatre at least once a year.
(4) Calculated as people who use a library at least once a month.
(5) Calculated as people who visit a museum at least once a year.
(6) People who visit a historic building at least once a year.
(7) People who go to the cinema at least once a year.
(8) People who read a daily paper more than once a week.
(9) People who read at least one book a year.
(10) People who look at television at least every other day.

raged in television since 1968, communications policy became the responsibility of a separate Ministry of Communications under Georges Fillioud rather than remaining under the aegis of the Ministry of Culture which might have been more logical in the light of technological change and the evolution of cultural habits. A wedge was thus driven between information (the press, radio and television) on the one hand and the creative arts on the other, ignoring the fact that for television and radio to compete successfully in world markets they needed to be highly creative. Increasingly socialist media policies were preoccupied with managing technological change. Thus the sale of video cassettes was heavily taxed and the import of video recorders kept artificially low nominally in an attempt to allow French manufacturers to catch up with the Japanese. (38) Meanwhile Canal Plus, a new pay-TV channel, was launched precisely in order to offer the kind of programmes such as films and sport that viewers were likely to purchase and to record. Much of this material was not French since imports were frequently cheaper and more popular. Then in 1985, two more television channels were launched, both private, and while one (La 5) had its schedules composed almost entirely of series, films and variety, much of which was imported material, the other (the Sixth) was a pop music channel.

The argument in favour of these measures was that technological change and international developments such as satellite broadcasting had rendered the concept of the public service, nationally based broadcasting system outdated and impossible to sustain. The arguments against were that in modernising and enlarging its distribution networks France had opened up a huge market for imports since no accompanying measures ensured that production would increase to fill the available slots. Indeed, in the case of the fifth channel, the cahier des charges had, in the teeth of trade union and film industry opposition, fixed the quota of foreign material at a level much lower than that allowed on the other TV channels.

The Socialists' policy for the cinema was similarly shot through with contradictions. They continued the policies of previous administrations in assisting exhibition and this enabled cinema audiences in France to remain unusually high, and they complemented such policies by measures for the regions, through the Agence Régional du Développement du Cinéma. But as regards production, they increased the sums available for the <u>avance sur recettes</u>, but reduced barring agreements which effectively enabled importers of foreign films to saturate the market and make quick profits. However, it was 1985 before any agreement was reached on film and television co-productions and on the television channels' obligations to enter into co-productions with the cinema industry, despite the fact that almost all European films are currently made within co-production agreements. The French film industry remains the most flourishing in Europe but it increasingly works with foreign companies because French TV has not been able to expand its production capacity.

The audiovisual policies of the Socialists would therefore seem to suggest that they experienced some difficulties in reconciling their conception of art and some of the most popular forms of culture. Indeed, the Ministry's attitude towards cinema is instructive in this respect, for in addition to the usual forms of subsidy channelled through the <u>avance sur recettes</u> which provides support for art cinema, the Ministry also became involved, as co-producer, in a number of one-off productions such as <u>Danton</u> and <u>Un Amour de Swann</u>, and the effect of this was not simply to increase the amount of subsidy available but also to mark off those projects which were considered 'creative' and thus worthy of support from the run-of-the-mill audiovisual output. (39)

There is a final area in which it would appear that the Socialists misjudged or misapprehended modern trends. Jack Lang's inaugural speech in the National Assembly spoke of the reconciliation between artists and the State: 'Désormais, il n'y aura plus d'un côté l'imagination des uns tendant leur sébille et le désespoir des autres fabricant des cocktails molotov. Désormais, le Pouvoir s'emploiera, lui aussi, à retrouver, sous les pavés, la plage'. By the summer of 1983 this hope had been dashed. In a series of contributions to <u>Le Monde</u> in July and August under the general heading <u>Le silence des intellectuels de gauche</u> it became clear that the majority of intellectuals were not prepared to endorse government policies simply because they claimed to be socialist and, perhaps more important, that the notion of a committed intellectual of the kind referred to by Jack Lang was fast becoming irrelevant. As Max Gallo put it: 'Cette génération moralise, juge, ricane et travaille dans le concret. Mai-juin 1981 n'est pas sa victoire, même si confusément c'est la défaite de ce qu'elle a toujours méprisé. Est-il sans signification que, pour une part, ... elle ait soutenu la candidature d'un clown, tant les élections et la politique lui paraissent dérisoires)?' (40) Perhaps therefore the greatest achievement of socialist cultural policies was to have laid to rest the myths of May 1968.

Acknowledgements

I am most grateful to the Service de Documentation of the Ministère de la Culture in Paris for allowing me access to their archives and providing me with numerous documents. Gil Delannoi, Marie-Ange Laumonier, Janine Mossuz-Lavau and Richard Nice all offered help and advice while Dominique Wallon was kind enough to grant me a long interview. The Polytechnic of the South Bank research fund supported my visits to Paris and Sue Jones, as ever, brilliantly performed the essential task of deciphering my manuscript.

Notes

Where no publisher is listed, e.g. for Lang's speeches, this indicates that a typescript was consulted in the Ministry of Culture.

1. See eg. F. Mitterrand, Politique 2, (Paris: Fayard, 1981), p.286.
2. The histories and critiques of this process are well known. In Britain they include R. Hoggart's The Uses of Literacy and R. William's Culture and Society; in France R. Barthes's Mythologies and P. Bourdieu's La Reproduction. For an overview see E. Ritaine, Les Stratèges de la Culture, (Paris: Presses de la FNSP, 1983).
3. 'The purpose of the ministry responsible for cultural affairs is to provide access for the greatest possible number of French citizens to the major works of mankind and above all of France; to make our national heritage available to the widest possible public and to encourage their enrichment by the creation of works of art and of the mind', (J.O., 26 July 1959, L. 7,413).
4. For Malraux's approach to cultural policy see V. Morin, 'La Culture majuscule: André Malraux', Communications, no. 14 (1969), pp.70-81; J. Mossuz, André Malraux et le gaullisme, (Paris: FNSP, 1970) pp.166-72.
5. Cf. A. Mesnard, L'Action Culturelle des Pouvoirs Publics, (Paris: LGDJ, 1969); A. Piatier, 'Une notion nouvelle: le développement culturel',

L'Expansion de la Recherche Scientifique, 21 déc. 1964, pp.12-16.

6. Cf. IVe Plan 1962-5 Rapport Général de la Commission de l'Equipement Culturel et du Patrimoine Artistique, (Paris: Documentation Française, 1961), pp.5-7.

7. 'It is the very principle of cultural democratisation which is challenged: the professionals condemn the artificial unanimity created by an oecumenical and non-conflictual approach to culture and the illusion that emotion generated simply by individual contact with works of art is a good thing', F. Bloch-Lainé (ed.), La France en Mai 1981, (Paris: Documentation Française, 1982), Vol. III, p.297.

8. La France en Mai 1981, Vol. I, p.225; cf. Fig. 6.3.

9. La France en Mai 1981, Vol. I, p.226.

10. Cf. Programme Commun de Gouvernement Actualisé, (Paris: Editions Sociales, 1978), pp.51-3 & 131-5; Mitterrand, Politique 2, pp.322-3.

11. For the text of this interview see C. Clément, Rêver Chacun pour l'Autre, (Paris: Fayard, 1982), pp.279-92. Mitterrand owns up to being 'a poor television watcher' and an infrequent cinema-goer and states: 'Socialist culture does and does not exist. It exists in one way in a social approach to problems and a concern to give expression to what we believe popular aspirations to be; above all in our desire to make culture intelligible to the greatest possible number of people and to those who are underprivileged. But within the field of culture itself we do not attempt to say that something one group wishes to paint blue ought to be painted red!' (p.281).

12. 'For the men of my generation the place in which we are now gathered (the Sorbonne) is a place in which the changes that we are now in government to carry through in daily life were first predicted and prefigured almost twenty years ago. There were many of us here ... and we hoped to build a new world quickly', Discours de Jack Lang à la séance de clôture du 45e Congrès du PEN Club International, 25 September 1981.

13. Clément, Rêver Chacun pour l'Autre, pp.63-92.

14. J. Rigaud, La Culture pour Vivre, (Paris: Gallimard, 1975), p.189.

15. C. Petit-Castelli, La Culture à la Une ou l'Action culturelle dans les Mairies Socialistes, (Paris: Club Socialiste du Livre, 1981), pp.21-7.

16. J. Lang, 'Discours à l'Assemblée Nationale', 17 November 1981.

17. It will be recalled that Rebérioux conducted a research seminar on the <u>expositions universelles</u> and their relation to technical culture and social change. This proposal occasioned an interesting conflict between Mitterrand as President and Jacques Chirac as Mayor of Paris which was later re-enacted over the issue of the Opéra de la Bastille when Chirac became Prime Minister in 1986.

18. 'Whereas in the 1983 budget proposals we are seeking 300 million francs for capital programmes in Paris, we are seeking 1.5 billion francs for capital programmes in the regions. This is a total reversal of the past situation: our proposals for Paris are more than matched by a considerable investment in every region in France'. 'Orientations budgétaires du Ministère de la Culture pour 1982', <u>Supplément à la lettre mensuelle d'information</u>, (Paris: Ministère de la Culture, 1 February 1982).

19. Cf. <u>Le Monde</u>, 1 December 1982, pp.1-2.

20. Cf. L. Boltanski, 'America, America. Le Plan Marshall et l'importation du management en France', <u>Actes de la Recherche et Sciences Sociales</u>, 38 (May 1981), pp.19-41.

21. J. Lang, 'Discours', 17 November 1981.

22. Cf. J. Lang, 'Intervention, le 17 September 1982 à la réunion des Ministres de la Culture des pays membres de la Communauté Economique Européenne, de l'Espagne et du Portugal à Naples'.

23. 'Culture is certainly universal but we are careful not to reduce everything to the same level ... Today we are aware that there is no single world culture ... The first cultural right is that of people to take their own decisions ... All our countries accept too passively a certain invasion of or a submission to images produced elsewhere, and to standardised and stereotyped music, which inevitably wear away national cultures and transmit a uniform lifestyle which it is attempted to impose on the planet as a whole. Basically, this is an attempt to interfere in the internal affairs of states, or, which is worse, a way of interfering with the minds of the citizens of such states ... Is our fate really to become the serfs of the huge empire of profit?' Intervention de Jack Lang à Mexico, 27 July 1982.

24. 'After the seasons of dogmatism and repetitiveness comes the time for inventiveness, and therein lies the ambition of the French plan. We wish to invest in technological training and in artistic and intellectual creativity. This is because we are

convinced that the culture industries are the industries of the future and therefore that investing in culture means investing in the economy'. Quoted in Le Monde, 15 February 1983, p.17.

25. Cf. La Politique Culturelle 1981-5. Bilan de la Législature, (Paris: Ministère de la Culture, 1986).

26. See P.-M. Menger, Le Paradoxe du Musicien, (Paris: Flammarion, 1983).

27. Cf. G. Delannoi, 'La Politique culturelle. L'Héritage et L'Innovation', Colloque l'Etat devant les cultures régionales et communautaires, (Association française de Science Politique, 23-25, January 1986).

28. Cf. F. Denel 'The INA Heritage', in J. Forbes (ed), INA French for Innovation, (London: BFI, 1984), p.17.

29. Cf. J. Dumazédier, 'Nous devons préparer l'avenir', L'Expansion de la Recherche Scientifique, 21 December 1964, pp.17-22.

30. J. Lang, 'Discours', 17 November 1981.

31. Cf. typescript available in the Ministry of Culture.

32. D. Wallon, 'Conférence de presse', November 1982.

33. Cf. La Politique culturelle 1981-5.

34. Most obviously the rise of the Front National and the impact this had on socialist policies relating to immigration.

35. Cf. Wallon's letter of resignation published in Le Monde, 22 May 1986, p.10.

36. A. Girard (ed.) Pratiques culturelles des Français. Description socio-démographique. Evolution 1973-81, (Paris: Dalloz, 1982) bears out the slow pace of change. Girard's department produces the most impressive set of cultural statistics in Europe and extrapolation from these is more legitimate than it might be from those of other countries. A similar message is conveyed by P. Dumayet (ed.), L'Impératif Culturel Rapport du Groupe de Travail Long Terme Culture, (Paris: Documentation Française, 1982), which reviews cultural policy since 1959 in the light of the preparation for the Ninth Plan.

37. P. Moinot (ed.), Pour une Réforme de l'Audiovisuel, (Paris: Documentation Française, 1981).

38. Hence the farcical requirement for all imported video recorders to enter France via the small customs post at Poitiers. More seriously, some commentators believe that a proliferation of private TV channels and cable networks is ultimately less

threatening to state control than the use of video recorders which permit person to person communication that by-passes state intervention.

39. Cf. H. le Roux, 'Les Années Lang. Abécédaire du cinéma français', Cahiers du Cinéma 381, (March 1986), pp.18-34.

40. 'This generation moralises, judges, sniggers and works on concrete projects. May-June 1981 is not its victory even though it in some way represents the defeat of what it has always despised. Is it not at least partly significant that the elections seemed so absurd to these people that they supported the candidacy of a clown?', Le Monde, 7 July 1983, p.7.

Suggestions for further reading

The bibliography on culture is vast both in French and English. However there is no real overview available in English. The following are a selection of the works which relate most closely to the material in this chapter. They are listed in alphabetical order.

1. Pierre Bourdieu, L'Amour de l'Art (Paris: Minuit, 1969) and La Distinction (Paris: Minuit, 1979) survey the public for art and attempt a social critique of artistic consumption and taste.

2. Communications, 14 (1969) is a special issue devoted to 'La Politique Culturelle' and offers a theoretical critique of the first decade of official cultural policy in France.

3. P. Duyamet (ed.), L'Imperatif Culturel. Rapport du Groupe de Travail Long Terme Culture (Paris: Documentation Française, 1982). This outlines the thinking behind the cultural policy planned for 1984-88.

4. P. Flichy, Les Industries de l'Imaginaire (Grenoble: Presses Universitaires de Grenoble, 1980). Though slightly overtaken by events nevertheless usefully places cultural policy in relation to technological change.

5. A. Girard (ed.), Pratiques culturelles des Français (Paris: Dalloz, 1982) a compendium of sociological and statistical information. This is the third such publication since 1959.

6. P. Moinot (ed.), Pour une réforme de l'Audio-visuel (Paris: Documentation française, 1981) contains the first socialist proposals for broadcasting.

7. E. Morot-Sir, 'Vers une conscience et politique nouvelles de la culture en France',

Contemporary French Civilisation, Fall-Winter 1983-4, pp.283-95.

8. C. Petit-Castelli, *La Culture à la Une* (Paris: Club Socialiste du livre, 1981) is a useful guide to cultural policy in socialist administered towns.

9. *La Politique Culturelle 1981-85. Bilan de la Législature* (Ministère de la Culture Service d'Information et Communication). This is a large folder containing fascicules setting out the Socialists' achievements in: Les Archives; Les Arts Plastiques; Le Cinéma et l'Audiovisuel; La Décentralisation et le Développement Culturel; Economie et Culture; Enseignement et Formation; Le Livre et la Lecture; Les Musées; La Musique et la Danse; Le Patrimoine; La Recherche; Les Relations Internationales; Le Théâtre et les Spectacles. It is thus an indispensable guide.

10. J. Rigaud, *La Culture pour Vivre* (Paris: Gallimard, 1975) a mid-1970s essay on the opportunities for cultural policy.

11. E. Ritaine, *Les Stratèges de la Culture* (Paris: Presses de la FNSP, 1983) offers a fascinating historical approach to cultural thinking on the Left.

Chapter Seven

FOREIGN POLICY: BUSINESS AS USUAL?

David A.L. Levy

Assessing François Mitterrand's foreign policy just one year after his election, Alain Duhamel concluded that, in foreign affairs, all Fifth Republic Presidents had pursued the same goals and carried out very similar policies. Such changes as had taken place were ones of presentation and tone rather than of policy as such. This view has now become more generally accepted, yet from the vantage point of 1981 it would have seemed surprising. (1) The Socialists themselves had promised that foreign policy would be an area for fairly dramatic change, and François Mitterrand's election success was greeted with apprehension by many of France's allies. The purpose of this chapter is to assess to what extent and why Mitterrand's foreign policy was indeed marked by change. First we focus on the Socialists' hopes for change; the critique of Valéry Giscard d'Estaing's foreign policy, and the main foreign policy initiatives of François Mitterrand's first year in office. Secondly, we look at the extent to which foreign policy during the remaining period from 1982-1986, demonstrates a continuation of these earlier ideas and initiatives, or rather a trimming of policy and a disavowal of strategies for change. Finally we will look at some of the factors underlying the evolution of socialist foreign policy between 1981 and 1986.

A Socialist Foreign Policy: The First Steps

As the 1981 elections approached the socialist critique of Giscard d'Estaing's foreign policy focused attention on its content, its style and its results. (2) Giscard's European policy was criticised for being too dependent on the Franco-German axis, and for its ineffectual defence of

Foreign Policy: Business as Usual?

French interests, both against the British with their demands for budget rebates, and against the threat posed to French farmers by the planned entry of Spain and Portugal into the Community. Policy towards the Middle East was accused of being dictated purely by a cynical desire to secure France a guaranteed supply of oil together with access to the lucrative arms markets of the Arab world. Many socialists, François Mitterrand among them, felt that Giscard's overtures to the Palestinians should not be carried out at the expense of good relations with Israel. In East-West relations socialists detected a similar lack of balance. They claimed that an obsessive concern to preserve détente with the USSR had, for example, prevented France from reacting to the Soviet invasion of Afghanistan in December 1979 in any but the most half-hearted way. Mitterrand thought that Giscard's East-West policy was both wrong - because it misread the political and military balance through underestimating Soviet strength - and that it was also unduly cynical in that it placed French desires for good political, and above all, economic, relations with the Soviet Union, before her duty to her allies and her wider obligation to preserve freedom and defend human rights. There was a very similar critique of Giscard's policy in the Third World. His aid policy was criticised for meanness and neo-colonialism while his economic and military support for some of Africa's bloodiest and least popular rulers was also condemned roundly. The issue here was one of style as much as substance. Like his predecessors, Giscard invested considerable time in maintaining close personal as well as diplomatic relations with African leaders. But his obvious enjoyment of the lavish hospitality, big game hunts and extravagant banquets offered to him by men such as President Mobutu of Zaire and the self appointed 'Emperor' Bokassa of the Central African Republic, was not appreciated at home. Indeed, the single foreign policy area which damaged Giscard more than any other in the 1981 Presidential elections revolved around the gift of diamonds which he had received from Bokassa. Giscard dealt with the issue badly and it turned into a scandal. Socialists pointed to the Bokassa affair as symptomatic of the more general failings of Giscard's foreign policy; a taint of corruption, amorality and cynicism, combined with a failure of political judgement.(3)

This was the situation which François Mitterrand set out to change. In place of the cynicism of the outgoing President, Mitterrand used his inaugural speech to promise that France would set itself no less an aim than to 'enlighten humanity's progress'. (4) Clearly, French socialism was designed for export. The Quai d'Orsay, formerly home to the Ministry of Foreign Affairs, was now renamed the Ministry for External Relations to underline the close links between the new domestic policy choices and their external implementation. The year from May 1981 was marked by a flurry of foreign policy initiatives, pronouncements, and above all, Presidential visits - all designed to underline the extent of policy change. We will look here at these initial changes in the four main areas of French foreign policy.

East-West Relations
In the approach to the 1981 Presidential elections both Moscow and Washington took comfort from the pundits' confident predictions of another term of office for Giscard d'Estaing. Moscow credited Giscard with the progress made in Franco-Soviet relations since 1974: progress which would be jeopardised by a Mitterrand victory. (5) The US for its part was wary of the radical language of large parts of the PS, and unambiguously hostile to the idea of seeing Communists enter a Western European Government for the first time since 1947. After Mitterrand's election when four Communists finally entered government, albeit in very junior roles, the US Government made its displeasure clear. (6) But events after the election were to prove that Moscow's fears had been better founded than those of Washington. François Mitterrand lost no time in swinging the ship of state in a markedly western direction; a change reflected both in a newfound warmth towards the US, its leader, and its strategic preoccupations, and in a deliberate cooling of relations with the Eastern bloc. One observer with close experience of both Giscard's and Pompidou's foreign policy sees this as the Socialists' single most dramatic change of course in foreign policy. (7)

François Mitterrand went out of his way to establish good personal relations with Ronald Reagan. The two men met on no fewer than six occasions during Mitterrand's first year in office. (8) At one such meeting the French President heaped praise on the US leader, remarking how he '... kept in mind the judicious advice, the care, the openness of spirit which you have shown whenever there was a question of discussing the fate of mankind'. (9) This friendship was not quite as improbable as it might have seemed. Although Mitterrand had led the PS into an alliance with the PCF at home, he had always been extremely wary of the Soviet bloc. He was a longstanding and sometimes isolated French defender of the Western alliance. When De Gaulle withdrew France from the unified military command of NATO in 1966 Mitterrand was among those who opposed the decision most vigorously. (See Chapter Eight).

In 1981 Mitterrand shared Washington's view that NATO was facing a crucial test over how it would respond to the Soviet Union's deployment of SS 20 nuclear missiles in Europe. Indeed, within a few days of his inauguration he used the occasion of a meeting with Helmut Schmidt to give the first public French support for the NATO decision to deploy Cruise and Pershing missiles in Europe if the Soviet SS 20s were not withdrawn. This French gesture was particularly appreciated in Washington. It was in West Germany that the hostility to the proposed new missiles was greatest, and the PS' sister party, the SPD was on the way to being won over to opposition to the NATO deployment. Over the following year and a half Mitterrand went to pains to remind the Germans of his firm belief that the new Soviet nuclear forces had 'upset the military equilibrium in Europe', and of how, in his words, 'I will not accept this and I agree that we must arm to restore the balance'. (10) French pressure reached its climax in January 1983 during the closing weeks of the West German parliamentary election campaign. Invited to address the Bundestag to celebrate the 20th anniversary of the Franco-German treaty of co-operation, Mitterrand used what might have been expected to be an almost entirely ceremonial occasion, to deliver a powerful plea for support for the NATO decision. The speech was interpreted, as indeed it was intended to be, as a clear statement of French preferences as to the outcome of the West German election. 'In the final weeks of the campaign, Chancellor Kohl drew full political capital from Mitterrand's tacit endorsement of his security policy, while SPD leaders spoke bitterly of French abandonment'. (11)

In addition to providing valuable French support for NATO's Intermediate Nuclear Force (INF) decision, Mitterrand also introduced a new coolness into France's dealings with the Soviet Union. Elysée officials reassured visiting American academics of the government's 'clear desire ... to move away from the policy of accommodation with the Soviet Union which characterised Giscard d'Estaing's diplomacy'.

(12) Communist ministers were only admitted to the government after they had signed a statement which amounted to a renunciation of Soviet foreign policy goals. For his part President Mitterrand made it clear that there would be no summit meetings, and relations between Paris and Moscow could not be 'normalised' until the problems caused by the Polish crisis, the presence of Soviet troops in Afghanistan and the Soviet SS 20 missiles were resolved. This new atlanticist orientation of French foreign policy was undoubtedly the product of socialist convictions - sixty years of a love-hate relationship between the two major parties of the Left had taken their toll - but it was also motivated by a sense of political tactics. Paris hoped that a strong atlanticist posture would allay Washington's fears about the 'democratic' credentials of France's socialist-communist coalition. (13)

North-South Relations

A distinctive, and in Washington's eyes, irritating, feature of the new government lay in its insistence that if in Europe the intensity of the superpower conflict forced France to stand with the US and against the Soviet Union, this was not necessarily the case elsewhere. (14) François Mitterrand's early pronouncements made it clear that his analysis and his solutions for the problems of the Third World were very different from those proposed by Washington. His visit to Mexico in October 1981 for the Cancun Summit saw him build on the anti-capitalist rhetoric of his own Socialist Party, and on the non-aligned traditions of Gaullist foreign policy. The new synthesis was designed to present France as being both in solidarity with, and one of the foremost advocates of, the cause of the Third World among the world's developed nations. Mitterrand marked off France's position from that of the US when he emphasised how:

> There is not and there cannot be political stability without social justice ... The East-West conflict cannot explain struggles for emancipation, any more than it can help to resolve them ... To all the combattants of liberty France sends her message of hope. (15)

Intellectually the new approach represented a triumph of ambiguity. At one level France presented itself as being motivated above all by a moral concern to help the Third World and denounced previous governments for subordinating aid policy to the export requirements of French industry. But François Mitterrand suggested that the new policy was also compatible with French self-interest since, as he put it, 'To help the Third World is to help oneself to get out of crisis'. (16) According to this logic, aid to the Third World would boost global consumption and thus help international economic recovery. At the same time, reducing inequality in Third World countries would make them better placed to resist the challenge of communism. As one commentator put it '... Third Worldism of the brain is complemented by a Third Worldism of the heart ...' (17) This kind of ambiguous reasoning, moving all the time between the moral, the pragmatic and the political seemed calculated to maximise support for the new policies while leaving government with a free hand as to the precise manner of their implementation.

The new language of liberation was reflected early on in the decision to develop relations with three Third World countries; Mexico, Algeria and India. Mexico was chosen as the most powerful democracy in Central America and as the best channel through which the Mitterrand government could present its views on the conflicts in the region. The decision to appoint Regis Debray, a former comrade in arms of Che Guevara and far left intellectual, as an Elysée adviser on Latin America was a powerful symbol of French differences with Washington in this area. France's first diplomatic initiative in the region - a joint Franco-Mexican declaration on the war in El Salvador which called for recognition of the guerilla forces fighting that government - irritated Washington and its clients. The French decision to provide Nicaragua, with military and civilian aid worth about $15 million in 1981 only succeeded in further incensing the Americans. (18)

The decision to develop relations with Algeria also marked a desire for change as socialists determined to purge the bitterness and guilt of the colonial era. The French President and External Relations Minister each visited Algiers before the end of 1981. What they brought back from their visits was a contract to purchase natural gas from Algeria at a rate substantially above the market price. Solidarity with the Third World, and a desire for reconciliation with a former colony were thus translated, for the Algerians at least, into hard cash.

Improved relations with India were advocated both for political and commercial reasons. Some progress had been made under the previous government but it was intensified under François Mitterrand. The new friendship brought commercial orders in its wake - for material for 200,000 telephone lines, for 40 Mirage 2000 jets, and for the provision of enriched uranium for the Tarapur nuclear power station - but there was less success on the political level. Supplying nuclear material to a country which refused to sign the nuclear non-proliferation agreement earned France a bad press. Meanwhile, India and France remained at odds in their perceptions of the major regional conflicts, in Afghanistan and in Cambodia. (19)

The new emphasis in France's bilateral relations was held out to be just one indication of a more profound change in French policy towards the Third World. Change was evident, firstly, in the choice of personnel. Claude Cheysson, France's first Minister of External Relations came to the job fresh from Brussels where he had been the EEC Commissioner responsible for negotiating the Lomé trade and aid agreements with African, Caribbean and Pacific countries. Similarly, Jean-Pierre Cot at the Ministry for Co-operation and Development at the rue Monsieur had become known as a committed Third Worldist during his time in opposition as the Socialist Party's foreign affairs spokesman. Both men supported enthusiastically the radical line which President Mitterrand had taken towards the Third World at the Cancun Summit and elsewhere. Cot in particular declared his determination to undertake what he called the 'decolonisation' of France's development policy. There was to be a move away from the old patron-client nature of French development aid. More money was to be channelled through multilateral agencies. The quality of aid projects was to be inspected more critically, with less money for large scale prestige projects and more for 'low tech', basic development work. Most important of all the aid net was to be widened to extend beyond France's former African colonies. The English and Portugese speaking front line states in Southern Africa - Angola, Mozambique and Zimbabwe - were to be singled out for special attention. Even more radical was the plan to diversify French aid efforts out of Africa and to start providing assistance elsewhere - in Asia, the Caribbean and in Latin America. In Paris, the old system whereby aid to former colonies was negotiated through a series of parallel networks controlled by the Elysée was to be ended. Instead, a new reformed Ministry of Co-operation and Development was to take overall charge for producing a rational and co-ordinated development policy, where relations with Francophone Africa would be just one of many areas of French interest. (20)

French aid to Africa was to continue, but on a different footing, with more concern for such issues as the respect for human rights within recipient countries. Jean-Pierre Cot boasted to journalists of how he never travelled to the Third World without first consulting his Amnesty International yearbook. Socialists declared that France was no longer to be the policeman of Africa, called upon to settle border disputes, and offering its military might to help prop up unpopular dictatorships. (21)

The new tone was shown just after the 1981 elections when French socialist leaders were given a rapturous reception at a UN conference on apartheid held in Paris. (22) The change was even more evident in November of the same year at the annual Franco-African Summit. The meeting was due to have been held in Zaire, but since the Socialists had been so vocal in their condemnation of the repressive regime of President Mobutu, it was thought more politic to hold this first Summit of the new, Socialist era, in Paris instead of Kinshasa. President Mitterrand's speech read like a manifesto for reform. He stressed France's new development policy, the harm caused by those who insisted on exporting East-West conflicts to the Third World, the need for increased aid, and France's support for those elements of the Lomé and other trade agreements designed to stabilise commodity prices for Third World exporters. (23)

Many of these promises were realised in the early months of the new government. Leaving aside aid to French overseas territories (which socialists had quite properly criticised previous governments for including in their figures on French aid) total aid was increased sharply from 0.36% of GNP in 1980 to 0.45% in 1981 and 0.49% in 1982, nearly on target to reach the level of 0.7% which Mitterrand had promised to give by 1988. An increased proportion of this aid was paid to multilateral agencies rather than directly to individual countries. The French contribution to the UN development agencies increased by 32% from 1981-2, at the same time as the contribution to the European Development Fund (devoted mainly to Africa) increased by 31%. (24)

The Middle East. Change was also the theme in France's relations with the Middle East. Giscard had been seen as pro-Arab. Mitterrand, by contrast was known as a friend of Israel. He had visited the country frequently, and his contacts in the Socialist International had led him to strike up friendships with several Israeli Labour Party politicians. In opposition he had criticised French involvement in Iraq's nuclear programme. And he had opposed the role played by France in the EEC's Venice Declaration of June 1980, seeing its insistence on the need for recognition of the Palestine Liberation Organisation, by Israel, as one sided. In office Mitterrand withdrew French support from the Venice Declaration, backed up the American sponsored Camp David peace process between Egypt and Israel, and emphasised that France would not recognise the PLO until the PLO, for its part, recognised Israel's right to exist. The Elysée kept a watchful eye on what it saw as the pro-Arab lobby in the Quai D'Orsay, taking a sceptical view of its advice on the Middle East, and examining diplomatic telegrams for sentiments hostile to Israel. (25) The previous government's decision to offer exemption from French anti-discrimination legislation to those firms which protected their Arab commercial interests by observing the trade boycott of Israel, was rescinded. Meanwhile, the new government launched a programme of economic, scientific and cultural co-operation with Israel.

Mitterrand's strong affinity for Israel did not blind him to the needs of the Palestinians. His aim was to aid a solution by restoring French diplomacy to a position of balance between the parties. The policy was reflected in the decision to allow Claude Cheysson to meet with the PLO (in August 1981) even as the French Government withheld its recognition. The same pattern was evident in the Presidential schedule of official visits to the region. The intention was to visit both Saudi Arabia and Israel before the end of 1981. The visit to Saudi Arabia took place (in September 1981) but Israel's bombing in June 1981 of the French built nuclear reactor in Iraq, and the death of a French technician strained relations. Menachem Begin's re-election in the same month also made it clear that Israel would be led by hardline Likud politicians rather than Mitterrand's friends from the Israeli Labour Party. The subsequent bombing of Beirut in July 1981 and annexation of the Golan heights at the end of the year led to the Presidential visit being put back to March of the following year and tempered Mitterrand's pro-Israeli

Foreign Policy: Business as Usual?

sentiments. When he finally did get to Israel he used his speech to the Knesset not only to remind his hosts of his friendly feelings towards their country but also to mention the need for them to recognise the Palestinians' legitimate right to self determination. In France and abroad the visit was hailed as a success. But the Israeli army's invasion of Lebanon in June 1982, signalled that Israel was not ready for compromise and seemed calculated to make President Mitterrand's attempts at balance in the region, difficult to sustain. (26)

Relations with the European Community

Surprisingly perhaps, the new government appeared to give little attention to France's relations with her closest neighbours, in the EEC. Community affairs had only featured in 10th and 11th place the 110 Presidential propositions, coming way behind proposals about Afghanistan (1st place), Latin America (2nd), Poland (3rd), the Middle East (4th), and Chad, Cambodia, Eritrea and Western Sahara (all in 5th place). (27) And during the first year in office the government seemed to have more time for East-West and Third World relations than for those with the European Community.

There were some initiatives. The new government attempted to break free of the Franco-German embrace, which they had criticised for becoming so stifling under Giscard. But the extent to which relations might be developed with alternative partners such as Britain, was severely limited by the Socialists' election commitment precisely to be tougher in their negotiations over the British budget contribution. More important was the Chandernagor Memorandum of October 1981 in which France called for the creation of a 'European social zone'; in essence the proposal that together the EEC should follow the reflationary French Socialist road, making the reduction of unemployment the first priority through the creation of new regional, industrial and social policy initiatives. French Ministers gained a respectful, but unresponsive hearing for their proposals. It appeared that the EEC was not the forum through which the French would succeed in converting either Mrs Thatcher or Chancellor Kohl away from monetarism and towards Keynesianism. (28) The French response was a rather petulant one - the government simply devoted less attention to EEC affairs, turning to other parts of the world where its proposals might gain a warmer reception.

175

Foreign Policy: Business as Usual?

'Realism' re-established: 1982-1986

Cautious socialists, Claude Cheysson among them, had said early on in the government's life that serious change would take time. They made the very reasonable point that everything could not be done at once. The reality though was that in foreign, as in domestic policy, the progress of time saw early moves for change being blocked or reversed rather than compounded, consolidated and extended. For some the process was one of retrenchment, for others realism, and for others still, betrayal. In this section the aim is to look at how this trimming and readjustment of policy took place in three different areas.

East-West Relations - The retreat from Atlanticism

From 1982 there were signs that François Mitterrand's honeymoon with Ronald Reagan might come to an end, and that France might move towards establishing more normal relations with the Soviet Union. It is quite possible to argue that these changes reflected not so much a fundamental alteration in François Mitterrand's political perspective but rather a sense of frustration at the limited success of his early policies. The reason that Paris had expended so much effort to convince Washington that it was a loyal ally, was at least in part because of its knowledge that the realisation of many of its domestic and foreign policy aims would be helped by American support. In 1982 the problem from the French point of view was that the price of proving one's Atlanticism was becoming more costly. Words - of support for Cruise and Pershing, and of criticism of the Soviet Union - were no longer sufficient. Washington demanded action as well, as it called on its allies to join in a series of boycotts and trade sanctions against the USSR.

The rift between the two countries came out into the open at the Versailles Economic Summit of June 1982. In the months before the Summit President Mitterrand had made some pointed remarks about the effects of US economic policies on her allies and his hope was that the French, both as hosts and as ardent Atlanticists, would get a favourable hearing for their proposals for international economic reform. (29) From a French perspective the need for change was urgent. High interest rates in the United States were pushing up the dollar and making French budgetary and trade deficits more costly to sustain. (30) Since imported oil was paid for in dollars the rise in the dollar had an immediate impact on the trade deficit. France had already carried out one devaluation and pressure was again mounting on the franc. But the Americans went to Versailles determined to reprimand rather than to reward the Europeans. The French in particular were chided for their inconsistency in their dealings with the Soviet Union, for their lukewarm reaction to the imposition of martial law in Poland, and the signing shortly thereafter of a substantial contract to buy Siberian natural gas. Washington had wanted the Summit to be a demonstration of allied diplomatic unity against the East, the Europeans by contrast had wanted a move towards economic harmony within the West. The result of these divergent approaches was a patched up end of Summit communiqué which swiftly fell apart as the parties engaged in mutual recriminations. The French had gained no economic support from Washington. Instead, President Reagan imposed an embargo against those European firms involved in supplying material for the Soviet pipeline, and increased pressure on the franc pushed France into her second devaluation. Claude Cheysson spoke for the Elysée when he mentioned the 'increasing divide between the Americans and the Europeans', complaining that, 'We don't speak the same language anymore. The Americans are totally indifferent to our problems ...'. (31)

In time these differences between the United States and her allies were smoothed over. But the crisis had a chastening effect. It made the French realise their limited scope for isolated action, pushed them closer towards their EEC partners and made them feel freer to develop relations with the Soviet Union. Moves to 'normalise' relations with the Eastern bloc started almost immediately after the Versailles Summit, but progress was slow. President Mitterrand announced his intention to visit three Warsaw pact countries later in 1982, but only one such visit actually took place (to Hungary in July). The death of Brezhnev in November seemed to open up the opportunity of improved relations with Moscow but the proposal from Yuri Andropov, the new Soviet leader, that British and French nuclear forces should be taken into account in the Geneva discussion on intermediate nuclear forces dampened these hopes. France was appalled at the idea that her independent forces should be the subject of discussions between the two superpowers from which she was excluded. François Mitterrand refused to concede any ground on this issue while pressing ahead with efforts to improve relations. Potential obstacles to this rapprochement, such as France's expulsion of 47

Foreign Policy: Business as Usual?

Soviet agents in early 1983, and the Soviet shooting down of a South Korean Airlines plane, were minimised by both sides. Two meetings between French and Soviet Foreign Ministers in 1983 were followed in June 1984 by President Mitterrand visiting Moscow, and then by the visit of Mikhail Gorbachev to Paris in October 1985. (32)

President Mitterrand tried to underplay the extent to which the improvement in relations with Moscow represented a policy reversal. On his visit to Moscow he caused a stir by using his meetings with the then Soviet leader, Constantin Tchernenko, and his speech in the Kremlin to mention the issues that still divided France and the Soviet Union. He called for the release of Andrei Sakharov, and a Soviet withdrawal from Afghanistan, while insisting on France's support for a nuclear balance in Europe and her refusal to have her weapons taken into account in the Geneva negotiations. This departure from the diplomatic niceties was hailed as a courageous move by French and foreign newspapers, even if Pravda censored the more embarrassing remarks about human rights from its account of the visit. (33)

This improvement in Franco-Soviet relations continued right up until March 1986. The rapid succession of sickly, geriatric leaders in the Kremlin (Andropov in November 1982, and Tchernenko in February 1983, before the younger and fitter Gorbachev took over in March 1985) allowed Paris to cite evidence of change in Moscow to those who accused her of abandoning the uncompromising stand of 1981. The argument would have seemed more convincing had the new men in the Kremlin shown any willingness to alter their policies in Poland, or Afghanistan. What was true was that by the end of 1983, with NATO's own INF weapons satisfactorily deployed, often against considerable opposition, there was a feeling that allied solidarity had been demonstrated on the key strategic issue and that the way was now open for talks with the Soviet Union about other matters. Even after the 1982 rows with Washington had passed the French were more cautious in their support for the United States. When President Reagan unveiled his Strategic Defence Initiative (SDI) the French felt no obligation to demonstrate Atlantic solidarity. (34) The Soviet Union, meanwhile, welcomed French criticisms of SDI and Mikhail Gorbachev chose Paris for his first visit to Western Europe (in October 1985). In December 1985 President Mitterrand's strange decision to become the first Western head of State to receive General Jarulzelski, four years after he had imposed martial law in Poland, seemed to symbolise the extent to which France's East-West policy had changed since the Presidential elections. By March 1986, France's position in this area appeared distinctly Giscardian, if not Gaullist.

The European Community: A New Priority. The change in France's East-West policy after 1982 was accompanied by a revival in interest in EEC affairs. It was not that EEC countries had become any more enthusiastic about Socialist plans for a workers' Europe, or for a co-ordination of economic policy in a reflationary direction. The change was rather the result of the socialists themselves realising the extent to which their own diplomatic and economic efforts depended on those of their partners in the EEC. By the end of 1983, when France was on the point of assuming the Presidency of the Community for the customary six month period, European affairs had been upgraded to become a prime area of concern in French foreign policy. The man appointed to be the new Minister for European Affairs in December 1983, was Roland Dumas, a close friend of the President. Meanwhile, François Mitterrand set himself the task of breaking the deadlock over the EEC Budget, practising a highly personal and interventionist style of leadership, holding no less than thirty bilateral meetings with his fellow Community leaders between January and June 1984. Even after the French Presidency ended, considerable energy was devoted to European affairs. Roland Dumas was promoted to be Minister for External Relations and French proposals for new areas of European co-operation came thick and fast. At one stage François Mitterrand even suggested holding a referendum 'on a European issue'. That idea was never followed up but the French proposal for technological co-operation - the ESPRIT project - was. Similarly the French-initiated Eureka programme became a European and civilian riposte to the American SDI military research programme.

There were four reasons for this change in French priorities whereby the EEC came to be regarded as a cornerstone of Socialist foreign policy. First, the French began to realise that successful diplomatic initiatives - whether on a new deal in North-South relations, for economic reform, or for a tougher line in East-West negotiations - required co-ordination with other countries, co-ordination which might be achieved through the EEC. Secondly, the domestic weakness of the French economy pushed her towards the EEC. The third devaluation, in March 1983, both brought home the extent of French economic interdependence within Europe and saw the conscious decision to accept that situation, by remaining within the European Monetary System (EMS) rather than choosing a go-it-alone protectionist economic policy. Thirdly, increased economic and trade tensions between the US and Europe generated a dynamic of unity within the Community. All the EEC nations were damaged by high US interest rates, by Washington's action against European steel imports, and by the application of American sanctions against countries selling technology for the Soviet gas pipeline. Finally, France's change of heart about the EEC stemmed from the realisation that the tedious fare of Brussels really _did_ matter. France _was_ concerned by the budgetary crisis, and in 1984 in particular, in the run-up to European elections questions about the budget, EEC reform, the CAP, and the terms for enlargement, needed to be taken extremely seriously. This new preoccupation with EEC affairs was meanwhile accompanied by a strengthening of the Paris-Bonn axis both in the economic and the military fields.

'Realpolitik' in the Third World
1982 also saw a turning point in French relations with the Third World as the high hopes and grand ambitions of the Spring of 1981 were reduced to more modest proportions. (35) François Mitterrand's readiness to attend the 1982 Franco-African Summit in Kinshasa, in spite of Zaire's continued poor human rights record, and his dismissal of Cot in December 1982, both symbolised the new, more pragmatic policy. Some remnants of the socialist's early North-South policies remained. French aid to multilateral agencies continued to increase, and in the EEC French support for the renewal of the Lomé trade and aid agreement with African, Caribbean and Pacific nations proved crucial. But otherwise after 1982 there remained little to show of the work started in 1981.

President Mitterrand felt the need to reassure journalists at the time of Cot's resignation that the conflict had not been one of Presidential pragmatism versus ministerial idealism in the Third World, but few were convinced. In 1981 when Cot was receiving African opposition leaders in his Ministry in Paris, the Elysée, for its part, was trying to improve

Foreign Policy: Business as Usual?

relations with states such as Gabon, Zaire, and the Central African Republic. In South Africa, the French trade mission continued its export drive and attempts to sell a nuclear reactor to Pretoria went ahead at the same time as Ministers in Paris made speeches denouncing apartheid. The Government seemed uncertain whether its trade policy towards the Third World should be determined by the traditional concerns of French industrial interests or by some new, more laudable, and ideally equally rewarding, principles. Meanwhile, political uncertainty produced bureaucratic confusion as the administrative machine was pulled in different and opposing directions. (36)

Christian Nucci's arrival at the Ministry of Co-operation marked a return to a more traditional pattern. He was far readier than Cot to acknowledge Presidential leadership. Under Mitterrand's guidance the rue Monsieur gave increasing attention to pleasing France's friends in Francophone Africa, and ceased to regard human rights violations as posing a serious obstacle to good relations. Disclosures resulting from the <u>Carrefour de Développement</u> scandal which emerged after May 1986, highlighted the use made by Nucci of special ministerial funds devoted less to development than to providing protection for unpopular African rulers, to paying the wages of their civil servants, and to getting Nucci himself re-elected. (37)

This move towards a more traditional policy in dealings with Francophone Africa was accompanied by a greater recognition of the limited means at France's disposal in its dealings with the Third World. French resources were just too small for her aid policy to make a great impact. A generous gesture towards one country - such as the decision to buy Algerian natural gas at 13.5% above the market price - might be hailed as 'the first step' in transforming North-South relations. The reality was that its costs were met from the aid budget, leaving that much less money to be spent on the requirements of other, possibly more needy countries. (38) As economic problems mounted within France, the increase in aid expenditure slowed down. Three successive devaluations of the French currency meant that African countries in the franc zone had to pay substantially increased prices for their imported oil, cancelling out advantages gained from socialist largesse. On the diplomatic front too France was forced to realise that its means did not match its international ambitions. In Central America, pressure from

Washington ensured that the largely symbolic military aid given to Nicaragua early on, was not renewed. France continued to support peace moves in Central America but chose the more modest path of lending its support to those of the regionally based Contadora group rather than trying to intervene directly as it had attempted in 1981. By 1984 President Mitterrand was even ready to receive America's democratic protégé in the region, President Duarte of El Salvador. Generally, French policy moved into a new, more modest, less wide ranging phase. (39)

After 1982 French efforts in the Third World were once again concentrated in her traditional area of influence, Francophone Africa. One of the key promises of the Socialists' 'Africa Project' was that under their leadership France would cease to be the 'policeman of Africa'. This policy of restraint was put to the test in June 1983 when news reached Paris that in the Chad Civil War, the town of Faya Largeau had fallen to the Libyan-backed rebel forces. For two months the French government seemed unsure how to react. Claude Cheysson was against any action, refusing evidence of Libyan involvement, and insisting that the Civil War was simply a conflict between two tribal leaders, a conflict in which France had no place. But others such as Nucci, Charles Hernu and Guy Penne (the Elsyée adviser on African affairs) argued that the fact that the intervention was Libyan-backed was the key issue, and that Chad was facing foreign aggression, which only French troops could effectively repulse. The dilemma was clear. To intervene would compromise France's image of solidarity with the progressive forces in the Third World, and might prove politically costly at home. But for France to stand outside the conflict would also be damaging. The United States urged France to resist the Libyan aggression, and Francophone countries in Africa took the same line, dropping hints that if the French could not be relied on as allies it might be necessary to look towards Washington for the guarantees denied them from Paris.

Finally, in August, after weeks of hesitation, a push south by the Libyan backed rebels forced Paris to launch a military action - Operation Manta - to check their progress. The intervention was a military success, but it left French forces exposed in Chad and effectively sanctioned the partition of the country in two, with a government controlled South and a rebel and Libyan controlled North. The French spent the best part of the next year trying to find a

Foreign Policy: Business as Usual?

way to withdraw, with honour. An agreement that all French and Libyan forces should leave the country by 10 November 1984 seemed to offer the solution. Five days after the 10 November deadline had passed, and as the Americans were producing evidence of a substantial Libyan presence still in Northern Chad, Mitterrand flew to Crete for a private meeting with Ghadaffi to try and resolve the problem. Ghadaffi's communiqué after the meeting declared that a new chapter in Franco-Libyan relations had been opened. But the reality was that Mitterrand's gamble had failed. As the French troops left the Libyans stayed, and the President's personal prestige emerged looking rather battered. (40)

There are four lessons to be drawn from the double failures of French foreign policy in Chad in 1983 and 1984. The first is that, faced with a crisis in an area where French interests were at stake, circumstances pushed the Socialists into reneging on their early promises never to intervene militarily in their former colonies. Secondly, the reluctance to follow this path, the days and months of doubt and hesitation, suggest that the transition was not easy and that reforming ideas still carried some weight even in the Elysée itself. Thirdly, if the ultimate choice was one of realpolitik it placed the need to retain French influence in Africa above any considerations of the goals towards which that influence might be directed. Finally, the Chad crisis revealed the extent to which French foreign policy was not so much guided by grand principles, as made - usually by Presidential initiative - in the midst of crises.

Understanding Socialist Foreign Policy

Domestic policy - and particularly economic policy - changed in response to external constraints. To what extent was that the case with foreign policy? Were the socialists pushed off course in foreign policy because of factors beyond their control? Such an explanation would suggest that France's room for manoeuvre became more limited under the Socialists than had previously been the case. All Fifth Republic Presidents since de Gaulle had pursued a foreign policy characterised by activism, independence, and above all voluntarism - the belief that France could exert an influence in international affairs way beyond that which could be reasonably expected given her resources and military power. The Socialists had enthusiastically embraced this vision, combining the

Foreign Policy: Business as Usual?

traditional belief in voluntarism with a new desire for a principled foreign policy, which would put moral considerations at the forefront of France's dealings with the international community. These were ambitious aims. A desire to defend human rights and national self-determination and to oppose inequality throughout the world meant that France had to try and exert influence in areas where she had none - in Central America, and South East Asia, for example. Elsewhere, where she did have influence, as was the case in Africa, she risked upsetting her friends. Notions of equity - of France as an honest broker - were equally hard to apply. A 'balanced' policy in the Middle East, whether in the Lebanon or the Arab-Israeli conflict, brought few rewards and many problems in its wake. Similarly the new Atlanticist posture brought costs as well as benefits.

To some extent then the Socialists were deterred from their initial aims because of the weight of external constraints. But other factors were even more important. When socialist principles were put to the test they were seen as just that - principles which did not necessarily give very useful guidance as to policy. Socialist thinking about foreign policy when in opposition had been designed more as a basis for criticising Giscard and for rallying the different factions within the Socialist Party than as a programme for government. Once in government socialists came face to face with the fact that policy choices involved sometimes heavy costs, and that not all the government or the party were agreed on how those choices should be made.

In the early stages of the government a deliberate ambiguity in policy making resolved these difficulties nicely. The ambiguity was evident at almost every level of the governmental machine, within the party, the government and at the Elysée itself. Thus, while Jean Pierre Cot took the President's defence of human rights seriously, and accordingly scaled down relations with traditional African allies of France such as Guinea, Gabon and Zaire, the Elysée was busy sending emissaries to these countries to assure them of France's continued friendship. Similarly, while François Mitterrand made overtures to the Israelis he left his Minister for External Relations to cultivate Arab governments and the PLO. It would be too easy to see these apparently contradictory moves purely as examples of clashes between the Elsyée and the Ministers concerned. Some incoherence in policy *was* due to differences of opinion or administrative inefficiency. But conflicts were also encouraged as an act of policy. Even among his own team of advisers at the Elysée Mitterrand encouraged a multiplicity of opinions, and perspectives, using presidential emissaries to accomplish overlapping missions, and instituting a wide variety of different channels of communication. (41) It was not that Mitterrand believed in relinquishing the Elysée's traditional decision making powers in the foreign policy field - if anything his own role was strengthened as he became the sole point of convergence for sources of information and policy debate. It was rather that he himself seemed torn between different policies, unsure of what policy to follow, keen that France should adopt a new, more principled image on the world stage without necessarily having to pay the costs of that stance.

Mitterrand's own indecision increased the impression of reversals and disappointments. And as policy wavered, the presidential predeliction for grand diplomatic initiatives which he was not always either able or even interested in following through, continued unabated. It was as though Mitterrand felt that foreign policy was conducted as much at the level of style as of substance, that rhetoric could itself change or influence a situation even when not followed up by any concrete actions. Thus in his speech to the European Parliament in May 1984, as President of the Council of Ministers, Mitterrand went to pains to show himself as a committed European, pledging support for reform of the EEC's institutions, and hinting at French support for a move towards majority voting in the Council of Ministers. Yet France continued to use its power of veto under the Luxembourg compromise. (42) Events of this kind suggested both an indifference to the gulf between the promises and performance of French foreign policy, and a reticence to undertake proper diplomatic preparation before French initiatives were unveiled. A similar lesson could be drawn from French behaviour at the first three Western Summits of the Mitterrand Presidency, at Ottawa, Versailles and Williamsburg. On each occasion more attention was devoted to the speechwriting than to the prior rallying of support for French proposals. Given the opposed economic approaches of the other nations present, the predictable result was that the French ideas increasingly fell on deaf ears, and the currency of the grand Presidential initiative became devalued.

Indecision, vagueness and lack of preparation, impeded the implementation of a consistent foreign policy. But the Socialists also made some serious miscalculations about the outside world. In particular, they underestimated their dependence on their allies. France's lone attempt at reflation relied either on a general upturn in the Western economies or on solidarity from her allies. The first failed to materialise, leaving the choice of allied support or the retreat into economic isolationism. Hopes that it would be possible to cash in on French Atlanticism and ask for US economic solidarity with France in return for France's strategic solidarity over the Euromissile issue, were dashed. Similarly the EEC countries made known their displeasure at the economic path chosen by the French at the same time as their support for the franc became more important than ever. In Africa too, France had underestimated the cost of her alliances. Pledges not to act as the policeman of Africa paid off on the international aid conference circuit where France was feted as the best friend of the Third World in the developed world. But where France had some influence, in Francophone Africa, a hands-off policy threatened to undermine that influence, pushing France's old allies into the arms of the Americans, and increasing the extent to which the East-West divide permeated the Third World.

Faced with these difficult choices Mitterrand opted for a path of 'realism', doing his best to maintain traditional French influence and continuing to pay lip service to the heady ideals of 1981. The change in emphasis was very much Mitterrand's own choice rather than the product of ministerial consultations. But he hesitated before opting for it, and at key moments of crisis, such as the Chad Civil War, he hesitated again about the manner of its implementation. In the end though, François Mitterrand moved to a position where he saw his task as being primarily to use foreign policy, not just for 'enlightening humanity's progress' but also for defending French self interest and influence in the world. Securing France's position abroad became ever more important as difficulties at home increased.

Notes

1. A. Duhamel, La République de Monsieur Mitterrand, (Grasset, Paris, 1982), p.201, S. Hoffmann, 'Gaullism by any other Name', also stresses continuity, Foreign Policy, no. 57, (Winter, 1984-1985), pp.38-57.

2. By 1981 the critique was far less specifically 'socialist' than previously. The radical third worldism, anti-americanism and anticapitalism of groups such as CERES was still present in the party - and was evident in the Projet Socialiste of 1980 - but it played very much a secondary role to the new emphasis on Atlanticism, East-West balance and western solidarity proposed by Mitterrand. The new, Mitterrandist synthesis is quite well described by J. Huntzinger, 'La politique extérieure du parti socialiste', Politique étrangère, vol. 47, no. 1, (1982), pp.33-44.

3. For a comprehensive review of Giscard's foreign policy see S. Cohen and M-C Smouts (eds.), La politique extérieure de Valéry Giscard d'Estaing, (Presses de la Fondation Nationale des Sciences Politiques, Paris, 1985). A shorter review is contained in A. Grosser, Affaires Extérieures: La politique de la France 1944/1984, (Flammarion, Paris, 1984), chapter 9.

4. Speech of 21 May 1981 contained in F. Mitterrand, Réflexions sur la politique extérieure de la France: Introduction à vingt-cinq discours (1981-1985), (Fayard, Paris, 1986), p.141.

5. For further details of Soviet attitudes towards, and support for, Giscard, see M.J. Sodaro, 'Moscow and Mitterrand', Problems of Communism, (July-August 1982), pp.23-5.

6. Grosser, Affaires Extérieures, p.289.

7. G. Robin, La Diplomatie de François Mitterrand, (Editions de la Bièvre, Les Loges-en-Josas, 1985), p.27.

8. Ibid., p.32.

9. Ibid., p.89.

10. S.F. Wells Jnr., 'The Mitterrand Challenge' Foreign Policy, no. 44 (1981), p.59.

11. R.S. Rudney, 'Mitterrand's New Atlanticism: Evolving French Attitudes towards NATO', Orbis, vol. 28, no. 1, (1984), p.83.

12. Wells, 'The Mitterrand Challenge', p.60.

13. Grosser, Affaires Extérieures, p.289.

14. The policy was spelt out most coherently by Jean-Pierre Cot in his article, 'Winning East-West in North-South', Foreign Policy, no. 46, (1982), pp.3-18.

15. Speech of 20 October 1981 quoted by M-C. Smouts, 'La France et le Tiers-Monde ou comment gagner le sud sans perdre le nord', Politique étrangère, vol. 50, no. 2, (1985), p.339.

16. Ibid., p.340.

17. D. Moisi, 'Mitterrand's Foreign Policy:

The Limits of Continuity', Foreign Affairs, Vol. 60, no. 2 (1981-1982), p.351.
   18. Smouts, 'La France et le Tiers-Monde', pp.350-351.
   19. Robin, La Diplomatie de Mitterrand, pp.62-3.
   20. See Smouts 'La France et le Tiers-Monde', passim.
   21. J.-F. Bayart, La politique africaine de François Mitterrand, (Editions Karthala, Paris, 1984), part 1, passim.
   22. Ibid., pp.24-5.
   23. Speech of 5 November 1981. Text in F. Mitterrand, Sur la Politique Extérieure, pp.366-79.
   24. Smouts, 'La France et le Tiers-Monde', p.347. However, the figure for 1985 of 0.55% of GNP suggested that by then the 0.7% target had been abandoned. See ADA, Bilan de la France 1986, (La Table Ronde, Paris, 1986), p.444.
   25. S. Cohen, La Monarchie nucléaire, (Hachette, Paris, 1986), p.215.
   26. Useful summaries of policy towards the Middle East may be found in T. Carothers, 'Mitterrand and the Middle East, The World Today, vol. 38, no. 10, (October 1982), pp.381-6, J. Marcus, 'French Policy and the Middle East Conflicts: Change and Continuity', The World Today, vol. 42, no. 2, (February 1986), pp.27-30, and Cohen, Monarchie nucléaire, pp.153-6. Mitterrand's speech to the Knesset may be found in F. Mitterrand, Réflexions, pp.335-46.
   27. For the background to socialist thinking on the EEC see, Y. Poirmeur and C. Pannetier, 'Les socialistes français, la crise et l'Europe', Le Monde Diplomatique (avril 1984), pp.2-3, and M. Newman, Socialism & European Unity (C. Hurst and Co., London 1983), chapter 3 passim.
   28. Robin, Diplomatie, pp.69-81. M-C. Smouts, 'The External Policy of François Mitterrand, International Affairs, vol. 59, no. 2, (1983), pp.162-4, F de la Serre, 'La politique européenne de la France: new look or new deal?', Politique étrangère, vol. 47, no. 1, (1982), pp.125-137, P. Moreau Defargues, '"J'ai fait un rêve...". Le Président François Mitterrand, artisan de l'union européenne', Politique Etrangère, Vol. 50, no. 2, (1985), pp.359-62.
   29. Robin, Diplomatie, pp.89-95.
   30. The French feeling that strategic solidarity was not being reciprocated in the economic sphere was voiced by F. Mitterrand in a speech in

Hamburg on 14 May 1982. The President complained that 'It is difficult to insist on a vigorous military alliance ... while with our dear ally, very dear ally, the feeling seems to prevail that, in the field of trade, peace does not exist.' Quoted by Smouts, 'External Policy', pp.161-2.

31. Quoted by Robin, Diplomatie, p.93.

32. Discussion preparatory to these state visits was initiated by the Soviet Union in February 1983. Robin, ibid., p.198-9.

33. L'Année Politique, 1984, (Editions du Moniteur, Paris, 1985), pp.228-9. The French President's speech is reproduced in full in Mitterrand, Réflexions, pp.167-170.

34. Other western powers, such as Britain, also revealed initial disquiet about SDI, but the French concerns were more actively voiced. Mitterrand's speech to the UN General Assembly in September 1983 called on both superpowers to hold back from the militarisation of space. Later, on the eve of the Presidential visit to Moscow, the French Government called into question the wisdom of any country even attempting to make itself invulnerable to nuclear attack, as SDI was supposed to achieve. For a full discussion of the shifts in French attitudes towards SDI see J. Fenske, 'France and the Strategic Defence Initiative: Speeding Up or putting on the brakes?', International Affairs, vol. 62, no. 2, (1986), pp.231-47.

35. See Bayart, Politique Africaine, parts II & III, D. Parkin, 'Plus ça change? France and Africa in the Fifth Republic', Politics, vol. 4, no. 2, (October 1984), pp.32-7, T. Chafer, 'Mitterrand and Africa, 1981-1984. Policy and Practice', Modern and Contemporary France, no. 23, (October 1985), pp.3-12, K. Whiteman, 'President Mitterrand and Africa', African Affairs, vol. 82, no. 328 (July 1983), pp.329-43.

36. M-C. Smouts, 'La France et l'industrialisation du Tiers Monde: une vision kaleidoscopique', Revue française de science politique, vol. 33, no. 5, (octobre 1983), pp.797-816.

37. Soon after Cot's departure Mitterrand restated his belief in Presidential supremacy in foreign policy as follows: 'It is I who determine the foreign policy of France, not my Ministers (...) Ministers are not forbidden to think or have views (...) It is inconceivable that a policy could be implemented without my agreement, more precisely without my impetus'. Le Monde, 20.1.1983, cited by Cohen, Monarchie nucléaire, p.37. For a useful

summary of the scandal see L'Express, 19.12.1986, pp.37-41.
  38. Smouts, 'La France et le Tiers-Monde', pp.342-4, 353-4.
  39. cf. Cheysson's comments on Radio France Internationale in September 1984 cited in ibid, p.353.
  40. This account rests largely on Cohen, Monarchie nucléaire, pp.47-8, 138-42, 146-53, and Elce & Hesse, La France et la crise du Tchad d'août 1983: un rendez-vous manqué avec l'Afrique', Politique étrangère, vol. 50, no. 2, (1985), pp.411-18.
  41. According to Cohen, Monarchie nucléaire, p.41, Mitterrand made greater use of personal emissaries and parallel diplomacy than any of his Fifth Republic predecessors.
  42. Debates of the European Parliament, 24.5.1984.

Suggestions for Further Reading
Good surveys of foreign policy produced early on in the Mitterrand Presidency include, P.G. Cerny, 'Mitterrand's Foreign Policy: Continuity and Vulnerability', Politics, vol. 3, no. 2, (October 1983), pp.3-8, M-C. Smouts, 'The External policy of François Mitterrand', International Affairs, vol. 59, no. 2 (Spring 1983), pp.155-67, and N. Waites, 'France under Mitterrand: external relations', The World Today, vol. 39, no. 6 (June 1983), pp.224-31. Stanley Hoffmann's article, 'Gaullism by any other Name', Foreign Policy, no. 57, (Winter 1984-1985), pp.38-57, provides a trenchant analysis of the first four years of foreign policy. A.W. DePorte, writing in the rival US publication, Foreign Affairs gives a rather less convincing but nevertheless useful account, 'France's New Realism', Foreign Affairs, vol. 63, no. 1, (Fall 1984), pp.144-65. Alfred Grosser's book, Affaires Extérieures: La politique de la France 1944/1984, (Flammarion, Paris, 1984) has the advantage of placing Mitterrand's foreign policy in the context of French foreign policy since the Second World War. The book stops in 1983-4 but little changed thereafter to invalidate its conclusions. 'Presidentialisation' and the role of high politics generally are dealt with in a revealing and compelling, but essentially anecdotal work by Samy Cohen, La monarchie nucléaire: Les coulisses de la politique étrangère sous la Ve République, (Hachette, Paris, 1986). An interpretation which

lays more emphasis on party as opposed to presidential initiative is Wayne Northcutt, 'The Domestic Origins of Mitterrand's Foreign Policy, 1981-1985', Contemporary French Civilization, vol. 10, no. 2, (Spring/Summer 1986), pp.233-67. The President's own account produced in the run-up to the March 1986 elections, F. Mitterrand, Réflexions sur la politique extérieure de la France: Introduction à vingt-cinq discours (1981-1985), (Fayard, Paris, 1986), could usefully be set against the highly critical and strictly chronological narrative offered by a former diplomatic advisor to Pompidou, and, briefly to Giscard too, G. Robin, La Diplomatie de Mitterrand ou le triomphe des apparences, 1981-1985, (Editions de la Bièvre, Les-Loges-en-Josas, 1985). A more balanced and varied collection of interpretations is contained in the invaluable special edition of Politique Etrangère, 1981-1985: Un premier bilan de la politique étrangère de la France, Politique Etrangère, vol. 50, no. 2, (1985). F. Joyaux, the director of the journal Politique internationale has joined forces with P. Wajman, to produce an edited collection of essays which look at past, present and future French foreign policy from a generally right of centre perspective, Pour une nouvelle politique étrangère, (Hachette, Paris, 1986). William Wallace, 'Independence and Economic Interest: The Ambiguities of Foreign Policy', in French Politics and Public Policy, (eds.) P.G. Cerny & M.A. Schain, (Methuen, London, 1981), pp.267-90 deals with an earlier period but nevertheless provides an interesting discussion of the conflicting aims of French foreign policy. Similarly, J-F Bayart, La politique africaine de François Mitterrand, (Editions Karthala, Paris, 1984), is of far more general use than its title alone might suggest.

Chapter Eight

DEFENCE POLICY UNDER SOCIALIST MANAGEMENT

Neville Waites

French Defence Culture

Military questions always present socialist parties with great difficulties and require sensitive handling if an effective defence policy is to be achieved. This is not because socialist parties always have a predilection towards non-violence and anti-militarism. That would be incompatible with a philosophy hinged on class conflict. Although socialist philosophy is aimed at the goals of human progress and world peace, it normally takes account of the need to overcome obstacles and opponents if necessary by force. The problem is to relate ends to means, international ideals to policies and action at the local or national level. Will a national achievement promote or prevent international socialism? The answer is elusive because nationalism, aptly called 'the modern Janus', is both healthy and morbid in its effects on socialism; its substance is 'always morally, politically, humanly ambiguous'. (1) Nationalism has provided as much political inspiration to the left as to the right in recent French history. Questions of national security and the nature and composition of the armed forces have therefore been frequently at the centre of passionate public debate, notably during the 1789 Revolution, the Dreyfus Affair and the Second World War. The disastrous defeat in 1940 brought the bitter experience of total dependence for the first time in French history. Rejection of the collaborating Vichy regime inspired a renewed republican ethos through a Resistance movement developed mainly by the Left with patriotic fervour that gave new life to the nation-in-arms tradition of citizen-soldiers abjuring authoritarianism at home and adventurism abroad, dedicated above all to defend the soil of France from an invader like their revolutionary ancestors in the triumphant levée en masse of 1793.

Warfare had become much more scientific by the time of the Second World War. A French atomic research team passed on their know-how to the Allies and thus contributed in a small way to building an atomic bomb by 1945. But their principal scientist, Frédéric Joliot-Curie had served in a Communist Resistance group, and the Americans therefore refused to share atomic research with the French. This man of the Left could only pursue his work through an independent national commitment, and in the 1950s socialist leaders continued this tradition when participating in multi-party governments that decided to develop atomic weapons.

Another important development under the Fourth Republic was that a strong sense of French cultural and political mission in the world involved socialist leaders among others in fighting long colonial wars that broke with republican tradition by sending professional troops to Indo-China and later keeping conscripts for long periods in Algeria. And this was undertaken while security at home in Western Europe depended on American and, from 1955, West German forces. Some socialists were among those favouring French integration into a European Defence Community, but that project was rejected by a majority in the National Assembly in 1954. It was this apparent willingness to allow French security to depend on foreigners, and of course failure to win costly colonial campaigns, that enabled de Gaulle to gather support for his rejection of the Fourth Republic in 1958.

The socialists soon went into opposition in the Fifth Republic, objecting to de Gaulle's extension of presidential powers, his right-wing economic policy and his self-congratulatory chauvinism when talking about a force de frappe of nuclear weapons that were not even operational until the late 1960s. Fearing what they saw as foolhardy militarism, some socialists poured scorn on de Gaulle's 'bombinette' and the party adopted a non-nuclear defence policy. Fearing also that de Gaulle's independent policies towards the European Community and the Atlantic Alliance would make France dangerously isolated, some socialists voted against leaving NATO in 1966 and the party's foreign policy emphasised a need to have close relations with neighbours and allies. Of course the emphasis on internationalism and disarmament was useful for political differentiation intended to increase electoral support for the party against the Gaullists. It is worth noting that de

Gaulle's vetoes in Brussels and his exit from NATO were followed by a decline in his electoral support. In 1971 the newly organised <u>Parti Socialiste</u> (PS) adopted a non-nuclear foreign and defence policy sharply opposed to official policy upheld by the Gaullists under Pompidou's government.

Thus the particular French historical experience of insecurity, wars and enemy occupation had created a defence culture within which the Left had at different times adopted a wide variety of positions along the continuum linking nationalism and internationalism in socialist philosophy. This experience inevitably gave rise to a number of different currents of opinion on foreign affairs and defence which would have to be taken into account by the new PS as it faced the problems of the 1970s. Categorisation of factions within socialist parties normally follows a continuum from revolution to reform, from left to right, on domestic political and economic issues. But positions on foreign and defence issues often create cross-currents. This is particularly true of the French PS because of the importance of defence culture in France which has created a distinctive internationalist-nationalist continuum on which the far left CERES faction was close to the classical Gaullists.

By the 1970s the PS contained five tendencies on defence policy, apart from the individual mavericks. (2) The far left CERES, in the first place, led by Chevènement and Motchane, sought security for France by means of a national sanctuary defended from external threats by a <u>force de dissuasion</u> of strategic nuclear weapons capable of a massive retaliatory strike against any aggressor; defence against internal subversion would be provided by small local militias making up a <u>force de mobilisation populaire</u> (FMP) rather than by classical army formations. Secondly, the 'Jacobin' tendency, led by Hernu who had always taken a special interest in defence, also sought security for the national sanctuary by means of a strategic nuclear <u>force de dissuasion</u>, but their less radical economic policy made them less worried about subversion than CERES and consequently more adaptable to classical army, navy and air forces. Thirdly, the 'European' tendency, led by Maurory, supported the nuclear <u>force de dissuasion</u> to keep the peace; but if war did break out France and her European allies would need an effective conventional and nuclear strategy, without depending on the United States, to ensure defence without suicide. According to this analysis, France alone could not provide economically and militarily for an adequate defence system and would find European neighbours more reliable allies than the United States. Fourthly, the 'Western' tendency, led by Pontillon and Huntzinger but also including the party leader, Mitterrand, believed that French security depended on a balance of power between East and West, and that so long as divisions into blocs persisted France and Europe would need support from the United States, whether in the form of strategic nuclear deterrence or tactical nuclear counterforce weapons or large conventional military formations, depending on the nature of any threat of aggression that might arise. Supporters of this tendency had either voted against leaving the NATO integrated military organisation in 1966 as in the case of Mitterrand, or believed that the Western alliance was vulnerable without a French commitment to co-operate closely with NATO forces against any attack. This tendency was uncertain about the value of French nuclear forces to the alliance, but doubted whether on their own they could provide an adequate deterrent. Fifthly, there was a complex non-nuclear tendency ranging from those who opposed the French nuclear force on political, economic or military grounds to those who opposed all nuclear weapons on ethical or religious grounds. This tendency was too diverse to have a leader, but its spokesmen were usually ex-members of the Parti Socialiste unifié (PSU) or Catholic activists like Viveret. It is interesting that Rocard, although having affinities with some members of this tendency, did not take a firm position on foreign and defence policies and would be hard to place there or in any other tendency.

Early in the 1970s the PS had a non-nuclear defence policy seeking closer co-operation with allied conventional forces. Thus the third, fourth and fifth tendencies discussed above were deriving the greatest satisfaction, and CERES was quiet because it backed an alliance with the Communist party which had a non-nuclear defence policy. The 'Jacobin' tendency was in the most difficult position because it was not prepared to follow the Communist party line and was unhappy with the majority PS policy, yet its leader, Hernu, was the chief spokesman of the Socialist Party on defence in the National Assembly. Hernu coped skilfully and energetically with this problem in public debates by letting the Communists take the lead in opposing strategic nuclear weapons while he satisfied the PS by opposing tactical nuclear weapons which he believed were a liability in encouraging deviation from the doctrine of massive retaliation. (3) At the same time in private PS discussions Hernu used his chairmanship of the PS Commission de Défense, created early in 1973 to formulate a defence policy acceptable to the various tendencies in the party while taking account of military opinion, both professional and conscript, to cultivate support for retention of the nuclear force. How Hernu's 'Jacobin' position on defence was converted from that of a beleaguered minority to one winning majority support within five years is a famous and well-documented story. (4) But less attention has been given to the changing circumstances of the 1970s that made Hernu's success possible. These are of interest first because they show how PS policy is determined, and secondly because different circumstances in the future might bring a reshuffle of PS tendencies and a revised defence policy.

Above all, it is important to appreciate the changes in policy which occurred <u>prior</u> to the assumption of power, for these foreshadowed much of the strategy adopted by the socialist government. Indeed in the realm of defence policy, the evolution which took place before 1981 was in many respects more significant than that which was subsequently to occur.

Opposing Giscard with Nuclear Defence
Assessing the determinants of Socialist Party defence policies, Hugues Portelli takes account of permanent features derived from geography, history and defence culture. But he also draws a valuable distinction between periods of opposition, when the influences of party activists, ideological spokesmen and pressure groups from churches and trade unions are usually predominant, and contrasting periods of power, when inherited decisions and situations encourage continuity, and the influences of military leaders and industrialists at home and of allies abroad are often predominant. (5) But a framework of analysis should not only include all these variables but also facilitate perception of prime influences, whether party political or societal, national or international, at various times. A refined framework of analysis is needed, for example, to explain why the French PS defence policy changed more while in opposition than when assuming power. A close examination of the circumstances in which the

Communist Party and the Socialist Party adopted nuclear defence policies in 1977-8 reveals a significant linkage between that change and changes in French domestic politics.

From 1979 to 1983, spanning the Left's accession to power in France, international developments increasing East-West tension to bring a new Cold War served to reinforce acceptance of a nuclear defence policy. From 1983 to 1986 stabilisation and renewed dialogue in East-West relations created conditions that allowed domestic politics once again to become a prime influence on French defence policy. And this feature of policy under the Left also characterised that of the Right when it returned to power after the 1986 elections. Closer consideration of these three distinct periods will show the changes to and from domestic and international determinants of policy.

In the first period, from 1974 to 1978, when the two largest parties of the Left underwent a profound transformation from non-nuclear to nuclear defence policies, their motivations were mainly derived from domestic politics. It is true that international developments during those years created problems for the Left. Its argument that the French bomb had a destabilising, negative impact on the Western Alliance was confounded in 1974 at the Ottawa summit when the Americans declared for the first time that it was a positive asset to the Alliance. Then in 1976 the PS trust in Alliance cohesion rather than national independence was severely shaken by the Kissinger doctrine of outright opposition to Communist participation in allied governments. Although this was aimed primarily at the Italians it also threatened the French PS strategy based on a common programme of the left, including the Communists. But PS policy did not change after these developments abroad; it was more responsive to specifically French influences.

The official defence doctrine of Gaullist France was set out most authoritatively in the defence White Paper of 1972. It was based on Genearl Poirier's theory of three circles, the first being France, a sanctuary defended by strategic nuclear weapons, the second being Europe defended by conventional forces including those of France, and the third being the world interests of France, especially in Africa, defended by small but highly mobile French conventional forces. But in practice this doctrine became incoherent and controversial. Firstly, the important emphasis on strategic nuclear weapons to sanctuarise France was diluted, arguably even destroyed, by the development of tactical nuclear weapons, notably <u>Pluton</u> which was deployed in 1974. A battlefield missle fired from modified tanks over a range limited to 120 kilometres, and positioned with French army units in West Germany, it fudged the distinction between the first two circles of French security and implied a shift from the doctrine of massive retaliation to the NATO doctrine of graduated response. But rather than a change of doctrine perhaps it resulted from the government's need to ensure army support as shown by its experience in the Algerian war and the events of May 1968. <u>Pluton</u> gave the army its nuclear weapon equivalent to those already possessed by the navy and air force and it gave satisfaction to the military-industrial lobbies. Opposition parties also needed to consider army support and so at this time Hernu, who enjoyed attending military manoeuvres and convivial gatherings of the military 'freemasonry', created a network of discussion groups to improve mutual understanding between PS politicians and members of the armed forces.

The second cause of military controversy was politically more important than <u>Pluton</u>. It was the Debré-Fontanet law of 1973 which upset many people by virtually abolishing deferment (<u>le sursis</u>) from the system of military conscription. Ironically, Debré was a stout defender of military service and his aim was to strengthen the nation-in-arms after the apparent decline in civic sense of duty as perceived in the events of May 1968. But his law of 1973 was felt to be oppressively rigid. Alienated public opinion turned its favour towards a voluntary system for the armed forces, a professional army, and also towards emphasis on the nuclear <u>force de dissuasion</u> which might provide France with sufficient security to enable her to dispense with large conventional forces and, by the same token, to dispense with conscription. That was why, at a time of international détente in the mid-1970s, French public support for nuclear weapons was increasing and encouraging people like Hernu to work for a change in the PS anti-nuclear policy. He was following rather than leading public opinion. (6) But the PS was reluctant to change its policy and, although its firm stance on the 'nation-in-arms' principle was popular, it was out of step with increasing public support for nuclear deterrence.

The PS after 1974 had considerable difficulty in achieving effective electoral differentiation from the right as led by Giscard d'Estaing with his programme for an advanced liberal society at home and closer co-operation with EEC partners and NATO allies abroad. But the PS was given both a lesson in political manoeuvre and an opportunity to apply it when the Right split in 1976. After resigning as prime minister, Chirac reorganised the Gaullists and the RPR harried Giscard on all fronts. On defence policy Chirac proclaimed the virtues of national independence based on strategic nuclear deterrence and condemned official government statements about enlarging the French sanctuary beyond the eastern frontier and spending relatively more on conventional weapons in order to co-operate effectively with allies, in spite of his previous support for such trends while serving both Pompidou and Giscard. Chirac had been an advocate of deploying <u>Pluton</u> in West Germany. From 1976 Chirac portrayed Giscard as a danger to national security because of his reduced emphasis on strategic deterrence. Chirac's change of policy suited the trend of public opinion and helped towards success for the RPR in the 1977 municipal elections, especially Chirac's election as mayor of Paris. And the following year RPR pressure drove Giscard to modify defence programmes to build a sixth strategic missile-carrying nuclear submarine, thus shifting his policy's emphasis away from conventional equipment back towards strategic nuclear weapons. But there were severe limits to Chirac's freedom to attack Giscard without damaging the Right as a whole and risking disadvantageous dissolution of the National Assembly.

The Left was much better placed for outright attack on Giscard provided it could play the national card against his liberal internationalism. The centralised PCF perceived Chirac's success and was able to move swiftly from an anti-nuclear defence policy to adopt the Kanapa Report in May 1977 which laid down a doctrine of multi-directional deterrence, providing national security independent of both superpowers. Its credibility was weakened, however, by conditions that it should not involve first use, nor anti-city strikes, nor presidential decision on firing. Nevertheless, this new PCF policy was one of the issues leading to friction and breakdown in the Left's Common Programme during that summer. The PS found it harder than Chirac and the PCF to change policy to take advantage of the public's preference for nuclear defence. Hernu had been pressed by the PS leadership to restrain his pro-nuclear polemics to avoid splitting the party;

199

and the CERES faction lost support at the Pau conference in 1975. But CERES played a key role in ensuring Mitterrand's continued party leadership, and was encouraged by public opinion and the PCF policy change to give more energetic support to Hernu. Mitterrand himself tried to paper over cracks within the Left and within the PS by proposing to have a referendum of the French people to decide whether to keep nuclear weapons. But coming in July 1977 when public opinion favoured nuclear defence, this proposal was a means of pressurising PS factions to move towards Hernu's policy. Now that the Americans regarded the French bomb as an asset to NATO the PS Western tendency on defence policy was sensitive to such pressure. And the inconsistencies of Carter's policy encouraged the PS European tendency to consider alternatives to the American deterrent. It is not surprising, therefore, that the PS central Bureau had a pro-nuclear majority by December 1977. The problem was to convert the party militants and supporters.

A special Convention on Defence in January 1978, called to agree on a new policy that would convince the military, unite the party and attract the electorate in the forthcoming legislative elections, resulted in a careful balance between international and patriotic principles derived from French socialist traditions. Emphases on the struggle for peace and disarmament were therefore balanced by the determination to organise an effective patriotic defence. And an emphasis on loyal co-operation with European and transatlantic allies was balanced by an insistence on the autonomy of French decisions on defence. As regards specific forces, commitment to the principle of abandoning army and air force nuclear weapons, and naval ones by means of a multilateral disarmament agreement, was balanced by commitment to the principle of independence from both superpowers by ensuring a French capacity for intervention that would make them take her will into account. The key point of change in PS policy was that naval nuclear weapons would be retained and modernised to ensure credibility unless other nuclear powers agreed to substantial disarmament. Despite the stress on a preference for disarmament the new doctrine was ambiguous, but an anti-nuclear amendment geared to a clearly alternative defence policy only got 30 per cent against 70 per cent support for the main motion, and even a fall-back position established by Viveret to prevent modernisation of residual naval nuclear weapons only won 26 per cent support. Hernu and CERES had won a majority, but there was a large opposition and 18 per cent of abstainers, which prevented the PS from playing the national or nuclear cards with any confidence in its unsuccessful 1978 election campaign. (7)

By the following year French defence policy had entered a new period. From 1979 to 1983 domestic political priorities and party manoeuvres were overtaken by major international problems that generated renewed tensions and rearmament to such a level that historians discussed comparisons with the years leading up to 1914, while political scientists and defence experts speculated about an imminent Third World War. (8) This was a period when a new oil crisis, revolution in Iran and Arab-Israeli conflict showed the high stakes at risk in the Middle East, when the United States intervened militarily in El Salvador, Grenada and Nicaragua, and when the Soviet Union intervened militarily in Afghanistan while also threatening to do so in Poland to bring her to heel. But above all it was the period of Euro-missile crisis. Soviet-American balance in strategic weapons seemed to many people to have been upset by a Soviet advantage in intermediate-range nuclear forces (INF) notably by deployment of highly accurate and mobile SS20 ground-to-ground missiles capable of 'clinical' strikes on West European missile bases and command centres. Some European leaders, notably Helmut Schmidt, the socialist Chancellor of West Germany, feared that a Soviet surprise first strike in Europe might confront the Americans with the choice between accepting Soviet control there or suicide. American strategic weapons might thereby be decoupled from Western Europe. Many French people similarly believed that Soviet 'clinical' strikes in France might decouple or undermine the submarine-based <u>force de dissuasion</u>. NATO leaders agreed in 1979 on a two-track policy of disarmament and rearmament: to persuade the USSR to withdraw SS20s but otherwise to counter them by installing US Cruise and Pershing II INF missiles in Western Europe by 1983. A protest movement emerged in Europe, notably in West Germany where the Greens and parts of the SPD sought to avoid a nuclear arms race and possible war by advocating renewed efforts for détente and a non-nuclear defence policy. In France President Giscard d'Estaing issued disarmament proposals in 1978, maintained a dialogue with the Soviet Union that included meeting Brezhnev in Warsaw in May 1980 and remained non-commital about the need for Cruise and Pershing missiles. Like

Schmidt in West Germany, Mitterrand in France led his Socialist Party to support NATO policy on INF missiles, believing that an East-West balance of power was essential to the integrity of the Western Alliance and to the security of his country. It was for this reason that the Euro-missile crisis reinforced the PS commitment to a nuclear defence policy and enabled Mitterrand to play the national card successfully against Giscard in the run-up to the 1981 presidential elections, projecting himself as a more effective defender of national and alliance security.

The international crisis also had the important effect of shifting the leadership in PS defence policy from the Jacobin to the Western tendency. Hernu published his view in 1980 that France need not concern herself with the Euro-missile crisis because her submarine-based <u>force de dissuasion</u> remained invulnerable to new INF weapons such as the SS20s. He even suggested that the Americans might have ulterior motives in the crisis, because their nuclear submarines were also invulnerable, and that they were really intent on tightening their grip on NATO allies in Europe. (9) The CERES leader Chevènement was also sceptical about the crisis, believing that the Soviet threat had been conjured up by Western military-industrial lobbies to achieve increased investment and production of armaments. Until this time Mitterrand had concentrated on merely holding the PS together on defence issues, leaving polemics to faction leaders, but the Euro-missile crisis led him to assert his leadership by insisting on international issues of prime importance to France. He argued that whatever ulterior motives some people had for exploiting the crisis, the Soviet threat posed by SS20s and the invasion of Afghanistan was intolerable for France as well as her allies. Blinkered concentration on a defence policy that sanctuarised France might tempt her to slide into neutralism. Her peace and security needed a balance of power in Europe, preferably with neither SS20s nor Pershings but if necessary with both, because France and her allies had to stand up to the Soviet Union to win respect and co-operation. This analysis was characteristic of the PS Western tendency. If there was criticism of the 1948 Brussels treaty and of the 1949 Western Alliance it was not in a spirit of negative rejection but rather one of seeking new moves to make them more effective. (10) Mitterrand took this firm stand on defence policy by July 1980 as a result of the international crisis, before becoming a candidate in the 1981 presidential elections. His strong support for the Western Alliance constrained Hernu subsequently to withdraw many remaining copies of his book from circulation. And the 1980 PS programme in <u>Projet Socialiste</u>, with its CERES-inspired emphasis on national defence, détente with Communist states and special relations with the non-aligned Third World, was laid aside in preference for Mitterrand's own 110 Propositions when it came to the election programme, which emphasised disarmament hopes but also defence through collective security. (11) Nuclear issues required caution to avoid offending some PS sensibilities, so development of new tactical weapons such as the neutron bomb was rejected. But Mitterrand made full use of the national and Western security cards in order to portray Giscard's initiatives to preserve détente as risking weakness and isolation, and this won many crucial votes from the right in the elections. Although domestic issues were paramount as usual, a 'secure' defence policy made the PS much more widely tolerable or even attractive. (12) Mitterrand's defence policy added a special significance to <u>la force tranquille</u>, the campaign slogan that carried him to the Elysée in 1981.

Power and Constraints

The recent evolution of the PS and the character of Mitterrand's leadership were sufficient to make continuity the keynote of socialist defence policy when in power. Portelli has also drawn attention to constraints on a party in government inheriting national traditions and conventions, and especially the equipment and personnel of a defence system central to the state apparatus. Then there are pressures arising from the hopes and fears of the military-industrial complex. But above all, in a period of international tension, there are pressures from allied governments not to rock the boat. (13)

As expected, Hernu was appointed defence minister. A short-tempered, decisive, hard-working, but humorous and convivial character, he was liked and respected by the military (perhaps more than by his four wives). His freemasonry experience gave him a taste for order, ceremony and secrecy, as well as many contacts in high places in civil and military life. He dispelled fears of upheaval by confirming General Lacaze as Chief of Staff of the armed forces and General Delaunay as army Chief of Staff, both

203

having reputations from good active service. The one big change to replace the head of the Service de documentation extérieure et de contre-espionage (SDECE) intelligence service Marenches with P. Marion, which soon led to over twenty staff changes, was seen as not only bringing in a long-standing freemason friend of Hernu but also promoting military experts to replace bureaucrats; the changes also may have been an attempt to reduce the penetration of French intelligence by the CIA and Mossad, the Israeli secret service. (14)

Whatever the pressures for continuity, some problems inherited from Giscard needed to be resolved. Controversies and confusion over the relative importance of strategic and tactical nuclear weapons were decided doctrinally in favour of the strategic force de dissuasion, though research into tactical weapons such as the neutron bomb was maintained pending decisions about future developments. Rejection of a graduated response, battle-fighting strategy by the Socialists in favour of deterrence, or non-guerre, meant a less important role for conventional forces than under Giscard. But rather than disrupting the army by manpower cuts implied by reducing conscription to six months, army problems of shaky morale were resolved considerably by improvements in pay and conditions and Hernu's early decision to keep the twelve-month service system, which helped to restrain rising unemployment. The fourth military programme begun by Giscard in 1977 was not due for completion until 1982, and it had already fallen behind target because of inadequate allowance for inflation, budget cuts under the finance ministry's deflationary policy and technical delays in the armaments industry. To underline the policy failures of the Right, Hernu announced that an extra year's expenditure would be needed to complete the programme by 1983.

In spite of problems and pressures facing the new government in a period of international crisis it tried to establish its left identity with courage tempered by realism. To introduce some morality into arms sales a denial of arms to fascist regimes was proclaimed. But many anxious governments had to be reassured, and sales maintained to offset the costs of French armaments industries, so that in practice only South Africa and Chile were subjected to special restrictions. Over 38 per cent of French arms production was being exported by the late 1970s and this was maintained by the socialist government after 1981 together with a continuing focus on the Middle

East markets. In one sense this reflected socialist support for advanced technology to keep France abreast of world competition, and arms proved to be the biggest capital goods export earner with, for example, a surplus of nearly 24 billion francs in 1983. In another sense it reflected the growing importance of the <u>Délégation générale de l'armement</u> (DGA), created in 1961 to direct all Defence Ministry departments responsible for providing munitions and equipment, and thereby controlling all arms industries by establishing the main orientations of French military industrial policy. As a focal point for military-industrial pressure groups the DGA, with a staff of over 73,000, was well placed to impress on the government the need to promote arms exports. (15)

The most overtly courageous assertion of the new government's left identity was the inclusion of four Communist ministers, notably Fiterman for transport. Mitterrand's decision to do this directly challenged the American doctrine laid down by Kissinger in 1976 opposing Communist participation in allied governments. Vice-President Bush visited the Elysée to warn Mitterrand that the tone and content of Franco-American relations could not be the same while there were Communists in the government. Apart from complicating French security during a critical period in international relations, this raised specific problems for French defence policy.

When Giscard d'Estaing decided in 1978 to build a sixth nuclear submarine, <u>l'Inflexible</u>, to be a new type with 16 missiles each carrying six hydrogen warheads, the technical difficulties were such that President Carter was asked to provide American super-computers. He complied in exchange for greater French co-operation with the Atlantic Alliance. In 1981 President Reagan halted the agreement because he objected to Communists in the new French government. Even in opposition Mitterrand had given strong support to the Atlantic Alliance, and during his first year in office he used four opportunities to meet Reagan to impress on him his commitment to Western security. His anti-Soviet diatribes left Reagan reportedly feeling 'pink' by comparison with Mitterrand. It was agreed to hold a NATO foreign ministers' meeting in June 1982 in Paris for the first time since before 1966 when France left the integrated military organisation. On 10 June 1982 Prime Minister Mauroy, who had overall responsibility for French defence organisation, addressed the NATO meeting with words especially for American ears, urging that they should underline the glaringly obvious lack of symmetry between the Warsaw Pact and the Atlantic Alliance. He added that to do this, 'We must show to what degree the Western world is capable of respecting the free development of each of the nations that compose it.' President Reagan was persuaded to reactivate the 1978 secret agreement and by August 1982 the first of eight Cray I supercomputers, worth 18 million dollars, had been sent to help French scientists solve hydrogen warhead problems. Additional supercomputers were delivered at a later date to help the French with new land, sea and air-launched nuclear weapons. Mitterrand had given the Americans public assurances that he took personal responsibility for national security. And Hernu had appointed General Forest as a special Defence Ministry commissioner to oversee military transport organisation in order to reduce dependence on Fiterman. (16)

Mitterrand's insistence on appointing and keeping Communist ministers in his administration struck an important blow for genuine pluralism in Western democratic political systems and set a precedent for France and comparable countries despite the Communists' decision to withdraw from government in 1984. The deal with the Americans showed certain limitations to French military capabilities. But it was part of an effective two-way street in the exchange of military equipment. By 1984 France was selling 180 million dollars worth of such equipment in a year and earning a net surplus. In 1985 France sold the huge GTE-Thomson RITA mobile subscriber equipment communications system to the American forces, and in return seemed likely to buy Boeing's E-3A AWACS for vital radar purposes. The SNECMA company was in the forefront of many other contracts with the United States, thus underlining the French Socialists' achievement in establishing the best defence relations for many years. (17)

By 1983 French armed forces found themselves in action alongside Americans overseas. Mitterrand's efforts to settle Arab-Israeli conflicts in the Middle East were more low-key than Giscard's, but his more positive support for American policy led him to contribute, for example, to a multi-national peace-keeping force in the Lebanon as well as to a United Nations force already posted ineffectually near the Israeli frontier, so that the total French troops reached nearly 3,000. Like the Americans they were accused of bias against Arab Muslims and after suffering nearly one hundred deaths from attacks were withdrawn from the Beirut area in 1984.

As David Levy shows in Chapter Seven, a similar attempt at a low-key policy in Africa, proved inadequate and was abandoned when Hernu sent in 3,000 French troops to halt the advance of Libyan-backed rebels from northern Chad to the capital. It was a long and uniquely complex civil war, but French intervention was necessary to uphold the credibility of their defence agreements with other African states, whose artificial frontiers made them fear partition almost as much as conquest resulting from any possible attack. Another reason for operation Manta was to pre-empt American intervention and the loss of France's special position in West Africa. The United States was anxious to stem the expansionist ambitions of Libya, apparently a Soviet client-state, and American money, arms and military advisers were appearing in parts of West Africa, including Chad. Hernu paid frequent visits to keep up the morale of French troops there, and in the Lebanon.

These overseas operations were also costly at a time of French budget and trade deficits. The decision to devote the 1983 military budget to making up the 8 per cent shortfall on equipment under Giscard's military programme, which had been largely to the detriment of the army, was overtaken by the general economic crisis. In 1982 17 billion francs of military credits were annulled involving suspension of orders for 25 Mirage jets, some armoured vehicles and artillery batteries. The 1983 defence budget kept spending constant at 3.89 per cent of GDP and 20 per cent of the credits were held back until December. This was the difficult context in which the socialist government introduced the fifth military programme law for the period 1984 to 1988.

Socialist Achievements

The work of any government should be assessed according to its ideology, its specific political objectives and its effective output, bearing in mind the geopolitical limitations of a state's size and strength. Technical or philosophical criticism should always take account of what alternative actions a government could, might, or should, undertake. These criteria will be used to assess French socialist government action according to the above categories, taken in reverse order.

During its first two years in power the effective output of socialist management of defence policy had amounted to little more than a holding operation in a time of economic crisis. Apart from minor improvements in service conditions and conventional equipment, the only significant change was the doctrinal commitment to build a seventh nuclear submarine as part of a priority for the strategic nuclear <u>force de dissuasion</u>. This was reaffirmed by the new programme law for the period 1984-8. <u>L'inflexible</u> would enter service in 1985 and work on the seventh submarine would start in 1988. Existing submarines would begin refitting with M-4 missiles developed for <u>l'Inflexible</u>. The controversial tactical nuclear missile <u>Pluton</u> would be replaced by 1992 with <u>Hadès</u> which had nearly three times the range at 350 kms. Decisions on a new warhead were deferred, but it was hinted that it might contain the neutron bomb. <u>Pluton</u> and all subsequent tactical weapons were renamed pre-strategic weapons and were to be based on national territory for use as ultimate warning according to the deterrence doctrine rather than for battlefield purposes. They would be placed directly under the control of the Chief of Staff of the armed forces in order to maximise the efficiency and flexibility of presidential decision-making.

The second major change concerned the conventional forces. They were to be reorganised to create a new <u>force d'action rapide</u> (FAR) comprising five varied and highly mobile divisions equipped with helicopters and anti-tank weapons. These 47,000 men, with headquarters at Maisons-Laffitte outside Paris, would be available for autonomous action in Europe or overseas according to presidential directives. The <u>gendarmerie</u> would take over territorial defence duties from the army and would include female volunteers. Reservists would be required to rejoin their units for a period during the first year after completing their service. Some conscripts could volunteer to extend their service to between 16 and 36 months. While keeping conscription to twelve months, these measures to improve mobilisation and civil-military links went some way towards the PS conception of a <u>force de mobilisation populaire</u> (FMP). But the conventional forces were to lose 35,000 men over five years, mainly from the army. The emphasis of the 830 billion franc programme was on equipment, 30 per cent of equipment credits being designated for nuclear weapons. On the conventional level, the Second Army Corps at Baden-Oos would get 100 extra tanks, and half of all existing AMX-30 tanks would be replaced by improved AMX-30B2 versions by 1988. The air force would get new Mirage 2000 jets from 1986 with medium-range missiles for a theatre role; and orders would be placed for an airborne early warning system (probably American AWACS). The navy's re-equipment would include a nuclear-powered aircraft carrier. All this would mean budgets rising from 3.91 per cent of GDP in 1984 to 4 per cent by 1988, and for the first time real spending-power would be maintained by a 6.2 per cent allowance for inflation in 1984 and 5 per cent for each subsequent year. (18)

A wide variety of assessments were made as to the effects of the new programme on the efficiency of French armed forces. In protest against cuts in manpower, the army Chief of Staff General Delaunay was one of several senior officers who resigned. But in view of Hernu's belief in the all-importance of strategic nuclear forces the army was perhaps fortunate to lose 7 per cent by natural wastage. The Gaullist theorist, General Gallois, was not alone in calling for a much smaller army. Many officers applauded the extra flexibility and mobility brought to the army by the FAR, but the retired General Méry bewailed the removal of helicopters from the Second Army Corps to the FAR. The official role of the army was to test the scale of enemy intentions and to demonstrate French will to resist. The FAR would be more able to serve those purposes at a chosen time and place than the forces stationed at Baden or Strasbourg. (19)

Even more controversy centred on whether the government would keep to the programme's financial commitments. By 1985 a complaint about delays in deployment of new tanks led to dismissal of General Arnold, commander of the First Tank Division. Chief of the General Staff, Lacaze, before retiring that year complained about economies forcing a five per cent reduction in training activities. Mesmin, a Giscardian deputy for Paris and member of the National Assembly Defence Commission, complained about inadequate and uncertain funding which had fallen from 16.5 per cent of the state budget in 1981 to 15.3 per cent in 1986, and from 3.85 per cent of GDP to under 3.8 per cent over the same period. A more fundamental analysis concluded that with the best will in the world the French could not afford to maintain and modernise adequate forces to give them effective defence of all their world interests. One view was that economic pressures alone would force France to make difficult choices and perhaps renounce her nuclear arsenal. (20)

A member of Hernu's <u>cabinet</u> at the defence

ministry countered such criticisms by issuing an analysis that broadly accepted Mesmin's statistics but argued that if budgets were examined in detail it became clear that spending on military equipment had increased by 2 per cent each year since 1981 and would rise faster in 1986. This was confirmed when a 2 per cent increase in real terms for defence was one of few exceptions to 1986 budget cuts in public expenditure. The truth was that the military programme scheduled the vast bulk of spending for the period from 1986 onwards to take account of economic difficulties in 1983 which would take time to resolve. Defence economies were made at the expense of training activities with tanks, planes and ships that were very thirsty for oil that was highly priced in dollars. General Lacaze said that military weaknesses would occur only if the restrictions on activity persisted, and so the 1986 budget increase together with the sharp fall in world oil prices would probably have solved the problem. But the effectiveness of the whole programme will always be a matter for speculation because the new right-wing government elected in 1986 refused to see it through and preferred to launch a new programme which was generously funded for equipment but significantly made no firm commitments for other forms of defence expenditure. (21)

The socialist government had undertaken to manage various strategic nuclear forces on land, sea and air; it had also kept up various tactical nuclear weapons totalling several hundred; and it was committed to various conventional forces including the FAR. This variety was intended to permit flexible response to complex and varied threats, and to allow for technical obsolescence while asserting the primacy of strategic deterrence. In any case, as seen above, not all tendencies of the PS were as committed to nuclear deterrence as the Jacobin and CERES groups. Varied commitments were no doubt encouraged by the military-industrial lobbies, and there was the prospect of reducing costs through exports or joint projects with allies.

The ultimate explanation for the government's strategic decisions lies in the politics of defence policy which were primarily international until after 1983. Mitterrand feared that the Euro-missile crisis might decouple France from her allies: the US reverting to isolationism or West Germany turning to neutralism. By 1981 new INF missiles were earmarked for bases in Europe and President Reagan was committed to maintaining a world role. But in Germany the SPD had rejected Schmidt's leadership and adopted a non-nuclear defence policy like the developing Green party. A sanctuarised France with only strategic nuclear weapons would have had no attraction for West Germany. To maintain West German confidence in allied support in 1983, when her elections were held just before delivery of Cruise and Pershing II missiles, France created the FAR which could operate alongside allied troops anywhere in West Germany in a matter of a few hours. Mitterrand's visit in 1983 not only contributed to the election victory of Kohl's CDU and to the installation of US missiles. It also led to the reactivation of the 1963 Franco-German treaty, particularly in the field of defence. This involved joint research and production in conventional weaponry but also consultation about the use of French nuclear weapons. This policy of tightening links with West Germany led on to one of increased European co-operation. Mitterrand was less convinced than colleagues such as Mauroy, Cheysson or Lemoine, the state secretary for defence, of the possibility of developing Western European Union into a basis for an integrated defence organisation. But he encouraged speculation in 1984 with speeches about new initiatives in the EEC for defence and advanced technology. A Franco-German agreement to produce a new military helicopter was hoped to be followed by projects for fighter aircraft and even space reconnaissance satellites. (22)

An active European policy was politically useful in the 1984 EEC parliamentary elections, and it pleased the European tendency within the PS. By this time PS rhetoric about co-operation with allies, as shown by the very title of a statement on <u>La Securité de l'Europe</u> adopted by the Party's <u>Bureau Executive</u> in June 1985, emphasised a possible European alliance rather than Atlanticism, in spite of CERES' fears to the contrary. But talk of collective security was at odds with a situation in which French nuclear forces and the FAR were based on national territory under strictly national control; and a suggestion that a demilitarised corridor could be created in Germany bore no sign of consultation with the German SPD and therefore appeared to be somewhat cavalier. French public opinion in June 1985 showed that 57 per cent believed France should intervene if West German security were threatened while 19 per cent did not; 40 per cent even believed France should identify her vital interests with West Germany and extend the nuclear guarantee while 24 per cent did not. A statement by Hernu at that time to the effect that France and West Germany had security interests in common was interpreted as an extension of French defence policy frontiers to the river Elbe. (23)

The socialist government had maintained French security by strengthening links with allies and using existing resources to create the FAR to improve the French contribution to the alliance defence system. This had been achieved during a period of international tension while holding the defence budget stable and even making savings in some sectors. French public confidence in their defences and alliances had never been greater. All this denoted considerable success for a socialist government within its national and international terms of ideological reference.

Nevertheless, important problems were bequeathed to its successors in government and to the PS in opposition. The development of varied and numerous tactical nuclear and conventional forces is bound to lead to the raising of the nuclear threshold. In one sense this might devalue strategic deterrence, and in another sense it might depart from a <u>non-guerre</u> policy and involve France and Europe in massive conventional destruction. A second problem is that advanced technologies lead to expensive choices of weaponry. Hitherto France has tried to oppose new developments such as SS20s, satellite ABM systems and President Reagan's strategic defence initiative (SDI) in order to protect French weaponry from obsolescence. But these efforts have failed, and Jolyon Howorth is not the only analyst to question the French ability to keep up proportional deterrence in competition with the superpowers. As seen above, much has been achieved with US co-operation; and Chirac is more willing to take the same road with SDI than Mitterrand. A third problem, particularly important to socialists, is the future of disarmament. France has traditionally regarded disarmament as a superpower responsibility, as if she were non-aligned. But the 1984-8 programme law not only made commitments to allies but also designated the Soviet Union as a specific threat. If French nuclear weapons, soon to expand to over 5 per cent of Soviet quantities, are committed <u>de facto</u> to NATO they must naturally be taken into account and if not could be a stumbling block in any disarmament talks. This has been pointed out by the West Germans. (24)

The PS must find solutions to these problems, not only as technical components of policy but even more to recover a left identity distinct from the Right now back in power, and to renew socialist ideology in an electorally attractive form. After several years in power there were signs that the PS had lost its sense of direction on defence matters. Arbitrary presidentialism, which had been associated by the Socialists with the nuclear force under de Gaulle, was never voiced more blatantly than by Mitterrand to the French people in a television interview on 16 November 1983 when he said that the keystone of deterrence strategy in France was the head of state himself. More serious still was the Greenpeace Affair in which a boat belonging to nuclear protestors was blown up in a New Zealand harbour by French secret service agents in order that nuclear testing could proceed at Mururoa Atoll in the South Pacific without interruption. This blatant infringement of international law, which also killed a man on the boat, caused a scandal resulting in the resignation of Hernu in September 1985 as the man responsible for secret service actions. Not only were there others in high places who were involved but did not resign, but the affair was also remarkable for the way in which the Left closed ranks with the right in condoning the sabotage in New Zealand because nuclear testing was in French national interest. It showed how big a gap had developed between the PS and international socialist opinion, and any subsequent renewal of PS ideology in opposition would require at least the bridging of that gap if its defence policy were to win international sympathy and support. (25)

Acknowledgements
I should like to thank staff at the International Institute for Strategic Studies, Mme. Perruchot at the French Embassy Service de Presse, and David Hanley at Reading University, for providing me with valuable research materials for use in writing this Chapter. Interpretations and any errors are entirely my own responsibility.

Notes
   1. T. Nairn, 'The Modern Janus', New Left Review no. 94 (1975) pp.17-18; see also P.D. Phillips and I. Wallerstein, 'National and World Identities and the Interstate System', Journal of International Studies vol. 14, no. 2, Summer 1985.
   2. This analysis of tendencies is partly derived from J. Howorth, 'Consensus of Silence: the

French Socialist Party and Defence Policy under François Mitterrand', <u>International Affairs</u> vol. 60, no. 4, Autumn 1984, pp.579-600; see also P. Buffotot, 'Le parti socialiste face aux questions de défense en France', in H. Portelli et D. Hanley (dir.), <u>Social-Démocratie et Défense en Europe</u> (Université de Paris X - Nanterre, 1985) pp.110-16. My analysis differs from others by avoiding terms such as 'patriotic', 'nationalist' or 'Atlanticist' which suffer from being too general or pejorative to be acceptable to PS tendencies.

3. An example was in the Senate defence budget debate in 1975 when the totally anti-nuclear PCF amendment was rejected by a show of hands and the PS amendment against tactical nuclear weapons was rejected by 190 to 89, reported in <u>Le Monde</u> 27 Nov. 1975, p.9.

4. Details are in C. Hernu, <u>Soldat-Citoyen</u> (Flammarion, Paris, 1975) and <u>Chroniques d'attente</u> (Tema, Paris, 1977); a full analysis is in P. Krop, <u>Les Socialistes et l'armée</u> (P.U.F., Paris, 1983) pp.85-114.

5. Portelli et Hanley, <u>Social-Démocratie et Défense</u> pp.8-9.

6. J-M. Lech, 'L'évolution de l'opinion des Français sur la défense à travers les sondages de 1972 à 1976', <u>Défense nationale</u>, Janvier 1977, pp.47-56.

7. Details of the 1978 PS convention on defence are in Krop, <u>Les socialistes et l'armée</u> pp.109-12 and in Buffotot, 'Le parti socialiste face aux questions de défense' pp.117-18.

8. Many publications reflected this atmosphere notably Gnl. Sir John Hackett <u>et alia</u>, <u>The Third World War, August 1985</u> (Sidgwick and Jackson, London, 1978), H. Carrère d'Encausse et F. de Rose (dir), <u>Après la détente</u> (Hachette, Paris, 1982) and frequent analyses in the press such as dossiers on the danger of nuclear war in <u>Newsweek</u> 22 June 1981 and 5 Dec. 1983.

9. C. Hernu, <u>Nous ... les grands</u> (Editions Fernand Galula, Lyon, 1980) 84pp.

10. F. Mitterrand, <u>Ici et maintenant</u> (Fayard, Paris, 1980) pp.232-5.

11. <u>Projet socialiste: pour la France des années 80</u> (Club Socialiste du Livre, Paris, 1980) 380pp.; for the 110 propositions see Cl. Manceron et B. Pingaud, <u>François Mitterrand</u> (Flammarion, Paris, 1981).

12. See the analysis of change in French public opinion towards support for the Western Alliance in

D. Capitanchik and R.C. Eichenberg, Defence and Public Opinion (Routledge and Kegan Paul, Chatham House Papers no. 20, London, 1983) pp.49-56; during the 1981 presidential election campaign there were two remarkable meetings at Chatham House in London at which J-P. Cot, a Rocardian PS deputy, emphasised weaknesses of all candidates including Mitterrand, and M. Couve de Murville, a Gaullist ex-prime minister, emphasised the reliability of all candidates except the Communists.

13. Portelli et Hanley, Social-Démocratie et Défense, pp.8-9.

14. D.B. Marshall, 'Mitterrand's Defense Policies: the early signals', Strategic Review, Fall 1981, p.46; 'Mitterrand and the Generals', Foreign Report 8 Oct. 1981, pp.5-6; for analysis of the French secret service see Middle East Aug. 1981 and Feb. 1982.

15. See analysis of E.A. Koldziej, 'French Arms Trade: the economic determinants', SIPRI Yearbook 1983 Chap. 13, pp.371-90; for Defence Ministry organisation and the role of the DGA see Ministère de la Défense, Dossiers d'information, 'L'armement en France', no.77, Mai 1985, and 'L'organisation de la défense de la France', no. 81, Mars 1986.

16. Details of the secret computer deal were reported two months before the April 1985 launching of l'Inflexible at Cherbourg, Guardian 5 Feb. 1985; for Forest's appointment see Foreign Report 8 Oct. 1981, p.6.

17. R. Marshall, 'France: the problems, the prospects', Defense and Foreign Affairs, May 1985, p.17.

18. Loi no. 83-606 du 8 juillet 1983 portant approbation de la programmation militaire pour les années 1984-8, Journal Officiel, 9 juillet 1983; see also L. Tinseau, 'Rapport...sur...la programmation militaire...1984-8', no. 1485 (Assemblée Nationale, Paris, May 1983); the best analysis of this programme law and its implications is in D.S. Yost, France's Deterrent Posture and Security in Europe (International Institute for Strategic Studies, Adelphi Papers 194 and 195, London, 1985), see especially no. 195 pp.26-32.

19. The discussion is summarised in Yost, no. 195, p.28ff.

20. G. Mesmin, '1986: l'année des choix décisifs pour la défense', Défense nationale, avril 1986, pp.49-65; J. Howorth, 'Resources and strategic choices: French defence policy at the crossroads',

World Today May 1986, pp.77-80.
21. F. Tiberghien, 'L'effort de défense depuis 1981' Défense nationale Nov. 1985, pp.31-70; Lacaze reported in Times 3 July 1985 and Telegraph 4 July 1985; the new programme of the Right was reported in Le Monde 6 and 18 Nov. 1986.
22. Discussion of Franco-German relations on defence is in A. Grosser, Affaires extérieures (Flammarion, Paris, 1984), pp.302-4; discussion of French views on European defence problems and co-operation is penetratingly developed by Diana Geddes in Times 28 Jan. 1985.
23. 'La Sécurité de l'Europe', Rapport adopté par le Bureau Exécutif du Parti Socialiste le 26 Juin 1985; report of IFOP opinion poll in Le Monde 28 Juin 1985; Hernu's statement was reported in Financial Times 28 June 1985.
24. Discussion of PS attitudes to deterrence and disarmament, emphasising the risks of trying to raise the nuclear threshold, is in J. Soppelsa, 'Défense: continuité dans le changement', in M. Guastoni (dir.), Gauche: premier bilan (Revue Politique et Parlementaire, Paris, 1985) pp.88-96; see also J. Alford, 'The place of British and French nuclear weapons in arms control', International Affairs vol. 59, no. 4, Autumn 1983, pp.569-74.
25. The most recent and accessible book among many published on the Greenpeace Affair was by Sunday Times Insight Team, Rainbow Warrior (Arrow Books, London, 1986); details of Hernu's resignation and an assessment of his career were discussed by David Housego in Financial Times 21 Sept. 1985; Hernu was replaced by Paul Quilès, previously minister for transport after Fiterman resigned in 1984, born in Algeria and son of an artillery officer, who was essentially a caretaker at defence until the fall of the socialist government in 1986.

Further Reading
For a reliable, comprehensive introduction to French military strategy and defence traditions see M.M. Harrison, The Reluctant Ally: France and Atlantic Security (Johns Hopkins University Press, Baltimore, 1981) or the brief summary in H. Haenel, La Défense nationale (PUF, Que sais-je? no. 2028, Paris, 1982). Full and penetrating discussion of recent developments during the Euro-missile crisis is in J. Howorth and P. Chilton (eds.), Defence and Dissent in Contemporary France (Croom Helm, London, 1984) and from a mainly military point of view in D.S. Yost,

France's Deterrent Posture and Security in Europe (IISS, Adelphi Papers 194 and 195, London, 1985). The wider implications of PS experience for international comparison are explored in H. Portelli et D. Hanley (dir.), Social-Démocratie et Défense en Europe (Université de Paris X - Nanterre, Paris, 1985). A very useful collection of Mitterrand's speeches while in power and a lengthy introduction explaining why, for example, he opposes Reagan's SDI, is in F. Mitterrand, Réflexions sur la politique extérieure de la France (Fayard, Paris, 1986). Apart from press and periodical articles detailed in the Notes above, the best collections of defence studies are by J. Barrat and D. David, 'France and World Security', in P. Morris and S. Williams (eds.), France in the World Wolverhampton Polytechnic, Association for Study of Modern and Contemporary France, 1985) and in F. Joyaux et P. Wajsman (dir.), Pour une nouvelle politique étrangère (Hachette, Paris, 1986). Finally, a useful summary of most of the socialist period in power is by F. Heisbourg, Défense et sécurité extérieure: 'la continuité dans la changement', Politique étrangère no. 2, 1985, pp.377-97. Finally, a recent publication in French, covering all aspects of defence policy is a special edition entitled 'L'Armée' in Pouvoirs no 38, 1986.

CONCLUSION - THE BALANCE SHEET

Michael Newman

In the preceding chapters the nature of the Parti Socialiste has been examined and its performance in government in a number of policy areas has been explained and evaluated. It is now time to ask, in words made notorious by Georges Marchais, whether the balance sheet is positive overall. Do the achievements of the government outweigh its failures? This apparently straightforward question raises some complex issues of perspective and value. For example, in Chapter 2 it was concluded that the reduction of inflation was achieved with less increase in unemployment than the international norm. Is this therefore to be regarded as a 'success' because it avoided the full consequences of deflation as experienced elsewhere, or a 'failure' because it betrayed electoral promises and socialist aspirations? Such problems of interpretation will be discussed further below, but let us first establish some central guidelines that supporters of a socialist/social democratic government might suggest for evaluating its record. (1) We can then judge the performance of Mitterrand's France with reference to these criteria.

First, such governments would be expected to be concerned primarily with the interests of the working classes and 'ordinary people' rather than the rich and powerful. Class inequality is a fundamental feature of capitalist society which social democratic and socialist parties normally promise to tackle. In addition their rationale is to promote the welfare of the masses through the maintenance of full employment, the provision of improved pay and conditions, and greater access to improved quality educational, housing and health facilities. More generally, the objective of such parties in the post-war era has been to improve the 'quality of life' of

Conclusion - The Balance Sheet

ordinary people.

Secondly, particularly in recent years, increased democratisation has been viewed as a crucial goal. This involves greater participation in decision-making and control over fundamental choices in life. Socialists and social-democrats therefore normally pledge themselves to break down traditions of authoritarianism, paternalism and bureaucracy, and to de-centralise the governmental structure. Furthermore, such parties normally oppose state involvement in issues of personal and sexual morality.

Such matters are related to a third element in the thinking of contemporary social democracy: the demand for equal opportunities. The growth of the women's movement, challenging traditional role stereotypes and demanding equality of access to positions of power and responsibility, means that a social democratic government is expected to make a major impact in furthering the rights of women. Similarly, such an administration would be urged to counter racism in the form of discriminatory practices, attitudes, and values.

Finally, social democracy is also held by its supporters to have relevance in the areas of defence and foreign policy. True, there are important national differences on the issues of peace and disarmament. In particular, while many West German, Dutch or British rank and file social democrats regard unilateral nuclear disarmament as a part of social-democracy, the PS, like the majority of the French population, has absorbed the Gaullist viewpoint that the possession of nuclear weapons is an essential component of 'national independence'. It therefore makes little sense to judge the PS government with reference to criteria which it would not accept (even if its position is not shared). Nevertheless, the PS and Mitterrand did make a commitment to promote disarmament and the record here can fairly be judged. On foreign policy, more generally, a social democratic government would be expected to oppose overt imperialism, to support 'progressive' movements, for example, for national liberation, and to make some contribution to international détente to diminish the danger of war.

If these are taken as broad guidelines for evaluating the performance of social democratic governments, how successful was the French socialist administration?

Conclusion - The Balance Sheet

Inequality and Working-Class Conditions
Although France in 1981 was one of the most unequal of capitalist societies, the socialist government made little significant impact on the distribution of wealth and the pattern of class inequality. (2) The reduction in the working week without loss of pay, the raising of the minimum wage, and the wealth tax constituted an increase in transfer payments to the working-classes but there was no radical restructuring of the taxation system, and the subsequent concern of the government to restore the rate of profit and stimulate business confidence counteracted the early attempts to diminish inequalities. (3)

Nor was this offset by any long-term improvement in working-class standards of living. Certainly, progress was made in the initial phase: the raising of benefits and minimum wages was accompanied by the introduction of a fifth week of paid holidays, which put French workers in an enviable position compared with those in the majority of European countries; the stimulation of the economy and special measures protected employment; and major efforts were made to improve access to health care and housing, while the government also attempted to deal with working-class under-achievement in schools, by reinforcing the comprehensive system, modernising the curriculum and reducing streaming. (4) However, the series of economic U-turns soon threatened most of these gains. Unemployment rose from just over two million in early 1982 to 2.4 million in 1984 and, in the latter year, average wage levels fell by 2.5 per cent, while austerity measures led to a tightening of benefits and increased contributions which cut back the early increases in the 'social wage'. Even in education and health care the government retreated in the face of both deflationary pressures and the right-wing backlash. Overall, then, the record was very mixed with the early advances largely negated, particularly after Spring 1983.

Democratisation
Since 1968 there has certainly been a change in France in which local initiative, variety of life-styles, cultural heterogeneity, and participation have increased. The socialist government did not therefore initiate the changes in this sphere, but it made conscious efforts to hasten them and some of its members took the doctrine of 'autogestion' very seriously. The Auroux reforms, decentralisation,

Conclusion - The Balance Sheet

Rocard's planning, and aspects of both cultural and social policy were intended to increase participation and local control over decision-making and were, as has been shown, partially successful. It is, moreover, still too early to judge their overall impact since some of the measures, particularly in the sphere of decentralisation, have not yet taken full effect. Nevertheless, it is clear that here too austerity undermined much of the reforming impetus and, in any case, the radical content was limited.

As Martin Rhodes shows, the Auroux reforms carefully preserved managerial privilege in decision-making and may even have weakened trade unionism in some respects. In addition to this, the government back-tracked when it feared that a bold initiative in workers' decision-making might actually strengthen the Communist-led CGT rather than the CFDT. (5) Similarly as Sonia Mazey shows, the decentralisation measures, though important in restructuring the 'one and indivisible Republic', actually incorporated the local socialist elite more fully into the decision-making system rather than opening up the structures to the 'masses'. (Paradoxically, the measures also provided an important new base for right-wing politicians). The limitations of the reforms are also demonstrated by Doreen Collins's discussion of the way in which the status quo in health care was, in its essence, preserved, by Jill Forbes's evidence that opera remained the most subsidised branch of the arts, and in her apt description of Mitterrand's view of culture as 'monarchical'. Nor did the French Socialists encourage forms of popular participation which were, for example, promoted by some Labour-controlled municipalities in Britain in the same period.

In general, then, the Socialists certainly increased democratisation by establishing some countervailing influences to the patron in industry and the prefect in local government. But the changes were not dramatic and here too the government gradually became more defensive. By 1986, it no longer emphasised 'autogestion' but the more traditional virtues of 'republicanism' and democracy.

Equal Opportunities

On the issue of feminism the French position has long been curiously complex. On the one hand, popular practices and attitudes remain patriarchal; on the

Conclusion - The Balance Sheet

other hand, France was the only country already espousing the principle of equal pay when the EEC was formed in 1958, and a fairly vigorous women's movement has pressed the political parties into action over a wide range of policy. The record of the Socialists in government was equally mixed. As Doreen Collins shows, they introduced extensive proposals on women's rights, including a requirement for private firms to prepare annual statements on the position of women in their employment structures and to provide a channel for promotion - a measure in advance of most comparable countries. Yet the traditional concern with the need for a higher birth rate cut across such notions of emancipation. Nowhere was this contradiction more apparent than on the issue of abortion, where Mitterrand's own intervention was necessary to ensure that the government reimbursed women undergoing the operation, after Bérégovy had retreated on this. Nor did the Socialists' own record on personnel in positions of responsibility suggest that the party was as committed to equal opportunities as its rhetoric implied: only one of the new prefects (later Commissaires de la République) was a woman and, for the regional elections of March 1986, very few women were placed in winnable positions on the party lists.

The position on racism was also ambiguous. In the early stages, the government adopted a far more liberal attitude than its predecessors, dropping Giscard's repatriation policy, implementing educational programmes to help immigrant communities, and allowing them the right to free association. Even then it refrained from a positive 'multi-ethnic' or anti-racist programme, which was contradicted by the francisme of the cultural policy. But prior to 1981 the Left had controlled most of the local authorities in which North Africans lived and had practised a form of institutionalised racism, with the argument that numbers must not exceed the French 'level of toleration'; and it was a Communist mayor - supported by the local Socialists - who had bulldozed an immigrant hostel in Vitry. All of this helped to promote immigration as a mobilising issue for the extreme Right and, when Le Pen, the leader of the Front National, took the initiative the government was forced on to the defensive. It lamely attempted to maintain a 'civilised' stance on the issue, but abandoned the earlier commitment to grant full voting rights to immigrant communities in municipal elections. (6)

Conclusion - The Balance Sheet

Peace and Détente

Even if the commitment of the government to the retention and strengthening of French nuclear weapons is not questioned, its defence policy hardly appears 'positive' in the sense sought by social democrats. As Neville Waites shows, the interrelationship between conventional and nuclear weapons remained undefined, and the degree of 'national independence' as against NATO involvement was unclear. Furthermore, there was, of course, the notorious destruction of the Rainbow Warrior in New Zealand so as to prevent a Greenpeace protest against French nuclear tests. Apart from the illegitimate nature of the attack itself, the issue raises two significant points. First, there is evidence that the Socialists had only limited control over the military and secret service. Secondly, despite the sacrifice of Hernu, the government made light of the incident, indicating that it regarded military 'needs' as sacrosanct. This epitomised the extent to which the traditionally right-wing themes of grandeur and strength have been absorbed by the PS. (7) The predominance of military considerations also had an economic aspect: French arms sales (encouraged by the notoriety of Exocet missiles in the Falklands war) remained the biggest single capital item in French exports and the socialist government was certainly not prepared to do anything to threaten the million jobs allegedly dependent on the industry. (8) It would be difficult to interpret any of this as making even a modest contribution to international peace, and it is probable that indiscriminate French arms sales and intervention in the Middle East subsequently encouraged Arab terrorists to make Paris the principal European target of their activities.

As David Levy shows, Mitterrand's foreign policy was hardly more successful in the terms defined by socialists or social democrats. The government disagreed totally with the American treatment of the Sandanistas and, at the beginning of its period in office, was prepared to stand out against Washington by granting modest arms supplies and aid to the beleagured Nicaraguan government. However, while verbal condemnations continued, concrete support was soon curtailed. Similarly, in its early days, the government sought a new relationship with ex-French colonies in Africa to replace the blatant neo-colonialism which had characterised the Giscardien era. However, this too was soon to change: Jean-Pierre Cot resigned, and the

Conclusion - The Balance Sheet

French government resumed its customary intervention in Chad. When French political and economic interests in colonial or ex-colonial territories were at stake, policy hardly changed, despite the rhetoric. (9)

The trajectory was similar with regard to the French role within its primary alignments - the EEC and the Atlantic Alliance. In the first year of the Mitterrand presidency, the French proposed a new spirit of reform in the European Community but, faced with a negative response, it abandoned any immediate prospect of change. It subsequently observed the EEC rules over tariff policies and subsidies to the steel industry, and sought as high agricultural prices as possible, while firmly resisting British demands for budgetary re-allocations. And in the Atlantic Alliance, the government followed a similar line to that of its predecessor: despite assertions of independence, actual co-operation was increased. The Americans prudently regarded French criticisms of US policy as partly for internal consumption and therefore compatible with a reasonable working relationship, particularly as the Socialists adopted a more hostile attitude to the Soviet Union than the previous administration. (10) When a crucial energy source such as the gas pipeline was involved, the French government was prepared to withstand American hostility and it often denounced Reagan's economic policy. But, in general, Mitterrand's France took an overtly anti-Soviet stance on most issues and a covertly pro-American one, partially masked by continuing attacks on US culture. The French Socialists now seemed to interpret 'mediation' and 'independence' as necessitating firm adherence to the Western Alliance. As Soviet-American relations were characterised by a new 'cold war', it would be difficult to argue that the French stance made a significant contribution to the promotion of detente.

Overall, then, the balance sheet indicates some modest achievements and some serious failures even if the criteria of judgment are within a social democratic perspective, rather than those that would be adopted by critics of the Right or Left. It is true that the government helped to modernise France and introduced humanitarian reforms - most notably the abolition of the death penalty. It was also relatively successful in 'managing' the severe economic crisis which dominated its period in office. But it did not make a significant <u>socialist</u> impact. Why were its achievements in this respect relatively limited?

Conclusion - The Balance Sheet

We saw earlier that the economy exercised a dominant role in that successive waves of austerity measures inevitably affected the government's performance in all spheres of domestic policy. Moreover, 'rigour' inevitably precipitated disillusionment with the government amongst the working-classes while reinforcing the opposition and exacerbating sinister threats on the extreme right. It is therefore appropriate to seek economic explanations for the government's limited success.

A number of studies, as well as Peter Holmes's contribution, have suggested that economic policy suffered from a lack of co-ordination between the agencies concerned, insufficient clarity about objectives and strategy, a lack of integration between banking and industry, and a weak role for planning. (11) All this, it is argued, led to confusion and a failure fully to exploit the opportunities that existed in an admittedly difficult situation. In addition, Peter Holmes argues that a fundamental mistake lay in the government's refusal to devalue early enough and by a sufficient amount, leading to more severe austerity than would otherwise have been necessary.

These arguments clearly have validity. Yet there is room for scepticism as to just how much difference better co-ordination or earlier devaluation would have made. In particular, would the avoidance of such mistakes have made a <u>fundamental</u> impact upon the government's ability to maintain employment and wage levels? If not, it is unlikely that the general record of Mitterand's France would have been substantially different, or would have been judged a greater success by the electorate.

A second economic explanation for the government's limitations - strongly emphasised by Peter Holmes - is that the initial radical phase was unrealistic. The argument here is that the pace of change at the beginning led to major subsequent problems over the balance of payments, inflation and international competitiveness, which forced the administration to adopt very severe austerity policies and to curtail reform. However, this point may indicate a contradiction between economic and political judgments.

From the perspective of sober economic analysis the first year may have seemed rash. Yet the reforming impetus and successes of the government in the spheres of decentralisation, social policy, industrial relations and cultural policy occurred, for the most part, during this early radical phase when budgetary matters were not the primary consideration. Reform <u>might</u> have been sustained for longer had the government paid more attention to economic constraints in 1981-82. But it is also possible that some of the more radical measures would never have been introduced at all had the government been 'realist' in the early stages. For anticipation of the subsequent difficulties might simply have strengthened the position of those who were subsequently to argue that reform was impracticable and that the main priority should be to restore profitability. (12) A more fundamental economic explanation of the problems, also developed by Peter Holmes, stresses the international constraints. With almost 25 per cent of GNP dependent upon foreign trade, as part of the international financial system, the EEC and the EMS, France was inevitably subject to pressures from the international capitalist economy. More specific factors compounded these general constraints.

In 1981 the French socialist government was the only major administration committed to neo-Keynesian expansionist policies in a climate in which the United States, Britain and West Germany were imposing deflation. The resulting import penetration and pressure on the franc led to borrowing abroad from sources - particularly the West Germans - who were able to bring about a reorientation of French policy in line with the prevailing international orthodoxy. Indeed Peter Holmes maintains that French economic performance between 1981-86 was determined far more by movements in the international economy than by any of the policies of the Socialist government.

If this is so, the Socialists' domestic failing can be attributed <u>primarily</u> to external pressures; and if Holmes is also justified in his suggestion that alternative economic policies would have proved ineffective, it means that even a major state like France exercises very limited autonomy in domestic policy.

A second kind of explanation for the government's limited achievements emphasises political factors. It holds that the Socialists were 'blown off course' not only by the mounting economic pressures, but also by the difficulties in domestic politics.

The government faced a general problem in that much of its support in 1981 was inherently volatile. With the Right in power since 1958, and Barre's austerity measures taking effect, a large sector of the population had turned to Mitterrand and the PS

Conclusion - The Balance Sheet

for 'changement'. However, this meant that many of those who had voted for the Left in 1981 were also a prey to mobilisation against the new government if it failed to fulfil their hopes, particularly in the economic sphere. The Socialists were therefore soon on the defensive. This was reinforced by the rise of direct action movements, subtly encouraged by the Right. The administration faced mass protest by farmers and lorry drivers even before the most publicised and de-stabilising protest: that of approximately 1.5 million demonstrators in support of the école libre movement in the summer of 1984. Such protest, coupled with electoral set-backs, enabled the Right to undermine the legitimacy of the government, particularly as a wave of terrorist attacks made 'law and order' a potent issue. Mitterrand recovered ground but in a defensive way: in effect he and the PS now rallied support around the Gaullist constitution, and the socialist elements in the original programme were buried in the quest for a form of republican legitimacy.

All this is true. Yet the argument that political pressures dictated a retreat ignores key elements in the situation. It suggests that, without the rising opposition of the Right, the government would have been more successful and, by implication, more radical. But is this so?

It is unlikely that some of the 'realist' socialist politicians were ever serious about elements in the party programme. The rhetoric about the 'rupture with capitalism' attracted communist support and kept CERES happy, but it is unlikely that it was ever regarded as meaningful by Mitterrand himself, or by Mauroy, Delors, Defferre and other key figures. For many of them the exercise of power, the conversion of the PS into a dominant party in the political system, and moderate reform were seen as the real goals. It is no doubt true that the wave of anti-government direct action and extreme Right mobilisation was profoundly worrying and did induce a defensive mentality. Yet even here, the mood partially reflected a lack of radicalism: from the start pro-government demonstrations of solidarity were discouraged, and the PS appeared to believe that its parliamentary majority was a sufficient guarantee that reform would be implemented. Although they would have liked to increase living standards and maintain employment levels more successfully than they were able, it is probable that many leading members of the government implemented the form of social democracy which they had always desired. They were not 'blown off course': the party rhetoric provided little clue to the path they wished to follow.

All these specific factors about the French situation help to explain the record of the administration. Yet a wider perspective also suggests that the French experience was similar to that of social-democracy elsewhere in three crucial respects. First, such governments have generally failed to make a major impact upon the fundamental structural features of capitalism. By 1981, this had been demonstrated by the fact that, despite their prolonged periods in power neither the Swedish social democrats nor the British Labour Party had made a significant difference to the ownership of wealth, class inequality, social mobility, or even the level of state expenditure. (13) Secondly, their domestic achievements have been dependent upon their relationship with the international economy and its general 'state of health'. The failure of British Labour governments in both the sixties and seventies to introduce domestic reforms while the international economy exerted deflationary pressures illustrated this point. And, thirdly, their impact upon foreign and defence policy has been very modest - a point epitomised once again by British Labour governments throughout the post-war period and also by the transformation of the foreign policy of the German SPD in the fifties as a pre-condition for the attainment of power. (14)

Such 'lessons' were available to the PS when it took charge of the administration and its subsequent experience in government was to reinforce them. It is therefore often suggested that the thrust of government policy would have been clearer and, arguably more successful and popular, had the essentially social-democratic nature of the party been established more precisely prior to 1981. In this case, it might be argued, voters and commentators could have expected a government which would show a marked degree of continuity with the domestic and external policies of its predecessors, while introducing limited reforms where possible. The problem, from this perspective, is that the party CLAIMED to be something different, thereby inviting disillusionment and harsh judgments about its failure to fulfil the aspirations it encouraged.

It is certainly true that, prior to 1981, the nature of the PS was unclear and that, during the first year in power, divisions between CERES and the PCF on the one hand, and Rocardiens and 'realists' on

Conclusion - The Balance Sheet

the other, were evident in policy initiatives. The underlying rationale of much of the economic strategy, for example, was, as Peter Holmes shows, a complex and indeterminate mélange of Keynesianism and leftism which made it difficult to institute appropriate policies or even to establish criteria for their success. Why then did the party fail to establish its identity and strategy prior to 1981? Two answers can be suggested: the first maintains that the PS adopted social-democratic policies only after its alternative strategy failed; the second holds that political and electoral considerations prevented a resolution prior to the exercise of power. Both contain some truth and can be considered in turn.

It was the influence of CERES and the Common Programme which led the PS in the seventies to adopt a left-socialism designed to transcend the 'failures' of social democracy. It was held that governments of the Left had been unable to achieve a fundamental transformation of capitalism for various reasons: because they did not genuinely seek extensive change, or had been pusillanimous when confronted with opposition from the privileged, or had failed to understand the workings of the system, or had been divided and weak. A French government of the Left, with a degree of mass mobilisation in its favour, could, by contrast, alter the whole nature of society by removing capitalist control from key sectors of the economy. As already noted, such ideas were held with varying degrees of sincerity and commitment, but all sections of opinion maintained that it was possible to bring about decisive changes without compromising in the way that social democrats had done elsewhere or in the Fourth French Republic.

The stance on international issues was more complex. The whole party argued that the attainment of socialism in France depended on a partial withdrawal from the constraining pressures of international capitalism and American dominance, but much of this reasoning was compatible with Gaullism. Moreover, there was an unresolved and crucial ambiguity concerning the EEC. No-one actually advocated withdrawal, but CERES (and the PCF) regarded the European Community as a capitalist institution which could impose constraints upon a French government of the Left, while the majority of the PS - and, above all, Mitterrand himself - were almost unconditional 'Europeans'. (15) We can illustrate the strategic shift in government by further considering the impact of the European issue.

Conclusion - The Balance Sheet

Prior to 1981 CERES had been forced to accept the majority view that the EEC commitment was fundamental both because of the extent of French integration into the Community and because a 'European' dimension was held to be a necessary support to a left-wing government in France. Once in power, the underlying tensions over the issue were masked by two further factors: the belief that an international economic revival was imminent, and the hope that the Community as a whole might be persuaded to adopt expansionist policies and to confront American and Japanese import penetration. In these circumstances, rather than imposing deflationary pressures on France, the European Community would bolster the socialist government's reflation. (16) However, when this optimistic scenario failed to materialise and the French turned to West Germany for financial support, unconditional Europeanism easily prevailed over CERES' form of left-socialism. True, CERES protested, particularly at the time of Chevènement's resignation in 1983, and advocated a more strident socialist policy, incorporating an element of protectionism. (17) But the rebellion was short-lived. Mauroy's assertion that 'to choose Europe is to choose rigour' signified the predominance of both the external and domestic aspects of traditional social democracy, as the French government maintained its international alignment 'within the rules of the game' and implemented austerity at home. The adoption of social-democracy thus followed the failure of a more adventurous alternative strategy.

However, the second, more 'political', interpretation is also relevant. As David Hanley shows, the success of the PS depended on its ability to absorb different currents of thought in such a way as simultaneously to attract the new middle-classes, to maintain working-class support in its traditional areas, and to undermine the appeal of the PCF. For these purposes a coalition of traditional social democrats and various forms of leftism, which used a radical vocabulary, was highly effective. By contrast, any thoroughgoing attempt to resolve the issue of whether the PS was marxist or social democratic prior to the achievement of power could have destroyed party unity. In a sense, both CERES on the left and Rocard on the right attempted to do just this and were out-manoeuvred by Mitterrand. For what would clarity have achieved? Had the Rocardiens triumphed they would presumably have argued that there was relatively little scope for structural

Conclusion - The Balance Sheet

changes and that the party should promise only 'realistic' reforms. But in this case both CERES and left-Mitterrandistes would have been alienated, the PCF would have been granted a more plausible case for its anti-PS campaign, and rank-and-file Communists may have seen less reason for voting socialist. On the other hand, clarity of the kind that CERES advocated was equally unattractive to Mitterrand, for this would probably have entailed a far closer alliance with the PCF, a belief in direct action as well as parliamentary methods, and a greater stress on class-warfare. Such clarity did not accord with Mitterrand's viewpoint and was unlikely to attract the kind of centrist support that he needed to attain a presidential victory, or that the PS needed to achieve a dominant position in the political system. It was more effective to profess, and for many socialists also to believe, that both the PS and France were unique and that a government of the Left could really make a decisive break with capitalism.

Viewed in this light, the shifts in policy over the life of the government take on a new significance: that which could not be clarified prior to 1981 was resolved 'on the job'. The 'realists' were always waiting in the wings and their day was to come as the government's economic difficulties mounted. From June 1982 until the appointment of Fabius as Prime Minister and the withdrawal of the Communists two years later, they assumed ever increasing dominance and implemented traditional 'moderate' measures.

It is therefore a moot point whether the ideological transformation of the PS occurred because of its confrontation with harsh realities, or because of the shallowness of the original stance. In either case, the experience of government was a necessary factor in the shift, and the suggestion that the party could have proclaimed itself as 'social-democratic' prior to 1981 is untenable.

Two further points about the transformation are significant. First, the relative ease with which the party was able to accept its new identity is notable. CERES' protests were muted as Chevènement rejoined the administration, taking a firm line on the need for discipline in schools and stressing the importance of patriotic education, and CERES itself assumed a relatively quiescent line. Indeed the conversion was far deeper than this: not only was there no formal rebellion against the government, as there was, for example, against the Wilson-Callaghan governments in Britain, but the party as a whole

Conclusion - The Balance Sheet

espoused the new orthodoxy of realism and modernisation. Secondly, the ideological spectrum of the French left <u>as a whole</u> had undergone a major shift to the centre by March 1986. True, the PCF was now bitterly condemning the PS as a faithful agent of capitalism which would always betray the workers, but the Communists were becoming a marginal force in French politics and were probably more deeply divided than at any stage in their history. (18) CERES, renamed <u>Socialisme et République</u>, was now taking a left-wing social democratic stance: the government, it claimed, had not gone far enough and had been unwilling to offend international capitalism by taking the necessary measures of defence. But it no longer believed that socialism was on the agenda and saw the immediate mission to be the proclamation of an assertive republicanism which would carry the masses towards socialism. (19) And the majority of the PS now adopted a position which can be characterised as right-wing social democracy: the government, it was argued, had implemented its reform programme and had achieved far more for ordinary people than would an administration of the Right. Nevertheless, no government could bring about miracles, particularly in the midst of an international recession. It was thus necessary to modernise and be 'realistic' as well as to reform.

There is a paradox in this ideological change. In the sixties and early seventies, the predominant view of the French Left was that mass social democratic parties in Britain and West Germany had failed because they had not decisively altered the structural features of capitalism and had been 'Atlanticist'. Between 1981-86 France, for the first time in its history, had a majority government which largely repeated the experience of social democratic governments elsewhere. Yet by 1986 the marxist style criticism which had been so widespread fifteen years earlier had become the viewpoint of a small minority and the predominant perspective was indeed social democratic.

A major social democratic party had been built and the nature of left-wing ideology transformed. (20) Whether one applauds or bemoans the change, this was undoubtedly one of the most notable achievements of Mitterrand's France.

Notes and References

1. These guidelines are intended only to provide a context for the evaluation. For fuller

Conclusion - The Balance Sheet

recent analyses of social democratic ideology, see W. Paterson and A. Thomas, (eds) The Future of Social Democracy (O.U.P. London 1986) and from a critical left-wing perspective, R. Miliband et al. Socialist Register 1985/6 (Merlin, London 1986).

2. For full discussions of inequality in France, see Jane Marceau, Class and Status in France (O.U.P. London 1977) and P. Morris (ed.) Equality and Inequalities in France (Proceedings of the 1983 conference of the Association for the Study of Modern and Contemporary France). See also J. Ambler, 'Is the French Left Doomed to Fail?' in J. Ambler (ed.) The French Socialist Experiment (ISHI, Philadelphia 1985), pp.14-15.

3. The purchasing power of social transfers rose by 4.5 per cent in 1981 and by 7.6 per cent in 1982 and the minimum wage, to which the salaries of 1.7 million workers were tied, was raised by 15 per cent in real terms between May 1981 and December 1982. Peter A. Hall, 'The Struggle to Define a New Economic Policy' in P. Cerny and M. Schain, Socialism, the State and Public Policy (Frances Pinter, London 1985), p.84.

4. For a full discussion of the education policy, see J. Ambler 'Equality and the Politics of Education' in Ambler, French Socialist Experiment.

5. Hall in Ambler, French Socialist Experiment, p.99.

6. For fuller discussions, see Martin A. Schain, 'Immigrants and Politics in France' in Ambler, French Socialist Experiment, and Alec A. Hargreaves, 'The Politics of Immigration in France' in Modern and Contemporary France Review No. 23 October 1985.

7. See David Hanley, 'The Perils of Grandeur - Greenpeace, the socialists and the State' Modern and Contemporary France Review No. 25 March 1986.

8. Hall in Ambler, French Socialist Experiment, p.93.

9. See Tony Chafer, 'Mitterrand and Africa: 1981-84, Policy and Practice' Modern and Contemporary France Review No. 23 October 1985. (The same reversion to traditional policy applied with regard to the often brutal intervention by France in New Caledonia).

10. The accommodation to the USA was symbolised by Mitterrand's willingness to sign a joint communique on the security of the Western world at the Williamsburg economic summit in May 1983.

11. This is a major theme of the valuable introductory chapter in H. Machin and V. Wright (eds)

Conclusion - The Balance Sheet

Economic Policy and Policy-Making Under the Mitterrand Presidency, 1981-84 (Frances Pinter, London 1985).

12. 'Realism' also reinforced an étatiste approach which alienated interest groups whose goodwill may have helped the government, and enabled opposition groups to cultivate the image of 'defenders of liberty'. See Mark Kesselman, 'Lyrical Illusions or a Socialism of Governance: Whither French Socialism?' in Miliband, Socialist Register, Suzanne Berger, 'The Socialists and the patronat' and Frank L. Wilson, 'Trade Unions and Economic Policy' in Machin & Wright, Economic Policy and Policy-Making.

13. For a very useful discussion of the evidence, see J. Ambler, 'French Socialism in Comparative Perspective' in Ambler, French Socialist Experiment.

14. This point has also subsequently been illustrated by both the Greek and Spanish socialist governments which have compromised very considerably on the opposition to NATO and American bases which they expressed prior to taking power in 1981 and 1982 respectively.

15. For further details, see M. Newman, Socialism and European Unity - The Dilemma of the Left in Britain and France (C. Hurst, London 1983).

16. The French Minister for European Affairs, André Chandernagor, presented such a case to the rest of the European Community in October 1981. See Le Monde 9 October 1981 for details.

17. For further discussion of CERES' performance in government and its criticisms, see David Hanley, Keeping Left: CERES and the French Socialist Party (Manchester University Press, Manchester) Ch. 6.

18. For a discussion of disunity within the PCF, see M. Newman 'Conflict and Cohesion in the British Labour Party and French Communist Party' West European Politics vol. 10 April 1987.

19. See Hanley, Keeping Left Ch. 6 and 'La synthèse de la République et du socialisme' Le Monde, 19 April 1986.

20. For a very interesting assessment of the long-term ideological implications of the 1981 victory for the French Left, see Tony Judt, Marxism and the French Left (O.U.P. London 1986), Ch. 5.

Appendix One

ELECTION RESULTS

Results of the Presidential Election of April 26 - 10 May 1981
First Ballot (26 April 1981)

Registered Voters	36,398,859	
Voters	29,516,082	(81.09%)
Abstentions	6,882,777	(18.90%)
Blank or void votes	477,965	(1.31%)
Valid votes	29,038,117	

Candidate	Votes	Valid Votes %	Registered Voters %
Giscard d'Estaing (UDF)	8,222,432	28.31	22.58
Mitterrand (PS)	7,505,960	25.84	20.62
Chirac (RPR)	5,225,848	17.99	14.35
Marchais (PCF)	4,456,922	15.34	12.24
Lalonde (Ecologist)	1,126,254	3.87	3.09
Laguiller (LO)	668,057	2.30	1.83
Crépeau (MRG)	642,847	2.21	1.76
Debré (Ind. Gaullist)	481,821	1.65	1.32
Garaud (Ind. Gaullist)	386,623	1.33	1.06
Bouchardeau (PSU)	321,353	1.10	0.88

Second Ballot (10 May 1981)

Registered Voters	36,398,762	
Voters	31,249,552	(85.85%)
Abstentions	5,149,552	(14.14%)
Blank or void	898,984	(2.46%)
Valid votes	30,350,568	

Candidate	Votes	Valid Votes %	Registered Voters %
Mitterrand (PS)	15,708,262	51.75	43.15
Giscard d'Estaing (UDF)	14,642,306	48.24	40.22

Table compiled from official results published by the Ministry of the Interior.

Results of the Legislative Elections of June 1981 and March 1986

June 1981 (votes cast in First Round) (1)				March 1986 (2)			
Registered voters	35,536,041			36,605,381			
Votes cast	25,182,262	(70.89%)		28,721,804	(78.46)		
Abstentions	10,353,779	(29.13%)		7,883,577	(21.54)		
Valid votes	24,823,065			27,485,667			
Party	Votes	%	Seats (3)	Votes	%	Seats	
Far Left	330,344	1.33	0	427,753	1.53	0	
PCF	4,003,025	16.12	44	2,740,972	9.78	35	
PS/MRG	9,376,853	37.77	285	8,702,137	31.62	210	
Other Left	141,638	0.57	0	287,177	1.03	5	
Ecologists	270,792	1.09	0	340,138	1.21	0	
Regionalists	–	–	–	28,045	0.10	0	
RPR	5,192,894	20.91	88	3,142,373	11.21	76	
UDF	4,756,503	19.16	63	2,330,072	8.31	53	
RPR-UDF union	–	–	–	6,017,207	21.46	147	
Other Right	660,990	2.66	11	1,094,336	3.90	14	
FN	–	–	–	2,705,336	9.65	35	
Other Ex. Right	90,026	0.36	0	57,334	0.20	0	
Total		100.0	491		100.0	575*	

* The 1986 election results shown above do not include the results of Wallis et Futuna and Saint Pierre et Miquelon which elected one Deputy each under the old two round electoral system.

(1) The electoral system used for the 1981 legislative elections was the single member constituency double ballot system. A candidate must win over half the votes cast to be elected at the first ballot, but only a simple majority to win at the second (held one week after the first). To go forward to the second ballot a candidate must win at least 12.5 per cent of the electorate at the first ballot.
(2) An electoral reform in April 1985 introduced proportional representation for the March 1986 legislative elections. Electors voted in a single ballot for departmental party lists. Each of the departmental constituencies has between 2 and 24 representatives (52 of the 96 departments have 4 or less Deputies). Seats were allocated at the departmental level to those lists winning at least 5 per cent of the constituency vote, according to the 'highest averaging' system.
(3) Figures include seats won on the second as well as the first ballot.

Table compiled from official results published by the Ministry of the Interior.

237

French Results of the European Elections of June 1984

Registered voters	36,880,688	
Votes cast	20,918,772	
Abstentions	15,961,916	(43.27%)
Valid votes	20,180,934	

Party Lists	Votes	%
PCF	2,261,312	11.20
PS	4,188,875	20.75
UDF-RPR	8,683,596	43.02
PCI	182,320	0.90
LO	417,702	2.06
PSU-CDU	146,238	0.72
ERE	670,474	3.32
VERTS (Greens)	680,080	3.36
EUE	78,234	0.38
REUSSIR	382,404	1.89
UTILE	138,220	0.68
I 84	123,642	0.61
FN	2,210,334	10.95
POE	17,503	0.08

Table compiled from official results published by the Ministry of the Interior.

Results of the Departmental Elections of March 1982

Registered Voters	19,000,860	
Valid votes cast	12,575,535	(66.18%)

Party	Candidates	Votes on first round	Seats Won or held*		% First Round Vote 1982	1979
Extreme Left	254	73,382	5	(+1)	0.58	0.85
PCF	1,977	2,000,345	198	(-44)	15.91	22.46
PS	1,897	3,737,015	509	(-5)	29.72	26.96
MRG	249	217,143	61	(-27)	1.73	1.89
Other Left	301	214,328	54	(-24)	1.70	3.16
Ecologists	177	55,589	0	(no change)	0.44	0.47
RPR	885	2,262,245	336	(+146)	17.99	12.34
UDF	915	2,344,221	470	(+69)	18.64	21.14
Other Right	1,027	1,645,994	380	(+59)	13.09	10.03
Extreme Right	65	25,273	1	(no change)	0.20	0.69

* These figures include seats won on the second as well as the first round. These results exclude the 14 Saint Pierre et Miquelon seats and one French Guyana seat.

Table compiled from official results published by the Ministry of the Interior.

Appendix Two

CHRONOLOGY OF MAJOR POLITICAL EVENTS IN FRANCE 1981–86

<u>1981</u>

10 May: François Mitterrand elected President of the Republic, winning 51.75 per cent of the votes cast.

21 May: Pierre Mauroy nominated Prime Minister.

24 May: Mitterrand, in meeting with the West German chancellor, Helmut Schmidt, publicly supports NATO's decision to deploy Cruise and Pershing missiles.

14 and
21 Jun: Legislative elections. The PS and non-Communist allies win 285 of the 491 National Assembly seats.

23 Jun: Pierre Mauroy forms a second government which includes four Communist ministers after the PS and PCF sign a 'political accord'.

30 Sept: The death penalty is abolished.

2 Oct: Legislation passed permitting the establishment of local private radio stations.

4 Oct: The franc is devalued by 3 per cent.

8 Oct: The French Minister for European affairs passes a memorandum to his EEC partners outlining the French government's proposals for the development of the European Community. (These proposals are not

Appendix Two

adopted).

20 Oct: Mitterrand attends the Cancun Summit in Mexico and confirms his recognition of anti-government guerilla forces in El Salvador and his support for the Nicaraguan government.

4 Nov: The number of unemployed rises above 2 million.

30 Nov: Jacques Delors, Minister of Finance calls for a 'pause' in socialist reforms.

18 Dec: Legislation is passed nationalising five industrial groups, 36 banks and two financial institutions.

1982

13 Jan: The length of the working week is reduced to 39 hours and an extra week's paid holiday introduced.

16 Jan: The Constitutional Court rejects several articles of the nationalisation legislation.

3-7 Feb: The XXIV Congress of the PCF at Saint-Ouen. Georges Marchais, re-elected as Secretary General, calls upon every Communist to behave as a member of a government party.

5 Feb: Legislation is passed granting Corsica a 'Special Statute'.

13 Feb: Revised nationalisations law is passed.

3 Mar: The enabling decentralisation law is passed.

14 and
21 Mar: Cantonal elections. Right-wing opposition parties now control 64 (+8) general councils. Left-wing parties now control 36 (-8).

16 Apr: Pierre Mauroy announces government measures to reduce employers' costs.

Appendix Two

18 May: The French lead other EEC states in over-riding an attempt by the British to veto a rise in agricultural prices.

21 May: Following the announcement that prices rose by 1.2 per cent in April, Pierre Mauroy says it is necessary to moderate wage increases.

28 May: Pierre Mauroy calls for a change in speed of socialist reform.

12 Jun: Second devaluation of the franc since May 1981.

13 Jun: The introduction of economic _rigueur_. Measures include a wages and prices freeze until 31 Oct. These measures are approved by the PCF.

22 Jun: Georges Marchais, Secretary General of the PCF denounces the wages freeze as unjust and economically unnecessary.

29 Jun: Mme Questiaux, Minister for _Solidarité_ is replaced by Pierre Bérégovy.

27 Jul: The first of the Auroux laws on workers' rights is passed.

8 Aug: Regional elections are held in Corsica.

8 Dec: Jean-Pierre Cot resigns as Minister for Co-operation and Development.

23 Dec: The PCF and PS sign an electoral accord for the municipal elections in March 1983 covering all but 11 communes.

<u>1983</u>

6 and
13 Mar: Municipal elections. Left-wing parties lose control of 31 of the 221 largest towns.

21 Mar: The franc is devalued for the third time in 18 months and the French seek support from the West German government, accepting the constraints stemming from the European Monetary System.

22 Mar: Pierre Mauroy forms his third government.

Appendix Two

Laurent Fabius replaces Jean-Pierre Chevènement as Minister for Industry and Research. Edith Cresson replaces Michel Jobert as Minister for Overseas Trade and Tourism. Michel Rocard, formerly Minister of Planning, becomes Minister for Agriculture.

25 Mar: A second phase of economic <u>rigueur</u> is announced.

1 Apr: The retirement age is reduced to 60 years.

22 Apr: Violent protests by farmers in Brittany against the fall in pork prices.

28 May: Jean-Pierre Chevènement criticises the economic policy of <u>rigueur</u> at the PS national convention.

28-30 May: At the Williamsburg Economic Summit, Mitterrand agrees to include a declaration on Western security.

10 Aug: 3,000 French troops are deployed against Libya in Chad.

11 Sept: The Opposition forms an alliance with the FN to win the municipal election at Dreux.

28-30 Oct: CERES accepts an amended majority motion at the PS Congress in Bourg-en-Bresse.

1 Dec: Summit meeting between PS and PCF to review the operation of the 1981 agreement.

21 Dec: Hospital reforms are introduced.

<u>1984</u>

4 Mar: Between 500,000 and 800,000 people demonstrate at Versailles in support of private (i.e. Catholic) schools.

16 Mar: Alain Savary, Minister of Education announces details of socialist plans to bring private schools under the control of the state.

243

Appendix Two

29 Mar: Government adopts the Industrial Restructuring Plan which entails substantial job reductions in naval yards, coal mines and steel industries. Accompanying social measures for areas affected include assistance to migrant workers wishing to return home.

2 Apr: Georges Marchais, General Secretary of the PCF, declares that the government has respected neither the letter nor the spirit of the PS-PCF agreement.

4 Apr: General strike in Lorraine in protest at proposed redundancies in the steel industry.

13 Apr: 35,000 steel-workers from Lorraine demonstrate against the proposed redundancies in the steel industry.

19 Apr: Mauroy secures a vote of confidence for the government's general policy by 329 votes to 156. The PCF votes in favour while expressing reservations.

24 May: In a speech to the European Parliament Mitterrand calls for a strengthening of EEC institutions and a weakening of the national veto.

29 May: President Mitterrand and the West German Chancellor, Helmut Kohl, announce agreement on the joint production of military helicopters and the easing of frontier restrictions between France and West Germany.

17 Jun: Elections to the European Parliament. The extreme right-wing Front National gains 10 of the 81 French seats with 10.95 per cent of the votes. The PCF gain 10 seats with 11.20 per cent of the vote. The PS wins 20.75 per cent of the vote and 20 seats. The RPR-UDF coalition wins 43.02 per cent of the vote and 41 seats.

21 Jun: Mitterrand, in talks with the Soviet leadership in Moscow, outlines the issues which divide France and the Soviet Union.

Appendix Two

24 Jun: The law on private schools is passed by the National Assembly at the first reading after the government makes it a vote of confidence.

24 Jun: More than one million people demonstrate in Paris in support of private schools.

5 Jul: The Senate demands a referendum on the issue of individual liberties (particularly in relation to private education).

12 Jul: Mitterrand announces on television that Parliament is to consider revising Article 11 of the constitution to permit a referendum on the subject of individual liberties.

17 Jul: Mitterrand replaces Pierre Mauroy with Laurent Fabius as Prime Minister.

19 Jul: The PCF announces its refusal to participate in a new government.

19 Jul: Laurent Fabius announces his government. Pierre Bérégovy replaces Jacques Delors as Finance Minister. Gaston Defferre, Minister of the Interior and Decentralisation (and since March 1983 also in charge of the Plan) is replaced by Pierre Joxe. Alain Savary, the Education Minister resigns and is replaced by Jean-Pierre Chevènement.

24 Jul: Fabius secures a vote of confidence for a declaration in favour of the modernisation of the economy.

8 Aug/
5 Sept: The Senate rejects the proposals passed by the National Assembly to change the Constitutional provisions regarding the use of referenda.

6 Sept: Roland Leroy, editor of L'Humanité declares that the PCF is no longer part of the majority.

15 Nov: Mitterrand meets Colonel Ghadaffi in Crete to discuss the conflict in Chad.

16 Nov: The number of people unemployed rises above

Appendix Two

            2.5 millions (an increase of 16.2 per cent in one year).

18 Nov: Almost 50 per cent of voters abstain after the <u>Front de Libération Nationale Kanak Socialiste</u> calls for a boycott of the election in New Caledonia. Despite the electoral victory of the pro-French party, the liberation movement takes control of much of the territory.

7 Dec: Roland Dumas replaces Claude Cheysson as Minister for Foreign Affairs.

<u>1985</u>

12 Jan: A state of emergency is declared in New Caledonia.

6-10
Feb: The XXV PCF congress at Saint-Ouen supports the call for a 'new popular majority' rather than political agreements with the PS.

10 and
17 Mar: Cantonal elections. Right-wing opposition parties now control 71 (+7) of the general councils. Left-wing parties control 28 (-10).

3 Apr: Government announces that proportional representation will be introduced for the 1986 legislative elections.

4 Apr: Michel Rocard resigns from the government in protest against the proposed electoral reform.

19 Apr: It is reported that the French government will refuse to participate in the American Strategic Defence Initiative (SDI: 'Star Wars' programme) and will launch a European Research Co-ordination Agency (EUREKA) instead.

25 Apr: The government postpones independent elections in New Caledonia until after the 1986 legislative elections.

28 Apr: Mitterrand confirms in a television interview that he will not resign after the

Appendix Two

                1986 legislative elections.

2-4 May: At the Bonn summit, Mitterrand refuses to endorse the SDI or to set a date for new GATT negotiations.

26 Jun: Parliament approves the electoral reform introducing proportional representation for the 1986 legislative election.

24 Jul: Laurent Fabius announces the suspension of all new investment in South Africa and the recall of the country's French Ambassador.

31 Jul: The government authorises the establishment of private television stations.

7 Aug: Mitterrand orders an inquiry into the role of French secret agents in the bomb attack on 10 July on the ship, the *Rainbow Warrior*. The explosion, which killed one Greenpeace campaigner, took place in New Zealand as French nuclear tests were about to take place in the Pacific.

26 Aug: The Tricot report on the Greenpeace affair absolves the government and French secret services of all responsibility for the attack.

12 Sept: Mitterrand visits Muroroa to reaffirm the French right to carry out nuclear weapons' testing there.

20 Sept: Charles Hernu, Minister of Defence resigns from the government after revelations in *Le Monde* about the Greenpeace affair. Paul Quilès becomes Minister of Defence.

22 Sept: Laurent Fabius confirms that members of the French secret services, acting on government instructions, attacked the *Rainbow Warrior*.

2-5 Oct: Official visit of Mikhail Gorbachev to France.

21 Nov: The PS and MRG sign an electoral agreement.

22 Nov: In a press conference, Mitterrand reaffirms the need for an autonomous French

Appendix Two

              deterrence strategy and a European space initiative, whatever the outcome of the US-Soviet summit.

4 Dec: In the National Assembly, the Prime Minister, Laurent Fabius declares that he is 'troubled' by the fact that General Jaruzelski, the Polish leader is being received by Mitterrand in Paris.

5 Dec: For the first time since 1970 the CFDT does not call upon its members to vote for the Left in the March 1986 elections.

20 Dec: Legislation is passed limiting to two, the number of 'significant' electoral offices an individual can hold after 1987.

<u>1986</u>

18 Jan: During 1985 the number of people unemployed fell by 3.5 per cent for the first time since 1969.

16 Feb: Recommencement of Franco-Libyan fighting and the despatch of a further 1,000 French troops to Chad.

16 Mar: In the legislative elections the RPR-UDF coalition parties together won 41 per cent of the votes and 276 of the 518 seats. The FN obtained 9.65 per cent and 35 seats, almost equalling the PCF which secured the same number of seats and 9.78 per cent of the popular vote. The PS (with the MRG) obtained 31.42 per cent of the vote and 208 seats.

INDEX

abortion 91, 222
administrative reform 113, 118
   see also Commissaire de la République, prefectoral system
Africa 167, 172-3, 181-2, 184, 197
Algeria 171, 181
Atlantic alliance 168-70, 176-7, 186, 211
   see also United States
Auroux, Jean 65, 70
Auroux laws 65-8, 220-1
   impact of 71-5 passim
autogestion 12-13, 220
   and CFDT 23, 67, 68-9
   and cultural policy 137
   and decentralisation 111
   and social policy 84

balance of payments 34-5, 46-7, 49, 50
banks 39
   nationalisation of 41-4 passim
Barre, Raymond 33-5, 62, 83
Beregovoy, Michel 87, 99, 222
Britain
   economic growth 50
   economic policy 226
   Greater London Council 119, 154
   local government reform 107
   see also Labour Party, Britain

Cancun summit 170, 172
Carrefour de Développement 181
Carrefour de la Communication 140, 155
catholicism 21, 23, 24
Centre d'Etudes, de Recherches et d'Education Socialiste (CERES) 8, 9-10, 16, 28, 37, 86
   abolition of 232
   and Socialist defence policy 194, 195, 200-1, 202
   see also Chevènement, Jean-Pierre
Ceyrac, François 60, 71, 74
Chaban-Delmas, Jacques 61, 105
Chad 182-3, 207, 223
Charte de la Santé 93
Chevènement, Jean-Pierre 28, 40, 41, 47, 231
   and Socialist Party defence policy 194, 202
   CERES leader 9, 16, 37
Cheysson, Claude 172, 174, 176, 177, 182
Chirac, Jacques 29, 33, 54, 61, 106, 119, 126
Commissaire de la République 103, 113, 120, 126
Comités d'Entreprise 56, 66, 74, 75, 97, 152
Common Programme of Government 9-10, 35-6, 199, 229
   and cultural policy 136, 137; audiovisual reform 155
   and decentralisation 110, 112

249

and social policy 83-4, 94, 100
  trade union support 61, 68
Confédération Française Démocratique du Travail (CFDT) 23, 58
  and Auroux reforms 68-9
  and economic recession 63
  support for Common Programme of Government 61
  support for socialist government 70-1
Confédération Française des Travailleurs Chrétiens (CFTC) 23, 58, 74, 75
  support for Auroux reforms 69
Confédération Générale des Cadres (CGC) 58, 71, 72, 73, 75
Confédération Générale du Travail (CGT) 23, 58, 72, 73
  and Auroux reforms 68-90
  relations with CFDT 63
  relations with PCF 64, 74
  support for Common Programme of Government 61
Conseil National du Patronat Français (CNPF) 58, 60
  and Auroux reforms 69, 71-2, 74
conseils d'arrondissement 118, 119, 127
Contrats de Plan 40, 44, 72, 117, 122
  see also economic planning
Corsica 103, 111, 113, 117, 124, 127
Cot, Jean-Pierre 172, 180, 181, 184, 223
culture
  and autogestion 137
  and President Mitterrand 136, 138-41
  cinema 158, 159
  cultural development 148-54 passim; and decentralisation 149-53; Convention de développement culturel 152; Direction du développement culturel 137-41, 149;
  internationalism 141-5 passim; Institut du Monde Arabe 140, 14
  libraries 146-7
  performing arts 145-6
  television 155-8
cumul des mandats 22, 106
  socialisation legisation on 118, 119-20

decentralisation
  and social security 98, 100
  and socialist cultural policy 149-53
  Deferre reforms 112-120 passim; impact of 120-4
  see also economic planning, regions
defence
  and French Socialist Party 194-203 passim
  nuclear defence 178, 193-9, 198-9, 204, 208
  see also Atlantic Alliance, east-west relations, euromissiles, Hernu, Charles
Defferre, Gaston
  and decentralisation 106, 112, 119, 124-5
  and Socialist Party 8, 9
Delors, Jacques 36, 38, 39, 54, 61, 70, 227
devaluation of franc 46, 47, 53, 180
doctors 91-4
Dreyfus, Pierre 40
Duhamel, Jacques 134
Dumas, Roland 179

East-West relations 167, 168-70, 176-7
economic planning 35, 39, 40, 44-5
  and decentralisation 112, 116-17
  VII Plan 33, 98
  VIII Plan 45, 49
  IX Plan 45, 90, 94, 98, 116-17
  see also Contrats de Plan
Education 13, 24, 85, 96, 97, 220

Index

elections
    European 19
    legislative 1, 2, 4, 18-19, 29
    local 4, 22, 111, 117, 134
    presidential 1, 2, 19
    regional 22
electoral reform 119
Employers' Associations 57, 58-9, 64-5, 69, 71-2
Epinay Congress 9, 15, 21
euro-missiles 169, 176, 201-2, 210-11
European Economic Community (EEC) 49, 53, 211, 226, 229
    and socialist foreign policy 175, 177, 179-80, 185
European Monetary System (EMS) 34, 46, 47, 180, 226

Fabius, Laurent 4, 16, 27, 54, 73
family allowance 84, 87, 89-90, 121
farmers 17-18, 167, 227
Fédération de l'Education Nationale (FEN) 23, 24
Fiterman, Charles 205
Force Ouvrière (FO) 23, 58, 64, 71
    and Auroux reforms 69, 70, 74, 75
foreign aid 167, 172-3
    see also Third World

Gaullism 106-7, 108-9, 133, 170, 194, 197-8
Giscard d'Estaing, Valéry 1, 2, 33, 134
    and defence 198-9, 201, 205
    and foreign policy 166-7
    and local government reform 107, 109
    election in 1974 10
Greenpeace Affair 213, 223
Guichard, Olivier 126

health care 85, 90-4 passim, 121, 220
Hernu, Charles 182, 194, 195-6, 201, 203, 213, 223
Hervé, Edmond 123
hospitals 85, 92-4 passim

housing 21, 85, 96

immigration 21, 96
    Immigrants' Council 97
    see also migrants
India 172
inflation 34, 35, 46, 47, 49, 50-1
Institut de Recherche et de Coordination Accoustique-Musique (IRCAM) 146
Institut du Monde Arabe 140, 144
Institut National de la Communication (INA) 147, 159
Israel 174-5, 184

Jospin, Lionel 16, 27
Joxe, Pierre 16, 27

Labour Party, Britain 13, 25, 154, 219, 228, 232
Lang, Jack 125, 136-7, 138, 141, 153, 159
Latin America 144, 172, 175
    El Salvador 171, 182, 201
    Nicaragua 171, 182, 201, 223
La Villette 138, 139
local government 21-2, 104-110 passim
    communes 103, 105, 117, 121-2
    departments 103, 105, 117, 121
    see also decentralisation

Maire, Edmond 23, 70
Maisons de la Culture 133
Malraux, André 132, 133, 134, 141, 143
Mauroy, Pierre 4, 70
    and defence policy 194, 205-6, 227
    position within Socialist Party 9, 16, 27
May 1968 133, 137, 160, 198
Mendès-France, Pierre 110
Middle East 174-5, 184, 201, 204-5, 206, 223
migrants 82, 84, 96-7, 127
minimum wage 38, 60, 84, 87
Mitterrand, François

Index

and cultural policy 131, 136
and defence policy 195, 200, 202-3
and Socialist Party 9, 10, 16
110 Propositions 35, 36, 68, 83-4, 112, 125, 136, 155, 175, 203
suport for Western Alliance 168-70, 205-6, 210-11
Mollet, Guy 8, 9
Musée d'Orsay 138, 140, 146

National Investment Bank 39, 41, 43
nationalisation 35, 37
and Common Programme of Government 10, 13
of banks 41-4
of industries 39-41
North Atlantic Treaty Organisation (NATO) 169, 178, 193-4, 195, 198, 200-2
North-South relations 170-4 passim
Nucci, Christian 181, 182

Old Age Pensions 83, 87, 98-9 passim, 121

Palestinian Liberation Organisation (PLO) 174, 184
Parti Communiste Français (PCF)
and CGT 23, 58, 64, 68, 71
and Common Programme of Government 35
and defence 195, 197-9
decline of 1, 2
relations with Socialist Party 8, 9, 11, 39, 71
Parti Socialiste Français
electorate 18-19
factionalism 15-16, 227-8
membership 19-21
organisation 14-17
ideology 25-8, 230-2
see also CERES
Philipponneau, Michel 110
Plan d'Occupation des Sols 117, 121
Poperon, Jean 8, 12, 16

prefectoral system 103, 104-5, 113
Projet Socialiste 112, 203

Questiaux, Nicole 86, 87, 99, 124
Quillot Roger 125

Railte, Jacques 93
regions
and cultural development 149-52
and economic development 122
Defferre reforms 116
Gaullist regional reform 108-9
regional elections 116
Renault 39, 40, 47
Rigout, Marcel 67, 124
Rocard, Michel
and decentralisation 110, 124
and defence 195
and economic policy 36, 39, 54; economic planning 44-5
position within Socialist Party 10, 16, 27, 230
Roudy, Yvette 97

Savary, Alain 8, 24, 125
Section Française de l'Internationale Ouvrière (SFIO) 7-9 passim, 17, 22, 28
social democracy 24, 29, 218-19, 228
Socialisme et République 16, 232
social security system 46, 53, 82-3, 186-9 passim
and decentralisation 117, 121
Soviet Union 167, 168-70, 176-9, 201
see also East-West relations
steel industry 24, 62

Third World 167, 170, 180-3, 203
and socialist cultural policy 140, 143-4
trade unions
and Common Programme of Government 61
collective bargaining 59-60, 65, 73

Index

weakness of 57-9
see also Auroux reforms

unemployment 33, 34, 46, 49-51, 56, 63, 220
benefit levels 94-6
United States of America 168-70, 176-7, 182, 205, 223, 226
and socialist defence policy 195
attitude to French nuclear deterrent 200, 205
see also Atlantic alliance, East-West relations, Western Alliance

West Germany
and euromissiles 169, 201-2, 210-11
economic performance 36, 37, 46, 47, 226
Social Democratic Party (SPD) 228, 232
Western European Union 211
workers' representation
women 221-2
and local government 127
and social policy 82, 84, 89, 97-8
within Socialist Party 20

DATE DUE